Organizational
Discourse

Organizational Discourse

A Language-Ideology-Power Perspective

Renata Fox and John Fox

Westport, Connecticut
London

Library of Congress Cataloging-in-Publication Data

Fox, Renata.
   Organizational discourse : a language-ideology-power perspective / Renata
   Fox and John Fox
     p. cm.
   Includes bibliographical references and index.
   ISBN 1–56720–605–0 (alk. paper)
    1. Communication in management.   2. Communication in organizations.
   3. Corporations—Public relations.   4. Ideology.   5. Power (Social sciences).
   6. Discourse analysis.   7. Sociolinguistics.   I. Fox, John.   II. Title.

   HD30.3.F69 2004
   658.4′5—dc22   2004052150

British Library Cataloguing in Publication Data is available.

Library of Congress Catalog Card Number: 2004052150
ISBN: 1–56720–605-0

First published in 2004

Praeger Publishers, 88 Post Road West, Westport, CT 06881
An imprint of Greenwood Publishing Group, Inc.
www.praeger.com

Printed in the United States of America

The paper used in this book complies with the
Permanent Paper Standard issued by the National
Information Standards Organization (Z39.48-1984).

10 9 8 7 6 5 4 3 2 1

To our son Ivan

Contents

Preface

When thinking of corporations, most of us take them—and their goods and services—for granted. We think of them simply as entities signified by names and acronyms such as Aventis, Honda, Microsoft, Nestlé, Shell, BMW, BP, GE, HP, IBM, and so on. This is a convenient and necessary illusion; in reality a corporation is a dynamic and eruptive process of movement, change, and production. The taken-for-granted impression of a corporation as an entity is a result of order imposed upon disorder. That which imposes order is, of course, power: "a *concentration of control* within an *asymmetrical* relation between upper and lower strata in any complex system" (Beaugrande 1997, 533). A power, we note, practiced not through coercion but through consent (e.g., Hogan 2001; Schiff 2003; Monbiot 2004)—that is, through cultural processes such as language and ideology.

Exactly how, then, do corporations (and people in corporations) use language and ideologies to practice power through consent? What is that language about? What are those ideologies about? What are the effects of those cultural processes on society?

Answers to these questions, it might be expected, would be found in organizational discourse (OD): a field of study focused on researching discourse—language in social action—in organizations and its influence upon organizational structure and behavior.

It was Peters and Waterman who, just over 20 years ago in their best-seller *In Search of Excellence*, made that first, albeit brief, explicit reference to the importance of discourse for an organization. "A true people orientation (within an organization)," they wrote, "can not exist unless there is a special language to go with it" (1984, 260). Today OD encompasses the research of topics such as stories, narratives and novels, rituals, rhetoric, metaphor, language games, texts, drama, conversations, emotion and sense-making, talk, plans and lists, power, gender, meaning-making, culture, and leadership in organizations (Grant and Oswick 1996; Grant, Keenoy, and Oswick 1998; Westwood and Linstead 2001; Tietze, Cohen, and Musson 2003). All of these topics are brought together in their central concern with the "organizational being."

Yet, OD is "poorly defined" (Grant et al. 1998, 1). The main reason for this, Oswick, Keenoy, and Grant (1997, 8) have argued, lies in the fact that discourse in organizations has rarely been "a primary focus" of management research. For years, it would seem, the discourse of organizations has been taken for granted, rather than being treated as "integral to effectiveness" and strategic to the corporation. Researchers' marginalization of the discourse of organizations, Grant and colleagues (1998, 4–5) have further argued, is attributable to at least four reasons: (1) the ubiquitous focus of literature in organizational studies on effectiveness and efficiency of organization; (2) methodological misconceptions; (3) a simplistic association between discourse analysis and forms of postmodern deconstruction; and, most important, (4) a "cultural preference for action over mere talk."

Overall, we agree. Yes, the discourse of organizations has been taken for granted. Yes, literature in organizational studies has been focused primarily on effectiveness and efficiency of organization. We, however, find it somewhat difficult to accept "cultural preference for action over mere talk" as an explanation for a poor definition of OD. Writings in both management and organization theory, whether touching on the subject of corporate communication in passing or analyzing it in depth, show an acute awareness of the importance of communication to organizations. Corporate managers are known to use all available opportunities to publicly communicate in speech and writing, which is a clear evidence of their appreciation of the "power of words." In fact, the first thing one notices about senior managers is that they, "besides talking shop-bids, mergers and takeovers . . . absolutely relish talking about themselves" (Fox 1999b, 261). And, finally, the entire management education process, notably MBA courses, increasingly stresses the fundamental importance of communication to management.

In our view, the weakness of present definitions of OD arises from neither the quantity nor the quality of related research. Instead, it arises from the almost total absence of research into the discourse of organizations from a language-ideology-power perspective. A systematic appreciation of how organizations use language and ideology to practice power through consent has yet to be formulated.

Our aim in this book is to give some momentum to OD from a language-ideology-power perspective. We have tried to do this in three ways. First, drawing on theoretical linguistics, sociolinguistics, critical discourse studies, the theory of ideology, the ethnography of communication, media studies, and organizational studies, we have applied theories and methodologies indispensable for describing discourse from a language-ideology-power perspective to the discourse of corporations and people in corporations. Second, building upon our understanding of the discourse of corporations and people in corporations from a language-ideology-power perspective, we have developed a general theory of the discourse of corporations and people in corporations from a language-ideology-power perspective. And third, using our general theory to explore attested examples of the discourse of corporations and people in corporations, we have addressed our previous questions. In sum, we have tried to formulate a new appreciation of the discourse of corporations as power through consent. If through that appreciation we have helped all involved in the discourse of corporations—practicing managers, corporate communication officers, scholars and, last but not least, students of management and organizational studies—to get to grips with that discourse, both in theory and practice, we shall be very pleased indeed.

Renata Fox
John Fox

Acknowledgments

The authors are indebted to their editors at Greenwood Publishing Group, Inc., Nicholas Philipson and Hilary Claggett, for their advice and encouragement.

The authors and publisher wish to thank the following who kindly gave permission for the use and reproduction of their public discourse: Accor (Web page), Airbus (Web page), Altana (Web page), Aventis (corporate advertisement "So that discovery can lead to healthier lives"), Bank One (corporate advertisement "If We Call a Rock a Stone Isn't It Still a Rock?"), BusinessWeek (Carly's Last Stand?, December 24, 2001, p. 68), Canon (corporate advertisement "Wildlife as Canon Sees It), Cathay Pacific (corporate advertisement "With the right connections, there's no telling how far you can go.), Coca-Cola (mission statement), Dell (mission statement), Mary Kay Cosmetics (mission statement), Harley-Davidson (corporate news, mission statement), Harvard Business Review (interviews "The Logic of Global Business: An Interview with ABB's Percy Barnevik," March-April 1991, pp. 95, 103, 104; "Leveraging Processes for Strategic Advanage," September-October 1995, p. 84; "Leadership When There is No One to Ask: An Interview with Eni's Franco Bernabé," July-August, 1998, p. 90; "Organizing for Empowerment: An Interview with AES's Roger Sant and Dennis Bakke," January-February, 1999, pp. 15, 117, 118, 119, 120, 121; "Starting Up in High Gear: An Interview with Venture Capitalist Vinod Khosla," July-August 2000, p. 100; "The Business Case Against Revolution: An Interview with Nestlé's Peter Brabeck," February 2001, p. 114; "Jack on Jack," February 2002, p. 93), Heineken (annual report 1999), Hewlett-Packard ("Why Support this Merger?," "Our Promise to Customers," "We are Ready"), Hitachi (corporate advertisement "Global Vision"), HSBC (corporate advertisement "Never underestimate the importance of local knowledge"),

IBM (THINK, "Poised for leadership," 1998, 1, p. 6, mission statement, annual report 1999, corporate advertisement "People who think. People who do. People who get it," corporate advertisement "Saks turned it on," business guidelines), ICIG (Strathclyde Statement), Kodak (mission statement), Long John Silver (mission statement), Marconi (mission statement), McDonald's (mission statement), Microsoft (mission statement), Nalco (Philosophy of Operations "Building Value"), **one**world™ (corporate advertisement "Some people just seem to know how to travel. Are you one of them?"), Patek Philippe (corporate advertisement "You never actually own a Patek Philippe. You merely look after it for the *next* generation."), Ricoh (Web page), Sabena (corporate advertisement "Have you flown Sabena lately?"); Shell (report "People, Planet & Profits," annual report 2001 "Shell in the United States"), UPS (corporate advertisement "I hugged all of them goodbye . . . "), US Airways (corporate advertisement "Upgraded Comfort in Every Class"), Vodafone (Web page).

PART I

Introduction

Defining a Research Perspective

In fact, thanks to our Associates, Wal-Mart was able to report record sales ($244.5 billion) and record earnings ($8.0 billion) in one of the most difficult business environments in recent years.

—*Wal-Mart President and CEO Lee Scott*[1]

AN INSTANCE OF CORPORATE DISCOURSE

Every Saturday morning, the corporation Wal-Mart holds a meeting usually attended by at least 500 Wal-Mart "associates" (employees), including members of senior management. Described by the British weekly *The Economist* as "part evangelical revival, part Oscars, part Broadway show" (Saturday morning fever 2001, 60), the meeting starts with a ritual roar of the company's slogan, "Who's number one? The customer. Always!" The purpose of the meeting, *The Economist* writes, is a comparison of weekly sales figures. Those with good figures are loudly acclaimed, cheered, and applauded. Those with bad figures have to stand up and explain. The meeting is concluded with a top executive's speech and more cheering.

Perceived as meaningful social action, Wal-Mart's weekly Saturday morning meetings are much more than a comparison of weekly sales figures: They are a reality which embodies underlying (asymmetrical) relations of power as part and parcel of that reality. Accepting Wal-Mart's reality, Wal-Mart's employees not only accept underlying relations of power, they, in fact, endorse the right of certain individuals and groups of individuals (within Wal-Mart) to define Wal-Mart's reality and underlying relations of power. Put another way, Wal-Mart's employees, through Wal-Mart's weekly Saturday morning meetings, are made a part of a design that transcends mere persuasion, a design that, to quote Nash (1992, 1), "assiduously" involves all as "accomplices" in a "conspiracy from which there is no easy withdrawal." That design, of course, is founded on an ideology: a "cognitive and behavioral system that sets priorities among 'ideas' (concepts, meanings, actions, and so on), and legitimizes certain ones as 'true,' 'proper,' 'natural,' 'correct,' 'valuable,' 'respectable,' and the like" (cf. Beaugrande 1997, 517). An idea fundamental to Wal-Mart's ideology is the corporation's commitment to the customer.

IDEOLOGY

The term "ideology" has a long and turbulent history. Eagleton (1985), for example, has listed some 16 definitions of the term. Coined in 1796 by the French writer and philosopher Antoine Louis Claude Destutt de Tracy (1754–1836), "idéologie" originally meant a methodic and scientific analysis of ideas. Later, during Napoleon's reign, Destutt de Tracy's ideas were rejected, and the term "ideology" gained a pejorative connotation. This negative understanding of ideology was further taken up by Marx and Engels in *The German Ideology* (1845–1847/1974). According to Marx's "dominant ideology" hypothesis, the dominant bloc in any society, controlling the means of mental production (e.g., religion, education, and communication), generates the dominant ideas. The function of these ideas, Marx contended, is to conceal conflict of the real interests of social classes and maintain the stability of a social order. The acceptance of dominant ideas by the dominated creates what Marx referred to as "false consciousness," that prevents the dominated from seeing the world as it really is.

Abandoning the notion of "false consciousness," Althusser (1971), in his comparative analysis of "ideological state apparatuses," redefined ideology as a set of cultural practices perpetuated through the church, the educational system, the family, and the law. The main function of these cultural practices, Althusser explains, is the division of individuals into groups to give them systematically different treatment. For Althusser, ideologies create us as persons; they "hail us" and "make us." Interestingly, Foucault, one of the leading social theorists of the second half of the twentieth century, tended to avoid using the concept of ideology, replacing it by the much wider concept of discourse.

Within mainstream ideology-related research, two stances are taken: critical and neutral. Researchers focusing on the power aspect of ideology treat ideology as a negative social force. Researchers adopting "more globalizing and intellectualizing approaches" toward ideology employ the term broadly, and are "noncommittal on the truth value of ideology" (Woolard 1998, 8). Ideology is seen as a means for society to "generate solidarity" (Berger and Luckmann 1991, 141), to remove "surface markers of authority and power" (Fairclough 1999b, 37), and to sustain stability between classes and blocs. An understanding of ideology that aims to establish ideology as a field of study is van Dijk's (2000) multidisciplinary framework for theorizing ideology. In van Dijk's view, ideologies are "principles that form the *basis*" of a group's beliefs and, as such, "allow people, as group members, to organize the multitude of social beliefs about what is the case, good or bad, right or wrong, *for them*, and to act accordingly" (p. 8). Clearly, such an understanding of ideology places discovering how (members of) social groups make sense of and communicate ideologies at the center of research into ideology. As van Dijk explains, "we need not only a definition, but also a detailed *theory* of ideology" (p. 9).

LEGITIMACY

Institutionalized and legitimized, that is, "objectivated as activity" (Berger and Luckmann 1991, 78) and "explained and justified" (p. 79) through Wal-Mart's weekly Saturday morning meetings, Wal-Mart's ideology enables Wal-Mart to practice power through consent. But Wal-Mart's ideology does much more: it serves as a "protective cover of both cognitive and normative interpretation" (p. 79) for the corporation's power. Under that "canopy," Wal-Mart's power carries conviction to all of the corporation's "associates," generation after generation. It too is legitimized.

Knowledge of the need to legitimize power (usually that of the state) is not new. Over 24 centuries ago, Thucydides in *History of the Peloponnesian War* (423 B.C./1998) discussed what makes power morally right. The legitimacy of Athens' coercive power to annihilate Melos was founded, of course, on "the law of the stronger." In the centuries to follow, the main problem to be addressed by theories of legitimacy was political stability. In *The Politics* (335–323 B.C./1998) and *The Nicomachean Ethics* (335–323 B.C./1998), Aristotle argued that the legitimacy of a government depends on the legitimacy of rewards (a theory known as "distributive justice"). The instability of a political system, Aristotle further argued, is, therefore, a consequence of the mechanisms by which that system distributes rewards.

Not until the early sixteenth century and Machiavelli's *The Discourses* (1517/1983) and *The Prince* (1532/1998) was the stability of a political system directly attributed to the legitimacy of government itself. Essentially a "conflict" theory, Machiavelli's theory of legitimacy assumes (1) rational self-interest to be a basis of both action and order; (2) the interests of the rulers and the ruled to be in conflict; (3) power to enforce rules; (4) "pure" power to be unable to persuade that a rule is "right"; (5) ideology, myth, and ritual to be necessary to legitimize rules and mask the real interests of the rulers; (6) "pure" power to be ultimately unstable unless legitimized; and (7) legitimacy to be fundamental to any social order (cf. Zelditch 2001, 42). Some three centuries later, based on Machiavelli's views on legitimacy as a precondition for the practice of power, Marx was to develop his dominant ideology hypothesis, to which we have previously referred.

At the beginning of the twentieth century Max Weber in *Economy and Society* (1918/1968) put forward one of the most influential theories of legitimacy to date. According to Weber, legitimacy can be attributed to three bases of authority: traditional, charismatic, and rational-legal. Traditional authority originates from an established system of beliefs. Wall-Mart's commitment to the customer, for example, is a part of such a system of beliefs of contemporary society. Charismatic authority is founded on an individual's extraordinary abilities and traits or, alternatively, her or his followers' beliefs that she or he possesses such abilities and traits. An excellent example of a charismatic leader, whose legitimacy was founded almost exclusively on his followers' beliefs in his qualities, is the late U.S. President Ronald Reagan. Finally, a rational-legal authority system is based on the laws of society: rules which are legally defined and rationally enacted. All of these three types of authority— traditional, charismatic, and rational-legal—can be intertwined in any given case. For the corporation (and the CEO) they provide a potent means to legitimize an ideology.

Post Weber a number of scholars have established dominant theories of legitimacy. For example: Parsons in "Authority, Legitimation, and Political Action" (1958), Berger and Luckmann in *The Social Construction of Reality* (1966/1991), and Habermas in *Legitimation Crisis* (1975). More recent research into legitimacy and power is increasingly multidisciplinary. One such field of study is the "psychology of legitimacy," that seeks to understand how "ideas, beliefs, and stereotypes serve to legitimize and delegitimize existing forms of social relations" (Jost and Major 2001, 24).

POWER THROUGH CONSENT

Legitimizing the corporation's power, Wal-Mart's ideology has the potential to create Wal-Mart's symbolic universe (cf. Berger and Luckmann 1991, 114): a matrix of all social and individual meanings that determines the significance of all group and individual experiences. Within that symbolic universe all corporation-related situations are integrated into one central reality of corporate life and ordered in such a way that that central reality retains "its paramount, definitive (if one wishes, its 'most real') quality" (p. 116). Through the definitive quality of that central reality all corporation-related experiences are legitimized and "put in their right place." Within that symbolic universe all of Wal-Mart's customers (and employees) are "transposed on to a cosmic plane and made majestically independent of the vicissitudes of individual existence" (p. 121). Is such a huge accumulation of power by a corporation, rivaling even governments, socially acceptable?

A product of history (Perrow 2002), "power" has held different meanings for different generations. In the past power was perceived as greed, a fact the historian Bernard Bailyn explains in his Pulitzer Prize–winning *The Ideological Origins of the American Revolution* (1967):

Most commonly the discussion of power centered on its essential characteristic of aggressiveness: its endlessly propulsive tendency to expand itself beyond legitimate boundaries. . . . Sometimes the image is of the human hand, "the hand of power," reaching out to clutch and to seize: power is "grasping" and "tenacious" in its nature; "what it seizes it will retain." (p. 56)

Today, under the influence of moral, political, and economic philosophers, power is seen as a virtue, an advantage and/or interest that, appropriately guided by the state, governs behavior, cognitive patterns, and the formation of social identity (McClelland 1963, 1971; Hirschman 1977; Tjosvold 1984; Fleischer, Hazard, and Klipper 2002). It is in this positive sense, for example, that power within organizations has been defined as "the ability to make things happen" (Kanter 1977), as a "resource which enables management to pull together people, technology, time and space" (Morgan 1990), and as the capacity to "enhance the organization positively in relation to its 'environment' or key problems" (Pfeffer and Salancik 1997).

On the other hand, according to *BizEthicsBuzz* (2000), some 72 percent of all Americans seem to believe that business has gained too much power, a belief Marjorie Kelly (2001), author of *The Divine Right of Capital*, shares:

Corporations today are governments of the propertied class, exercising power over Americans that is greater than the power once exercised by kings. They are governments that have become destructive of our inalienable rights as a people. (p. 187)

Because a corporation's power is practiced through consent, the social issue at stake is not really about corporations exercising too much power over people. Rather, it is about people accepting corporations practicing power through consent, and about the social acceptability of corporations manufacturing consent.

It was the influential American journalist Walter Lippman who in 1922 first articulated the importance of manufacturing consent in democratic societies. Consent engineering, Lippman wrote, "is not a new art. It is a very old one which was supposed to have died out with the appearance of democracy. But it has not died out. It has, in fact, improved enormously in technic, because it is now based on analysis rather than on rule of thumb" (cited in Achbar 1994). A quarter of a century later, Edward Bernays (1947) was also to argue that the engineering of consent is "the very essence of the democratic process" and that "the freedoms to make the engineering of consent possible, are among the most cherished guarantees of the Constitution of the United States" (cited in Achbar 1994).

Breaking away from traditional scholarly thought, in the late 1980s, Edward Herman and Noam Chomsky in their well-known "propaganda model," expounded in *Manufacturing Consent: The Political Economy of the Mass Media* (1988), gave a new meaning to the term "manufacturing consent." Leading social actors, for example, governmental bodies, systems of education, corporations, etc., wishing to be integrated into society's institutional framework, Herman and Chomsky argued, see manufacturing consent as a primary task. The key force of this process, that "in a world of concentrated wealth and major conflicts of class interests" cannot be accomplished without "systematic propaganda" (p. 2), Herman and Chomsky further argued, are (elite) mass media. Including/excluding and supporting/opposing, mass media, Herman and Chomsky conclude, legitimize the hegemony of a dominant bloc.

Although it is often excluded from mainstream public media debate, and criticized for its basic assumptions on self-censorship and the ideological role of mass media, Herman and Chomsky's propaganda model is being increasingly seen by scholars as forceful and convincing, and as providing a valuable perspective on contemporary society (Klaehn 2002, 147–182). Collison (2003), for example, has used the propaganda model to examine the nature of corporate propaganda (and mass media), particularly in the United States, over a period of nearly 100 years. According to Collison, the mass media are not just used by corporations, they are a "manifestation of corporate power with fundamentally the same interests and concentrated oligopolistic structure as other areas of commercial activity" (p. 872).

Is, then, Wal-Mart's practice of power through consent socially acceptable? In today's society in which physical violence has been replaced by "symbolic violence" (Bourdieu 1977) founded on implicit mechanisms of social control that invite a complicity of social actors—yes, it is. In today's society in which symbolic violence works because the power of the dominant bloc enables dominant discourses (for example, the discourses of consumerism, wealth creation, sport, entertainment, music, fashion, education, economic unification) to drown out other discourses and seduce "the holders of dominated linguistic competencies to collaborate in the destruction of their instruments of expression" (Bourdieu 1991, 49)—yes, it is. In today's society in which consumers have consented to being "consented"—yes, it is.

RESEARCH INTENTION

Worldwide, there are 65,000 transnational corporations with 850,000 foreign affiliates. Together, they employ some 54 million people, have sales over $19 trillion, and create roughly one-tenth of world GDP and one-third of world exports. Like Wal-Mart, all of these corporations use discourse to practice power through consent. Like Wal-Mart, all give immense importance to that discourse, visible in the colossal budgets they allocate to their "most common corporate communication functions": advertising and image building, corporate culture and change, media relations, investor relations, global communication, communication policy, internal communication, communication technology, crisis communication, corporate citizenship and ethics, executive communication, leadership and communication, and public relations (CCI Corporate Communication 2004, 8). Of Fortune 1,000 corporations 18.6 percent spend over $10m a year on corporate communication, 2.3 percent $7.5–10m, 5.8 percent $5–7.5m, 43 percent $1–5m, 17.4 percent $0.5–1m, and 11.6 percent up to $500,00 (p. 4, Figure 10).

In this book we explore how corporations use discourse to practice power through consent. To do that, we:

1. Define a discoursal practice of corporations.
2. Explore and describe that discoursal practice from a language-ideology-power perspective. All discoursal practices in a corporation involve social situations, social processes, social relationships, and social roles, which embody language, ideology, and power.
3. Establish a general theory for that discoursal practice from a language-ideology-power perspective. All discoursal practices in a corporation imply some set of abstract ideas that give meaning to and shape those practices. These ideas may not necessarily be a part of a corporation's and corporate management's declarative knowledge. Nevertheless, whenever a corporation and corporate management are involved in a discoursal practice, they are inevitably acting on ideas. Put together, these ideas provide the basis for a theory.
4. Analyze the linguistic form and content of that discoursal practice from a language-ideology-power perspective. Linguistic analysis encompasses the analysis of individual written text samples and the analysis of text corpora compiled from a large number of written text samples. Individual texts are subjected to minute sociolinguistic[2] analysis and related to social context. Text corpora are subjected to computational analysis to provide statistical evidence of real choices of language vis-à-vis language as a virtual system.
5. Develop a metalanguage for the discussion of that discoursal practice from a language-ideology-power perspective.
6. Set a path for the future development of OD (as a field of study) from a language-ideology-power perspective.

ORGANIZATION OF THE BOOK

In this introduction we state, explain, and discuss our research perspective, undertaking and intention. The rest of the book is split into six parts.

Part II, The Corporation, consisting of four chapters, defines corporate public discourse (CPD) as a discoursal practice of corporations and puts together a theoretical framework for its exploration from a language-ideology-power perspective. Chapter 2, Corporate Public Discourse, shows in detail how CPD works to enable a corporation to practice power through consent and looks at previous research related to CPD. Chapter 3, A Corporation's Ideology, describes Shell's CPD. Chapter 4, CPD's Nomenclature, defines CPD's metalanguage. Chapter 5, CPD as Capital, analyzes IBM's CPD and describes IBM's ideology.

Part III, Corporate Management, consisting of four chapters, focuses on corporate management and on the ways CEOs use CPD to legitimize themselves and their ideologies. Chapter 6, The Corporate Management Discourse Community, applies the concept of a discourse community to CPD. Chapter 7, A Disclosure of Power, explores the media interview of AES Chairman Roger Sant and AES CEO Dennis Bakke. Chapter 8, A Disclosure of Leadership, relates to the media interviews of Pepsi-Cola President and CEO Craig Weatherup, former General Electric CEO Jack Welch, and Hewlett-Packard

CEO Carleton S. Fiorina. Chapter 9, A Disclosure of Social Position, analyzes the media interview of Eni CEO Franco Bernabé.

Part IV, Media of CPD, consisting of two chapters, is based on the fact that in today's society virtually everything (including the corporation) is expected to become an immediate object of communication. Chapter 10, Writing, elaborates reasons why, from a language-ideology-power perspective, writing is the preferred medium of CPD. Chapter 11, Mass Media and CPD, discusses the ways mass media define CPD.

Part V, Quantitative Analysis, consisting of two chapters, moves away from instances of CPD onto text corpora of CPD. CPD, it is argued, is socially situated in a probabilistic rather than a categorical way and employed more or less, rather than being present or absent. Chapter 12, Five CPD Default Genres, gives in detail the theory and methodology for a corpus-based approach for exploring CPD from a language-ideology-power perspective and uses this approach to describe the corporate mission statement genre, the CEO media interview genre, the corporate business guidelines genre, the corporate media advertisement genre, and the corporate annual report genre. Chapter 13, Five Corporate Web Pages, explores text corpora compiled from the Web pages of the corporations Accor, Airbus, Altana, Ricoh, and Vodafone to describe and compare their ideologies.

Part VI, Specific Research Perspectives, consisting of five chapters, contains selected topics of research into CPD from a language-ideology-power perspective. Chapter 14, The Corporate Metaphor, analyzes the CEO's use of metaphor in her or his media interview. Chapter 15, Globalization, uses the CPD of a number of corporations to explore CPD within the context of globalization. Chapter 16, Gender, refers back to CEO Fiorina's media interview to relate CPD to gender issues within the corporation. Chapter 17, The CEO's Media Interview, refers back to CEO Bernabé's media interview to show how the CEO's media interview has transformed into a drama. Chapter 18, Promotionalization of CPD, shows how promotion has become a communicative function of CPD.

Part VII, Postscript, consisting of Chapter 19, Adjourning the Exploration, brings together our observations, ideas, and conclusions on CPD from a language-ideology-power perspective and places them within the context of the future of OD.

NOTES

1. Wal-Mart's 2003 Annual Report, p. 2.

2. As a discipline, sociolinguistics was established in the early 1970s. This, however, does not mean that studying language in society is an invention of the 1970s. The study of dialects and the relation between language and culture has a long tradition. Today sociolinguistics is an ever-expanding interdisciplinary field of research. In contact with sociopsychology, pragmatics, discourse analysis, ethnography, and dialect geography, it is being applied to areas such as language varieties, media communication, educational issues, language policy, language, and identity (for domains of sociolinguistic research see, for example, Coulmas 1997).

PART II

The Corporation

2

Corporate Public Discourse

Human knowledge is limited not just because humans lack the diligence or their instruments lack the precision, but because *the set of knowledge about phenomena is indefinitely large,* and because *every phenomenon is connected to a still wider or deeper context.* In return, human knowledge is also *unlimited* precisely because its *current coverage can never be complete or final,* and because *new connections can always be made among phenomena.*
—*R. de Beaugrande (1997, 86)*

DEFINING CORPORATE PUBLIC DISCOURSE

The discoursal practice of corporations and corporate management we intend to explore in this book is what we refer to as corporate public discourse (CPD). Instances of CPD are a corporation's mission statement, a corporation's statement of general business principles, a corporation's media advertisement, a corporation's Web page, a corporation's annual report, a corporation's business guidelines, a corporation's news bulletin, a corporation's employee magazine, a corporation's merger and acquisition announcement, a CEO's media interview, a CEO's media address, and so on. The term CPD brings together three key concepts of today's society: "corporate," "public," and "discourse."

Corporate

By "corporate" we mean related to social entities that possess the power to affect and change whole societies. We take a corporation to be a community of stakeholders: groups and individuals affecting and affected by "the achievement of an organization's purpose" (Freeman 1984, 52) and having a legitimate claim on the organization (Hill and Jones 1992). Stakeholders include customers, employees, management, stockholders, creditors, suppliers, and the community, as well as competitors and even nonhuman entities such as animals or the natural environment (cf. Starik 1994). Each stakeholder group has different objectives: buying products, employment, performance, return on investment, repayment of principal and interest, selling materials/products/services, community interests, environmental protection, and so on. A corporation cannot choose the stakeholder group with which it interacts; it has to engage into meeting the demands of all of such groups, "whether it wants to or not" (Schilling 2000, 225). A corporation that fails to meet stakeholders' needs ceases to exist (Clarkson 1995).

The importance of stakeholders to corporations and the need for a stakeholder theory was first articulated by Freeman (1984) in his book *Strategic Management: A Stakeholder Approach*. A stakeholder theory, Rubinstein and Kochan (1996) contend, moves a focus from shareholders as the most privileged constituents of an organization onto stakeholders. Redefining a distribution of political rights—and empowerment—within the organization, stakeholder theory introduces a strong political turn into organizational studies (cf. Phillips 2003).

Public

By "public" we mean that which is open, visible, and available to all to accept or refuse. Publicness, Habermas argued in his book *The Structural Transformation of the Public Sphere* (2002, 1–2), first published in 1962, is a "clouded" concept. For example, an event, is public when open to all. If, however, a building is public, this does not necessarily mean that it is accessible to all. The publicness of a "public authority" such as the state is about the promotion of the public welfare of its members. And in the case of "public reception," publicness is aimed at inviting public recognition. Yet, none of these usages of publicness, Habermas emphasizes, relates to the most commonly employed meaning of public: a "carrier of public opinion," available to all to express their views and, under the influence of mass media, inevitably contrasted with "private."

As Habermas foresaw, in today's society the notion of publicness has definitely been redefined by mass communication and mass media. Publicness no longer involves a common spatial-temporal setting. Instead, it is understood as openness and visibility that extend beyond the boundaries of any nation-state (Thompson 1996, 236).

A consequence of publicness is a shift from a controlling to a regulatory state, manifested in what Urry (2000, 198) has referred to as a "polling culture": a culture generated by a huge number of surveys and polls giving people the opportunity to express their opinions. Practically overnight, the public space has turned into a "public stage" (p. 180) upon which the key virtues of society are being tested and recognized.

An evidence of corporations' awareness of the importance of publicness is the dramatic expansion of the corporate annual report. According to the November 2002 report *Trust Us*, published by a consultancy, SustainAbility, over the past two years corporate reports have increased by 45 percent in volume and grown to a "frightening" 86 pages apiece (Irresponsible 2002, 60). The reason for the enlarged corporate annual report, *Trust Us* suggests, is the general assumption that in the public space companies are seen as "inherently immoral" unless they prove the opposite.

Widely accepted as a public declaration of a corporation's ethicality, the corporate annual report has given rise to a rapidly expanding field of research known as "social and environmental accounting" (SEA) (cf. Gray, Kouhy, and Lavers 1995, 47–77; Mathews 1997, 481–531; Deegan 2002, 282–311; Adams 2002, 223–250). According to SEA research, corporate reporting is motivated more by corporate management's desire to legitimize the organization, than by the need to disclose information to stakeholders. When it comes to corporate reports, investors, so it seems, are "more likely to be shocked by honesty than appalled by deceit" (Kane 2004, 163).

Discourse

By "discourse" we mean language as meaningful social action: a key instrument of individuals' and groups' participation in social roles, social contexts, social situations, and social processes. Discourse is also a "linguistic objectifier" (Berger and Luckmann 1991, 91) through which individuals and groups learn how to participate in social roles, social contexts, social situations, and social processes.

In its early stages of use, the term "discourse" was understood as confined to spoken language (e.g., Sinclair and Coulthard 1975). Not until later did it become a label for all forms of spoken and written, and formal and informal interaction (Potter and Wetherell 1987). Put together, definitions of discourse are either structural (treating discourse as an autonomous system) or functional (emphasizing the social function of discourse) (Schiffrin 1994, 20–43). Ironically, the key trait of structural definitions of discourse—their focus on code and the way patterns of language are shaped and arranged—is at the same time their main weakness. Treating discourse as a mental (rather than societal) phenomenon, structural definitions support *"disconnectedness"* and mask the *"unity* and *continuity* of human utterances" and, consequently, "authorize an *academically accredited failure to connect"* (Beaugrande 1997, 42). Functional definitions of discourse, on the other hand, inquiring into how language elements and patterns are used as a means to an end, underline acts and events and recognize elements of discourse and the relations between those elements in terms of their contribution and function within the social situation. Yet, in spite of researchers' efforts to render an accurate definition, "discourse" remains an awkwardly "fuzzy" concept (cf. van Dijk 1997, 1), massively overused in daily interaction, frequently abused by mass media, and extensively exploited by the humanities and the social sciences.

THE FOUR CONCURRENT FUNCTIONS OF CPD

Viewed from a language-ideology-power perspective, CPD performs four concurrent functions: institutionalization, legitimization, capitalization, and inculcation of ideas constitutive to a corporation's ideology. To explain those functions, we analyze an example of Patek Philippe's CPD: its well-known corporate media advertisement "You never actually own a Patek Philippe. You merely look after it for the *next* generation."[1]

The main idea upon which Patek Philippe constructs its ideology is tradition: a social value so ingrained in society that it has become an "institutional formula" (cf. Berger and Luckmann 1991, 87–88) of everyday reality encapsulating other social values and conventional knowledge of the "real," experienced world. Taken for granted and never questioned, tradition functions as a myth: one of those "devoutly accredited accounts of how the 'world' must be" (Beaugrande 1997, 3), which, as any other myth, provides people with a "communal viewpoint, a focus for thought," and serves as a "binding-force" within time and space (McLeish 1996, 11).

Offered to stakeholders via the mass media, Patek Philippe's corporate media advertisement institutionalizes the idea of buying a Patek Philippe "for the *next* generation" as fundamental to Patek Philippe's ideology. Calling upon the convention of tradition, Patek Philippe's corporate media advertisement legitimizes the idea of buying a Patek Philippe "for the *next* generation" as fundamental to Patek Philippe's ideology.

Institutionalized and legitimized, the idea of buying a Patek Philippe "for the *next* generation" represents a form of capital—social, symbolic, cultural, and economic—that can be employed by a social actor (e.g., Patek Philippe) to secure "a power over the field (at a given moment)" (Bourdieu 1985, 724). Social capital is defined by access to and positions in social networks. Symbolic capital is found in the capacity to define and legitimize cultural values consisting of specific religious, philosophical, cultural, and social ideas. Culturally determined, learned, and practiced, values offer reasons for ways of behavior and self-perception. Values govern human motivations, which are based on the need for achievement, affiliation, and power (McClelland 1963, 1971). Values are important not only for what they represent, but because they have the potential to create consensus.

This does not mean, though, that values are immune to change. On the contrary, influenced by major social changes, for example, globalization, the end of the welfare state and the fall of communism, the renaissance of art, literature, and spirituality (Naisbitt and Aburdene 1990), traditional cultural values are undergoing a significant shift. In America, the value of family loyalty and sacrifice, for one, is in serious decline (cf. Loudon and Della Bitta 1993; Schiff 2003). Similarly, in Japan, both the idea of lifelong loyalty to the company and respect for seniority are diminishing in favor of more competitive and self-oriented behaviors (An alternative to . . . 2001, 52). And in an enlarged and increasingly multiethnic Europe, a whole new set of values, beliefs, and attitudes is rapidly emerging. Cultural capital is represented by education and expertise. Economic capital has the form of financial assets. A field is a net-work of social relations in which struggles take place over resources, stakes, and accesses (Bourdieu 1990). Fields provide individuals with "positions of possibility" constitutive to their social positions and possession of power. Reflecting relations of power, "positions of possibility" are in a constant state of flux.

Employed as symbolic capital, the idea of buying a Patek Philippe "for the *next* generation" defines the social value of a Patek Philippe: the buyer acquires not just a time-measuring device, but a name, a symbol, a lifestyle. Contemporary society is a society of different worlds in which members of that society play different roles. Acutely aware of all those worlds, including their own, people consciously detach themselves from their roles in the world. They increasingly act out and play those roles: they internalize realities, not as their realities, but as realities to be used for specific purposes. To paraphrase Gary Zukov (1980, 328): Their reality is what they take to be true. What they take to be true is what they believe. What they believe is based upon their per-ceptions. What they perceive depends upon what they look for. What they look for depends upon what they think. What they think depends upon what they perceive. What they perceive determines what they believe. What they believe determines what they take to be true. What they take to be true deter-mines their reality.

Employed as economic capital, the idea of buying a Patek Philippe "for the *next* generation" provides Patek Philippe with financial gain. Finally, an instance of advertising aimed at permeating the whole of society, Patek Philippe's corporate media advertisement inculcates the idea of buying a Patek Philippe "for the *next* generation" as fundamental to Patek Philippe's ideology.

RESEARCH RELATED TO CPD

Research related to CPD is found in three fields of study: the ethnography of communication, organizational studies, and linguistics.

The Ethnography of Communication

The first research to take a critical perspective on power within organiza-tions—examining not only the relationship between discourse and power, but also how that relationship produces, maintains, and reproduces underlying asymmetrical relations of power—was carried out by ethnographers. Two such classical studies are: Burawoy's *Manufacturing Consent: Changes in the Labor Process under Monopoly Capitalism* (1979) and Clegg's *Power, Rule, and Domination* (1975). Based on participant-observer methods, these studies show how relations of power within organizations are reproduced through sets of interpretive frames which workers incorporate in their work to make sense of everyday routines. Another well-known ethnographic study on power within an organization is Rosen's article "You asked for it: Christmas at the bosses' expense" (1988) in which a company's Christmas party is analyzed as an organizational event. The Christmas party, Rosen explains, helped to structure the company's social reality and, in doing so, served to systematically cultivate, enable, and obscure "an underlying network of instrumental relationships."

Organizational Studies

In the 1990s, researchers in the area of organizational studies (in particular human resource management) started to critique the practice of power in organizations through deconstructing words, stories, and text. A powerful stream of research was thus created that aimed to reveal how discourses in organizations "involuntarily undermine their purported assertions" and reappropriate themselves "into a reconfigured web of meanings" (cf. Beaugrande 1997, 65).

Deconstructing the rhetoric of human resource management (HRM), Karen Legge (1995) presents it as a phenomenon largely realized through the language of "tough love," which "glosses the potential tensions between 'external fit' and commitment to 'soft' human resource management values" (p. 90). Legge identifies major groups who have a vested interest in hyping HRM, and shows how, ultimately, language is used to serve "managerial triumphalism" (p. 325). For Sisson (1994, 15) as well, most key words of contemporary HRM (e.g., total quality management, empowerment, employability, team-working, training, development) are nothing but platitudes, tailored to mask the austere reality (doing more with less, making someone else take the risk and responsibility, no employment security, reducing an individual's discretion, manipulation) of a managerial prerogative in the service of capitalism. An expression of concern for the discernible gap between HRM rhetoric and the reality of the organization has been voiced, too, by Gratton and colleagues (1999). While companies believe they have "embraced the tenets of a commitment-based approach" (p. 203), reality experienced by employees, these authors maintain, seems to be the opposite, leading to a perception of increased central control and decreased commitment.

The rhetoric of promise and customer care is the topic of Munro's (1994) case study on rhetoric employed by middle-ranking line managers. According to Munro, such rhetoric is mostly used for an individual's career enhancement. How managers use a rhetoric of "backgrounding" or "highlighting" a team member or "distinctive contributions" to gain potential supporters has also been demonstrated by Storey (1992). Finally, drawing upon a case study of a subsidiary of a large multinational, Francis (2002) has argued for the treatment of HRM as a discoursal potential that can be used by managers to persuade employees to accept a particular worldview.

An activity of the organization often subject to a deconstructionist approach is change (Boje and Dennehy 1994). Knights and Morgan (1991), for example, have suggested strategic management to be an essentially linguistic construct. Dovey (1997) too has described the discourse of transformation as deceptive, masking the true intention of the capitalist elite, which aims to maintain hegemony.

The so called "bottom-up language" of organizational change management, typified by expressions such as "unofficial business," "being parsimonious with the truth," "management by stealth," has attracted much research attention (e.g., Marshak 1993; Ford and Ford 1995; Palmer and Dunford 1996). Bottom-up language of organizational change management, Butcher and Atkinson (2001) have suggested, challenges existing mindsets, instills meaning into the bottom-up approach, and legitimizes and values underground managerial activities "that could be used to better effect." More recently, research into the bottom-up language of organizational change management has expanded to include an understanding of ways in which ideologies are employed by management to construct a reality through the use of specific symbols that, in turn, legitimize and defend change (e.g., Demers, Giroux, and Chreim 2003; Watson 2003). For the first time, the analysis of the entire discourse of an organization has been called for.

Another activity of the organization commonly linked to language and hegemony is total quality management (TQM), a process that generates structures and a culture of quality to pervade the whole of the organization (Legge 1995, 219). The principles of TQM govern not only all working relationships within the organization but also relationships with suppliers and customers. As might be expected, TQM has been linguistically deconstructed by a large number of researchers (e.g., Gee 1990; Gowen 1996; De Cock 1998; Zbaracki 1998; Downs and Eastman 2001) who generally see the discourse of TQM as a tool corporate management uses to hegemonize. TQM discourse, it seems, defines a perspective from which employees, "enchanted by quality discourse" (Gee et al. 1996, 25), view their organizations, their places of work, and their management. Terms such as "self-direction," "empowerment" (Lankshear 1994), "project directors," "team leaders," "facilitators" (Gee 1994), "designers" (Senge 1990), and "partners" (Frank and Hamilton 1993; Gee 1994), it is maintained, create a sense of democracy and individual power, even if they do not exist.

Deconstruction has been done too on the language of global competition which, as Matthews (1998) explains, aims to make globalization desirable by including "teamwork as well as rivalry." The result has been a replacement of the "predatory tropes" of the 1980s, such as "cross-border acquisition," "control," "asset stripping," "making assets sweat," "corporate raiding," and "unbundling," by the "softer, less abrasive images" of the 1990s, such as "alliances," "integration," "networking," "responsiveness," "learning," and "leverage."

Deconstructing corporate mission statements, Mazza (1999) has sought a link between an organization's narrative strategies and its legitimization. Organizations, Mazza has shown, use mission statements to interpret legitimacy as either power or conformity. Where profit and market shares are dominant, the angle of interpretation will be power; where alignment and integration dominate, the angle of interpretation will be conformity (pp. 75–76).

Finally, discourse as both a means of constructing meanings in an organization and a medium through which those meanings can be explored, has prompted several researchers (e.g., Czarniawska 1997; Mumby and Clair 1997; Gabriel 1998, 2000; Humphreys 2002) to interpret the organization as narrative. The basic idea proposed is that stories told with an organization not only provide access to particular aspects of an organization's reality (e.g., corporate identity, an organization's legitimacy and power), but, more important, create that reality.

Linguistics

It was not until the late 1990s that linguists started to give their attention to discourse in organizations. A linguistic research explicitly deconstructing discourse within organizations is the seminal project *Talk at work*, edited by Paul Drew and John Heritage (1998). Bringing together conversation analysis and interaction in institutional settings and joining sociolinguistics and pragmatics with the ethnography of organizations, *Talk at work* insightfully reveals relationships between social contexts and social actions in organizations. Another project addressing linguistic aspects of discourse in organizations is *The Construction of Professional Discourse* (Gunnarsson, Linell, and Nordberg 1997). This project brings together a number of disciplines such as applied linguistics, social psychology, anthropology, and sociology to explore various aspects of the historical development of discourse, the use of discourse in professions, and discourse as a means of social negotiations.

An interesting approach toward researching the discourse of organizations is Fox's (1994, 1997, 1999a, 1999b) corpus-based analysis of management ergolect (ME).[2] The ME corpus consisted of three subcorpora: one compiled from scientific texts on corporate management, one from professional publications in the field of international management, and one from written managerial discourse (media interviews, corporate managers' professional and scientific papers, and corporate reports). Corporate management, Fox showed, employs language, notably key concepts, metaphors, and professionalisms,[3] primarily for sociorhetorical purposes: to create a positive identity of the individual and the group. The key constituents of management ergolect, Fox emphasized, are functional and can be defined only through the agreed objectives of the management community: wealth creation, leadership, corporate identity, and corporate culture.

Other linguistic research possibly involving the discourse of organizations is mainly confined to the role of English as a "lingua franca" (Firth 1990, 1995, 1996), communication patterns within the corporation (Barbara et al. 1996), corporate culture (Nickerson 1998), and cross-cultural aspects of corporate communication (Limaye and Victor 1991; Berger and St John 1993; Holden 1993; Trompenaars 1993; Scollon and Scollon 1995).

Finally, although numerous linguists do view the discourse of organizations as worthy of their attention, the discourse of organizations has yet to be liberated from the fold of Business English, which—being massive, fuzzy, and without an identifiable core grammar and lexis (Dudley-Evans and St John 1998, 65)—seems to be a "movement led more by the offer of teaching materials than scientific research" (St John 1996, 15). For years insisting on the traditional title "Business English," ESL/EFL teaching materials have been drowning issues of the discourse of organizations in business and commercial matters. Not until the end of the 1990s did authors of ESL/EFL textbooks start to show an awareness of the social importance of the discourse of organizations (e.g., Cordell 1999; Crowther-Alwyn 1999; Evans 1999). Emphasizing the sociorhetoric dimensions of communication in organizations, for example, social rituals, social ties, and social power, English for international business has at last moved toward the reality of the organization.

Interfacing Organizational Studies with Linguistics

Focused mainly on the political function of discourse, that is, on how content is subordinated to goals, authors in organizational studies quite correctly see language as a vehicle of reality, as an instrument for realizing personal interests, and as a catalyst for change. However, having their disciplinary base outside linguistics, most of them treat language informally and implicitly. We are not surprised. People are generally inclined to take language for granted and omnisciently express their opinions on linguistic issues. They believe they "know" about language simply "because they use it all the time" (Corder 1973, 21). Such popular theories have been referred to as "informal": they are not explicit and expressed "in a strictly logical form, and consequently may well contain hidden inconsistencies and contradictions." In this sense, all informal theories about language are simply unscientific.

As regards the status of language in organizational studies, little, so it seems, has changed in organizational studies since Holden's (1987) survey of mentions of language topics in a corpus of 463 English-language texts on international management, business, and marketing.[4] A very small proportion of the surveyed texts referred to language issues and none to linguistics as a field of reference. When mentioned, language topics were handled with "perfunctory brevity and frequent ignorance of linguistic fact" (p. 233).

Possibly, the reason why organizational studies have never managed to productively interface with linguistics lies in linguistics being overburdened by a formalism that restrains the integration of linguistic analysis with other disciplines (cf. Fairclough 1999a). Regrettably, linguists are not supplying "models of language" that would enable researchers in organizational studies to turn the "insights of linguists into comprehensible and usable forms" (p. 210). Still, the need to introduce linguistics as a theoretical frame into organizational studies has been articulated by a number of researchers. Cossette (1998), for example, sees language "as a key factor in understanding organizational life." Musson and Cohen (1999) have too emphasized the exigency of including language skills into the management curriculum. More recently, several scholars (e.g., Dhir and Góké-Pariolá 2002; Livesey 2002; Feely and Harzing 2003) have underscored the importance of sociolinguistic theory and critical discourse analysis to organizational studies.

CONCLUSION

The discoursal practice of corporations explored in this book is CPD. Viewed from a language-ideology-power perspective, CPD performs four concurrent functions: institutionalization, legitimization, capitalization, and inculcation of a corporation's ideology. Fundamental to a corporation's ideology is a legitimized idea that constitutes a corporation's capital to secure "positions of possibility."

To date, CPD has not been systematically explored from a language-ideology-power perspective, but then, neither has OD. At the best, there has been some related research into OD—mostly from a deconstructionist perspective—by ethnographers, researchers in organizational studies, and linguists.

To research CPD from a language-ideology-power perspective calls for the integration of theoretical linguistics and other related fields, for example, sociolinguistics, critical discourse analysis, and ethnography of communication into organizational studies, which should enable the development of appropriate models and theories.

NOTES

1. *The Economist*, November 16, 2002, p. 7.

2. Fox adopted the term "ergolect" from Pickett (1989, 5), who had coined it as a more adequate label for "Business English." The use of "management ergolect" offered two advantages: it served both as a generic term for the many facets of the language of management and as a replacement for the traditional linguistic terms "register," "jargon," and "technical language," which were either inadequate or imprecise. "Register" could not be used as, clearly, "management ergolect" is not a language variety "according to use" in a Hallidayan sense, determined by its nature of activity and expressing diversity of social processes, such as the division of labor. Also, some authors (e.g., Quirk 1968; Trudgill 1988; Hudson 1998) use the term "register" in the sense of style or jargon, which renders it imprecise. "Jargon," on the other hand, often carries negative connotations (Warner 1962; Quirk 1968; Leech 1981). Finally, "technical language" is primarily related to specific communicational needs of a particular industry (e.g., automotive, pharmaceutical, banking) and excludes the social and situational dimension of the language user.

3. Professionalisms, known too as "corporate graffiti" and "business buzzwords," are words of self-description used by people in organizations to refer to persons, objects, phenomena, and circumstances of the corporate world (Fox 1996, 1999a; cf. also Johnson 1990). Mainly metaphoric (e.g., "bear hug"—domination of a partner company, "shark"—a predator company in a hostile takeover, "killer bee"—an advisor who helps a company to fight off a takeover, "skunkworks"—

flexible work arrangement providing creative workers 24-hour access to their workplace, "take no prisoners"—leaving business competitors dead, not wounded), professionalisms constitute a body of images people in organizations use to communicate within the corporate environment.

  4. Checking a number of representative sources on management and organizational studies (e.g., de Bono 1985; Enz 1986; Peters and Austin 1986; Dorfman and Howell 1988; Evans and Russel 1990; Hui 1990; Cohen, Fink, Gadon, Willits and Josefowitz 1992; Bateman and Zeithaml 1993; Dickson, Saunders, and Stringer 1993; Weihrich and Koontz 1993; Ivancevich, Lorenzi, and Skinner 1994; Punnett and Shenkar 1996; Reichheld 1996; Basi 1998; Kanter 2001; Young 2001; Schermerhorn, Hunt, and Osborn 2002; Shenkar and Luo 2002; McKern 2003), we found them to decidedly underline the importance of communication to an organization, yet disregard language issues.

3

A Corporation's Ideology

Ideological power, the power to project one's practices as universal and "common sense." is a significant complement to economic and political power . . .

—*N. Fairclough (1999b, 33)*

A TOTAL CORPORATE COMMUNICATIONS APPROACH

Traditionally, corporate identity was understood as simply a benefit to the corporation. Today, corporate identity is understood as an essential strategic management tool applied both internally and externally (e.g., Balmer 1993, 1997, 1998; Marwick and Fill 1997; Morison 1997; Gray and Balmer 1998; Balmer and Wilson 1998; Gioia et al. 2000; Balmer and Greyser 2003). Corporate identity is now seen as a "reality and uniqueness" (Balmer and Gray 2000, 256) of an organization integrally related to its image through corporate communication, which forms a "nexus" between an organization's identity and its strategic objectives (p. 260).

The inseparability of corporate identity, corporate communication, corporate image, and corporate reputation has been captured in a total corporate communications approach "whereby everything an organization says, makes and does is seen to communicate" (p. 260). Such an understanding of corporate identity, Balmer and Gray argue, has been further legitimized and promoted by the formation of the International Corporate Identity Group (ICIG) and their issuance of "The Strathclyde Statement" (p. 262):

Every organisation has an identity. It articulates the corporate ethos, aims and values and presents a sense of individuality that can help to differentiate the organisation within its competitive environment.

When well managed, corporate identity can be a powerful means of integrating the many disciplines and activities essential to an organisation's success. It can also provide the visual cohesion necessary to ensure that all corporate communications are coherent with one another and result in an image consistent with the organisation's defining ethos and character.

By effectively managing its corporate identity an organisation can build understanding and commitment among diverse stakeholders. This can manifest in an ability to attract and retain customers and employees, achieve strategic alliances, gain the support of financial markets and generate a sense of direction and purpose. Corporate identity is a strategic issue.

Corporate identity differs from traditional brand marketing since it is concerned with all an organisation's stakeholders and the multi-faceted way in which an organisation communicates.

Defining a corporation's identity as an articulation of an organization's "values," as that which differentiates "the organization within its competitive environment," and as a strategic issue to "build understanding and commitment among diverse stakeholders," the Strathclyde Statement unquestionably views a corporation's identity as a "social" or "group" identity, rather than as a "personal" identity. Whereas group identity is governed more by identification processes related to group membership, personal identity is governed by personal experiences and biography.

From a language-ideology-power perspective, the Strathclyde Statement's understanding of a corporation's identity as a group identity is important for one reason: projecting a corporation's identity as a shared representation of ideas, it equates a corporation's identity with a corporation's ideology. As van Dijk argues (2000, 120), a group shares not only knowledge, attitudes, and ideology, but also a "social representation" that defines its identity or "'social self' as a group." Thus, a group, van Dijk further argues, equates its identity with its ideology.

SHELL'S IDEOLOGY

Over the past decade, a number of corporations have used a total corporate communications approach to construct their ideologies. One such corporation is Shell. Conspicuously exposed through the mass media, Shell's ideology encompasses the whole globe. It is institutionalized, for example, in Shell's corporate media advertisements shown on satellite and cable channels, including CNN, BBC World, Star World and Star News, Eurosport, ESPN, CNBC, and the Discovery Channel. A Shell corporate media advertisement "Profits and Principles" is regularly placed too in *National Geographic*.[1]

To describe Shell's ideology, we explore Royal Dutch/Shell's statement of objectives taken from the corporation's report "People, Planet, and Profits":

The objectives of the Royal Dutch/Shell Group of Companies are to engage efficiently, responsibly and profitably in the oil, gas, chemicals and other selected businesses and participate in the research and development of other sources of energy. Shell companies are committed to contribute to sustainable development.[2]

To state its objectives, Shell used the verbs "engage," "participate," and "commit." Stating those objectives, Shell revealed its beliefs, attitudes, and emotions.

Shell's beliefs originate in the knowledge and experience of relations among objects, attributes, and benefits. Objects are the places, persons, or things about which Shell holds beliefs. The object of Shell's belief is a sustainable environment. Attributes are the characteristics or features that an object may or may not have. An attribute of a sustainable environment is wellness. Benefits are the outcomes that attributes may provide. A benefit of a healthy environment is an improved quality of life.

Shell's attitude is the way Shell thinks, feels, and behaves about objects, attributes, and benefits. It is closely linked to Shell's behavior and the corporation's interaction with the world symbolized in Shell's commitment to sustainability.

Finally, Shell's emotions are the instinctual motivations and responses accompanying its activities. Shell expresses its emotions through the phrase "committed to," which signals not only a decision to do something, but also an intent of letting people know about the decision. Generally co-occurring with words referring to something good, necessary, and desirable, the phrase "committed to" invites approval independent of the actual *nature* of the commitment.

Why did Shell decide to build its ideology on a commitment to sustainable development? Because, as a corporation engaged in the oil, gas, and chemicals business, Shell has to build sustainability into everything it does. In the late 1980s, it was already clear that the rhetoric of sustainable development provided an elegant solution for global corporations confronted with the environmental challenge and held responsible for the ecological crisis (Sklair 2000).

The breakthrough in persuading the world to view the environment as global came in 1992 at the Rio Earth Summit, which institutionalized the concept "sustainability" and helped replace the idea of "conservation" by the idea of "sustainable growth." Clearly, this new perspective well suited global corporations, which felt threatened by increasingly pressing environmental groups. Since the Rio Earth Summit, sustainability has been treated as a leading global value founded on the basic assumptions of the preciousness of nature. In July 2000, the United Nations Secretary-General Kofi Annan invited leading companies to join the Global Compact Initiative to create an environment of responsible business. Presently, the Global Compact has about 1,400 members.

Unquestionably, Shell knew of the basic assumptions behind global sustainable development: Nature is precious and fragile, and nature is threatened by both science and the global marketplace; therefore, nature has to be protected.

It was in 1997 that the Royal Dutch/Shell Group publicly committed itself to operating in a manner consistent with sustainable development and for the first time institutionalized the corporation's commitment to sustainability. Today Shell's commitment to sustainability is incorporated into every aspect of the corporation, including capital allocation, technology ranking, and contractor selection.

To show how Shell employs its commitment to sustainability as social, symbolic, cultural, and economic capital, we refer to the corporation's 2001 annual report "Shell in the United States."[3] Used as social capital, Shell's commitment to sustainability legitimizes Steven L. Miller's social positions as chairman, president and chief executive officer, enunciated in his letter introductory to the annual report. Some 14 references to Shell's commitment to sustainability are made by CEO Miller. Employed as symbolic capital, Shell's commitment to sustainability legitimizes Shell's corporate culture, which is linked to sustainability through references to Shell "employees regularly teaming up with other volunteers to build houses with Habitat for Humanity" (p. 16). Employed as cultural capital, Shell's commitment to sustainability legitimizes Shell's expert cooperation with the California state government in developing (sustainable) methanol-fuelled vehicles (p. 10). Last, employed as economic capital, Shell's commitment to sustainability legitimizes socially responsible investments in Royal Dutch/Shell, rated first in the energy sector 2001 of the global Dow Jones Sustainability Index (p. 7).

As we have shown, Shell's CPD, just as Patek Philippe's CPD, performs four concurrent functions:

1. Institutionalization of Shell's commitment to sustainability as an idea fundamental to the corporation's ideology.
2. Legitimization of this idea through the social value "sustainability."
3. Capitalization of Shell's commitment to sustainability as a legitimized and institutionalized idea fundamental to the corporation's ideology.
4. Inculcation of Shell's ideology.

Permeating the whole of the corporation (and its environment), Shell's ideology offers Shell great benefits. "Conclusive, complex and consistent" (Brunsson 1986, 30), Shell's ideology provides a good basis for managerial action. It, for example, reduces the ambiguity of situations within Shell, solving a great part of the choice problem and enabling Shell's management to concentrate on performance. It also constitutes Shell's potential to govern the selection principles of social norms and values, as well as, to use van Dijk's (1996, 177) term, the "structural organization of social representations" within Shell. But most important, the potential of Shell's ideology to legitimize Shell's power holders, makes it, as Weber (1918/1968) has argued, the leading component of employees' motivation. Needless to say, Shell's ideology, like other corporate ideologies, is a part of the ideology of the dominant bloc,[4] which, treating social hierarchies as natural, justifies status differences inherent to an essentially hegemonic, capitalist logic of efficiency (Bendix 1956).

ORGANIZATIONAL POLITICS

Within organizational studies, a corporation's ideology is treated as a domain of organizational politics. Although numerous authors have researched the political nature of organizations (e.g., Fligstein and Freeland 1995; Fligstein and Mara-Drita 1996; Davies, Schoorman, and Donaldson 1997; Ghoshal and Bartlett 1998; Fleischer et al. 2002) and persistently emphasized the importance of such research, the political constitution of organizations remains one of the few underdeveloped topics in organizational theory (Alvarez 1999). In the past often described as "back-stabbing" and an "instrument of self-interest and turf-wars," organizational politics is now increasingly seen as essential for effective management and "synonymous with managerial adeptness" (Butcher and Clarke 1999, 9). If used in a principled way and in the interest of an organization, organizational politics, it is maintained, is an asset rather than a liability.

It was Robert Michels who in his book *Political Parties: A Sociological Study of the Oligarchical Tendencies of Modern Democracy* (1915) first viewed management as a locus of power and as the most crucial level at which political behavior within the organization emerges. However, not until the 1960s, when, focusing on interdepartmental politics, Cyert and March (1963) developed a behavioral theory of the firm (for research into departmental power in organizations see Crozier 1964; Pfeffer and Salancik 1978; Bacharach and Lawler 1980), did organizational politics start to receive systematic research attention. According to Cyert and March, an organization can not be properly understood unless both formal and informal relations of power are taken into account.

Cyert and March's theory served too as the basis for a "garbage can" model in decision making, developed by Cohen, March, and Olsen (1971). Managerial decisions, these authors claimed, result from a complex interaction between four independent streams of events: problems, solutions, participants, and choice opportunities. Because of the independent nature of these events, they interact randomly. The result is "a collection of choices looking for problems, issues and feelings looking for decision situations in which they might be aired, solutions looking for issues to which they might be the answer, and decision makers looking for work" (p. 2). The "garbage can" model suggests decision making to be anything but a rational, nonpolitical process.

For Eccles and Nohria (1992), the essence of management is contained in principles of "robust action" consisting of a lack of certitude, a need for flexibility, political ability, a sense of timing, good judgment, use of rhetoric, and working multiple agendas. These principles suggest that gaining other parties' cooperation is mainly founded on a manager's political and rhetorical skills. Highlighting the importance of empathy, Fligstein (1997) too stresses the political dimension of the organization. In Fligstein's view, the competency of empathy surpasses the ability to relate to others, relying instead mainly on developing participants' identities in line with a desired course of action. Again, Fligstein emphasizes a repertoire of political skills, such as interpreting reality for the group, networking, building alliances, and display-ing power in the belief that the appearance of power will generate power itself.

Although all of these authors do provide insight into the political constitu-tion of organizations, that insight fails to go beyond simplistic descriptions of actors' political skills. Very likely, the reason for this is their not having grasped the true role of language in organizations. Political action within organizations, which is simply the practice of power through consent, is not created through a repertoire of political and rhetorical skills (which, admit-tedly, are important), but through an ideology. And because the receptacle of ideology is language, the only way to explain the political constitution of organizations is through an exploration of organizational discourse from a language-ideology-power perspective.

CONCLUSION

Shell's corporate ideology is successful for two reasons. First, it is inculcated in Shell's stakeholders through a total corporate communications approach. Second, it meets stakeholders' expectations of Shell as an oil company com-mitted to sustainable development and, in doing so, encourages their cooper-ation. In this sense, Shell's ideology constitutes an interactive model of com-munication in which both the sender (Shell) and the receiver (Shell's stakeholders) simultaneously participate in the construction of Shell's ideol-ogy. More precisely, Shell not only produces its ideology, it also partly receives it. Vice versa, Shell's stakeholders not only receive Shell's ideology, they also partly produce it. As the "sender," Shell has the big advantage of not only being able to choose how to present its ideology to receivers, but also to define receivers' understanding of that ideology. Shell's resource to do this is CPD.

NOTES

1. Over 40 transnationals (among which are American Express, BMW UK, British Petroleum, Canon, Carlsberg, Honda, Kosta Boda, Patek Philippe, Rolex, Texas Instruments, Toyota, and UBS) are advertising partners of *National Geo-graphic*. Their help, as *National Geographic* tells its readers, "makes possible the National Geographic Society's mission of education, exploration and research."

2. The Shell report "People, Planet, and Profits," 2000, at www.shell.com/shell-report.

3. At www.shell.com/home/royal-en/downloads/shell_report.

4. Overstating its "proven" petroleum reserves, about which Shell's stakehold-ers learned in January 2004, Shell's management went against that ideology.

4

CPD's Nomenclature

Language has to interpret the whole of our experience, reducing the indefinitely varied phenomena of the world around us, and also of the world inside us, the processes of our own consciousness, to a manageable number of classes of phenomena: types of processes, events and actions, classes of objects, people and institutions, and the like.

—*M. A. K. Halliday (1978, 21)*

A PUBLIC STATEMENT

To perform its four concurrent functions—institutionalization, legitimization, capitalization, and inculcation of Shell's ideology—Shell's statement of objectives was placed in the public sphere, that is, in Shell's report "People, Planet, and Profits." There is an interdependence between Shell's statement of objectives and Shell, in the sense that the statement positions Shell and, vice versa, Shell positions the statement in relation to an objective world in which Shell intervenes. Anything can serve as a corporate public statement: corporate architecture, office furniture, or dress code, as well as CPD.

Assuming a material form, a corporate public statement becomes an artifact. Whether physical, visual or written, corporate artifacts are much more than "rational solutions to comprehensible problems" (cf. Brain 1995, 193). They are profoundly social in the sense that they both reflect and engage social context. Corporate artifacts are made by human beings, they act as representatives for human beings, and shape human behavior. People accept artifacts because artifacts position them and their actions in a social context and ensure, to a certain extent, the reproduction of circumstances that made that action possible (Bourdieu 1990).

All artifacts undergo a process of stabilization that results in a final definition of an artifact's content and form, and approximately guarantees its success (Bijker and Pinch 1987). An artifact's content and form embody a practical sense, which is a part of the habitus: a set of "mental or cognitive structures through which people deal with the social world" (Bourdieu 1989, 18). Habitus is not only a "structuring structure" but also a "structured structure": It both structures the social world and is structured by the social world (Bourdieu 1977). As a product of a specific set of living conditions embodying social roles and relationships, habitus is a force that organizes both social practices and people's perception of those practices. A part of the habitus, artifacts maintain and reproduce the circumstances that made them possible. Thus, it may be justifiably assumed that as Shell's reports "People, Planet, and Profits" and "Shell in the United States" stabilized in content and form, they helped stabilize the social field in which they were produced, the practices that produced them, and the social relations implied in their production and use.

THE CPD COMMUNICATIVE EVENT

A corporate public statement constitutes a communicative event, which is the basic unit of CPD. A CPD communicative event includes CPD, its participants, and the environment of CPD's production and reception, "including its historical and cultural association" (cf. Swales 1991, 46). A CPD communicative event is strategic (fundamental to the formulation and implementation of a corporation's ideology), preplanned (a product of a corporation's network of formal communication), and recorded (tangible, consistent, and public). A CPD communicative event's formalization defines options and implies the possibility of a stricter social control of the communicative event.

A CPD communicative event is driven by a set of communicative purposes or communicative objectives, which, along with the nature of the statement, situational context, and social relations between participants, determine the schematic structure of the event and constrain choice of content and style. A CPD communicative event has two communicative purposes: general and specific. The general communicative purpose defines the goal of the event, while the specific communicative purpose defines its content. The general communicative purpose is common to all CPD communicative events, whereas the specific communicative purpose is particular to a CPD communicative event. The general communicative purpose of a CPD communicative event is to enable the practice of (a corporation's) power through consent.

The specific communicative purpose of a corporation's mission statement is to state the corporation's reason for existence. The specific communicative purpose of a corporation's annual report is to document the actions taken by a corporation to meet economic, environmental, and social responsibilities. The specific communicative purpose of a corporation's statement of general business principles is to discern fundamental principles that govern a corporation's conduct of its affairs. The specific communicative purpose of a corporation's business guidelines is to advise employees on desirable behaviors within a corporation. The specific communicative purpose of a corporation's media advertisement is to sell a corporation's products/services. The specific communicative purpose of a corporation's philosophy of operations is to define a corporation's relationships with customers, employees, shareholders, and communities. Finally, the specific communicative purpose of a CEO's media interview is to paint the CEO's vision of the corporation.[1]

THE CPD GENRE

A class of CPD communicative events sharing the same specific communicative purpose constitutes a CPD genre that redefines a CPD communicative event at a higher level of abstraction and relates the CPD communicative event to other corporate CPD events in the same class.

A genre is a social construct. It is a product of human action, which is inevitably self-conscious and enormously diverse. Throughout the history of civilization, a variety of genres, for example, administrative, scientific and literary, emerged to satisfy various social needs. As society developed and communicational needs became increasingly diverse, these fundamental genres evolved to meet those needs. The administrative genre evolved into legal, personal, diplomatic, and business genres. The scientific genre evolved into academic and popular scientific genres. And the literary genre evolved into prose, poetry, and drama genres. Contemporary society is characterized by an ever-growing number of new genres.

The concept of a CPD genre—a functional category "assigned on the basis of use rather than on the basis of form" (cf. Biber 1991, 170)—provides corporate management with a socially recognized frame for realizing communicative purposes. More exactly, through CPD genres corporate management constrains a communicative event to overtly indicate a communicative intention (cf. Swales and Feak 2000, 7; Grabe and Kaplan 1997, 211).

A CPD genre may be highly frequent (e.g., corporate news), periodical (e.g., corporate annual reports), or comparatively infrequent (e.g., corporate mission statements). Corporations naturally generate a diversity of communicative events to meet specific communicative purposes, which fosters the emergence of new CPD genres. Certain CPD genres such as the corporate mission statement, the corporate annual report, and the corporate business guidelines, have become stabilized in content and form. We refer to these genres as CPD default genres.

LANGUAGE

Patek Philippe's media advertisement and Shell's statement of objectives were able to perform their four concurrent functions owing to the unique qualities of the medium they used. Language is the most important human sign system and the "fundamental human mass medium . . . through which all other media speak" (Schudson 1995, 29). Unlike other sign systems, language, Berger and Luckmann (1991, 52) remind us, can become an "objective repository of vast accumulations of meaning and experience, which it can then preserve in time and transmit to following generations." Not only does language construct abstract symbols, it also "brings them back" and presents them as "objectively real elements in everyday life" (p. 55). Through language "an entire world can be actualized at any moment" (p. 54).

The ability of language to construct symbols and relate them to society assigns it a number of roles: ideational, textual, personal, interpersonal, contextual, processing, and aesthetic (Biber 1991, 33–36; cf. also Halliday 1978; Jakobson 1960). The ideational role of language refers to its propositional content: the selection of facts. The facts contained in Shell's statement of objectives state the reasons for the existence of Shell. The textual role of language relates to the "packaging" of facts; it marks focus and creates cohesion (the connection of words within a sequence). A property of an entity and therefore objective, cohesion supports coherence (connectivity of underlying content), which is a facet of an audience's evaluation of an entity and therefore subjective (cf. Beaugrande and Dressler 1981; Hoey 1991). Expressing Shell's beliefs, attitudes, and emotions, Shell's statement of objectives creates a focus for stakeholders. Through its precision and brevity, it attains cohesion. The personal role of language marks group membership and attitudes toward facts. Used as a banner behind which the whole corporation aligns, Shell's statement of objectives performs a personal role. The interpersonal role of language marks role relationships and attitudes toward participants. Shell's statement of objectives, by definition, is an invitation to stakeholders for cooperation. The contextual role of language marks setting, purpose, and scene. In the case of Shell's statement of objectives, the context was the report "People, Planet, and Profits." The processing role of language concerns production- and comprehension-related requirements of a corporation's communicative event. Shell's statement of objectives, for example, requires a stakeholder's knowledge about sustainability. The aesthetic role of language relates to the addressor's and addressee's attitudes and preferences about language, style, and expected rhetorical effect. Shell's statement of objectives both follows standard patterns (a generally accepted configuration of linguistic, stylistic, and rhetorical features) and develops a distinctive, Shell-specific language [to engage efficiently, responsibly and profitably . . . participate in the research and development of . . . committed to . . . sustainable development] to communicate Shell's ideology. Visually, Shell's statement of objectives was made prominent by its positioning (at the top of the report's inside cover page), choice of font, and bold type.

A CONCEPT

While accessing meanings in a corporation's CPD, stakeholders rely on a shallow layer of knowledge, which is "carefully and projectibly defined"

(Dahlgren 1992, 196) and is held in concepts and propositions. Concepts are "prototypes, i.e. clear typical cases," for example, "tradition" and "sustainability." Propositions are carefully worded statements, for example, "Shell companies are committed to contribute to sustainable development." Most of the time, concepts and propositions are close enough to the truth to make reference possible. Both concepts and propositions give stability to people's shared world knowledge.

A concept is not a word. Although links between words and concepts are conventional, the existence of a concept is not (Lyons 1978, 110). All languages and language varieties possess words for concepts formed through direct observation. When confronted with a particular expression, language users tend to activate approximately the same cognitive content: a configuration of knowledge, which can be recovered "with more or less unity and consistency in the mind" (Beaugrande and Dressler 1981, 4). This focus on relevant data, which "converge into interobjectivity among experiences with the same object" (Beaugrande 1997, 91), is a concept (Figure 4.1).

A concept consists of elements of knowledge that, in varying degrees, contribute to its identity. Elements essential to the very identity of the concept constitute determinate knowledge. Elements true for most but not all instances of the concept constitute typical knowledge. Elements that happen to be true of random instances constitute accidental knowledge (Beaugrande and Dressler 1981, 85–86). People define concepts through combinations of elements of knowledge. For example, when ABB CEO Percy Barnevik in his *Harvard Business Review* interview "The Logic of Global Business" (Taylor 1991, 90–105) said

Global managers are made, not born. This is not a natural process. We are herd animals. We like people who are like us. . . . Naturally, as a CEO, I set the tone for the company's management style. With my Anglo-Saxon education and Swedish upbringing, I have a certain way of doing things.[2]

he conceptualized a global manager through typical knowledge [Global managers are made, not born. . . .We are herd animals.], determinate knowledge [I set the tone for the company's management style. . . . I have a certain way of doing things.], and accidental knowledge [With my Anglo-Saxon education and Swedish upbringing]. Conceptualizing a global manager as a configuration of knowledge, CEO Barnevik gave stability to his and his stakeholders' shared world knowledge.

Figure 4.1
A Concept

TEXT

The linguistic product of a CPD communicative event is text, which can consist of anything from one word to hundreds of words. Our understanding of text is built on professor de Beaugrande's ideas about language, text, and discourse, developed in his book *New Foundations for a Science of Text and Discourse* (1997). According to Beaugrande, it is essential to view text as a communicative event "wherein linguistic, cognitive and social actions converge, and not just as a sequence of words that were uttered or written" (p. 10).

To be described as a convergence of linguistic, cognitive, and social actions, text needs to be thought of as a text-world model: "the total array of knowledge" (Beaugrande 1997: 128) activated while processing a text. Thought of as a text-world model, text gives information about entities, states, events[3] and processes. An entity (e.g., the corporation, the CEO, stakeholders) has identity and properties and is capable of participating in a process of which the basic premise is a state. A state represents a stage in the evolution of an entity. A change from one state to another is an event. A process is connected to cognitive and social knowledge about how events happen or who does what (Figure 4.2).

Within a state, the entity stands in relation to its environment and possesses properties inherent to the entity—attributes, and properties derived from attitudinal judgments about the entity—values. In an event, an entity is either agentive or affected. The agentive entity is a force-possessing entity that, by performing an action, creates change and affects other entities. The affected entity (a target) is an entity whose situation is changed by an event or action in which it is neither an agent nor an instrument (Beaugrande and Dressler 1981, 95).

If Shell's statement of objectives is viewed as a text-world model, Shell will be seen as an entity engaged in a state, or, rather, an entity standing in relationship to its environment. Shell possesses attributes and values. The event Shell is engaged in is sustainable development: Shell is an agentive entity affecting a target entity—the environment.

To provide a perspective on processes within the text-world model, Beaugrande (1997, 196) offers a scheme of discourse processes made up of categories and subcategories. The categories (and their subcategories) should not, however, be seen as neat and distinct. Rather, because a functional description of language is always nondeterministic (p. 207), the categories are built around "prototypical verbs" and their "favored collocations." In this sense, a

Figure 4.2
States and Events

$$State_1 \ldots State_2 (Event_1) \ldots State_3 (Event_2) \ldots State_4 (Event_3) \ldots State_n (Event_{n-1})$$
$$\xrightarrow{\hspace{4cm}}$$
$$Change$$

functional categorization of language, covering the seemingly unlimited possibilities of authentic discourse, is much more flexible than a traditional grammatical categorization. The gains of adopting a functional approach toward language that allows processes in the text-world model to be linked with social knowledge and everyday life are invaluable.

Beaugrande distinguishes among four main categories of discourse processes: endocentric, exocentric, representative, and expressive. Endocentric discourse processes relate to an entity's "mental" or "data-based activities" and include: perceptive processes representing sensory actions (prototypical verbs: see, watch, listen); cognitive discourse processes, which are performed whenever "knowledge is attained, stored, recovered, used" (prototypical verbs: know, find out, hear, learn); and volitional discourse processes involving wanting and doing (prototypical verbs: want, hope).

Exocentric discourse processes usually have a target, an affected entity, and include dispositive discourse processes, which are conspicuously obtrusive with an agent directly affecting a target (prototypical verbs: do, make, give); productive discourse processes, resulting in an entity that did not previously exist (prototypical verbs: create, manufacture, build); enactive discourse processes, whereby an initiator "consciously engages in an obtrusive self-centred activity rather than disposing over or producing another entity" (Beaugrande 1997, 218) (prototypical verbs are those relating to self-directed corporeal behavior: blow [a nose], yawn, cough), and developmental discourse processes in which an entity becomes or changes (prototypical verbs: grow, get, become). Endocentric discourse processes and exocentric discourse processes are the two most important categories of discourse process in Beaugrande's scheme. Exocentric discourse processes, for example, are exclusive to Shell's statement of objectives, which stresses Shell's productive role to "engage," "participate," and "contribute."

The third category of discourse processes, representative discourse processes, is connected not with events and actions, as in the case of exocentric discourse processes, but with the states and relations of entities. Representative discourse processes express identity and connectedness in terms of "properties, relations or significance" (p. 197) and include existential discourse processes, expressing the existence of an entity (prototypical clause core: there + be /is/); circumstantial discourse processes, relating to circumstances, especially weather (prototypical clause core: it + be /is/was); identification and attribution discourse processes, in which "the subject identity is identified" (p. 222) (prototypical use: definitions) followed by a listing of the subject identity's attributes; evaluative discourse processes evaluating the relative merits of an entity to an attitude; and possessive discourse processes, delimiting possession (prototypical verbs: own, have). Marked by the verbs "own" and "look after," Patek Philippe's corporate media advertisement is a typical example of a possessive discourse process.

The final categories of Beaugrande's scheme of discourse processes are expressive discourse processes that externalize inner states and include emotive discourse processes and semiotic discourse processes. Emotive discourse processes express the outward inner feelings of a feeler (prototypical verb: feel + sad/angry/happy . . .). Semiotic discourse processes are either activity-centered, in which case they foreground behavior (prototypical verbs: talk, speak), or message-centered (often including quotation marks), in which case they foreground communication (prototypical verbs: say, tell).

Viewed as a text-world model, a text, evidently, is much more than a collection of words. It is a collection of interconnected data drawing upon a person's store of experience and knowledge, which are organized through a set of basic postulates: identity, connectedness, temporality and locality, observability, dimensionality, and predictability (Beaugrande 1997, 80). These postulates are founded on the premise that "the world must be 'knowable' and 'experienceable' if it is to be 'known' and 'experienced', and vice-versa—things must have identity to be identified, observability to be observed, and vice-versa. Otherwise, humans couldn't attain a convergence among data and a consensus among observers" (pp. 80–81).

THE LEXICOGRAMMAR

The text-world model is related to a text through the lexicogrammar: a unity of lexical and grammatical resources. The term "lexicogrammar" was created by systemic functional linguists (notably Halliday 1978) who rejected the traditional, formalist division between grammar and lexis. In Hallidayan terms, the lexicogrammar represents a "form level" of language, which acts "as the integrative system," taking configurations from all the components of the semantics and combining them "to form multilayered, 'polyphonic' structural compositions" (p. 134).

CONCLUSION

Establishing a nomenclature—a set of hierarchically positioned and systematically named units—is a first step in our exploration of CPD. The basic unit of CPD is a CPD communicative event: a strategic, preplanned, and recorded act of communication driven by a general communicative purpose and a specific communicative purpose. The general communicative purpose of a CPD communicative event is the construction of a corporation's ideology to enable the corporation to practice power through consent. A specific communicative purpose regulates the ideational content of a CPD communicative event. A class of CPD communicative events sharing the same specific communicative purpose constitutes a CPD genre. The linguistic expression of a CPD communicative event is text, which is a unity of linguistic, cognitive, and social actions. Text is related to a corporation through the text-world model. The text-world model is related to text through the lexicogrammar.

NOTES

1. The CEO's vision has to be articulated over and over again. As CEO Tom Jermoluk of @Home once put it: "At least 50% of my job is being evangelist—with our employees, the Street, the press, my partners. There are up times and down

times, but it's keeping everybody believing that there really is a pot of gold at the end of this rainbow—I don't mean in a money sense, I mean in the accomplishment of the vision" (Colvin 1999, 43).

2. *Harvard Business Review*, March-April 1991, p. 95.

3. "Event" as a part of the text-world model should not be confused with a communicative event that belongs to the real world.

5

CPD as Capital

Knowledge of the social world and, more precisely, the categories that
make it possible are the stakes par excellence of political struggle, the inex-
tricably theoretical and practical struggle for the power to conserve or
transform the social world by conserving or transforming the categories
through which it is perceived. . . .This work of categorization, i.e., of making explicit and of classification, is performed incessantly, at every
moment of ordinary existence, in the struggles in which agents clash over
the meaning of the social world and their position within it.
—*P. Bourdieu (1985, 729)*

IBM'S CPD

To show how a corporation uses its CPD as a medium of social, symbolic, cultural, and economic capital, we turn to the corporation IBM. The beginnings
of IBM date back to 1915 and the Computing-Tabulating-Recording Company,
which in 1924 Thomas J. Watson, Jr., president of the company, renamed International Business Machines. In a booklet titled *A Business and its Beliefs: The
Ideas That Helped Build IBM*, published in 1963, Watson, then chairman of the
board of IBM, wrote: "I believe that if an organization is to meet the challenges
of a changing world, it must be prepared to change everything about itself
except those (basic) beliefs" (Schmidt 1995, 85). Today, IBM is one of the
world's largest information technology companies, covering 150 countries
worldwide and employing over 300,000 people. The corporation is known too
for its CEOs, who have become landmarks in the corporate world. One very
famous former CEO of IBM is Lou Gerstner.

CEO GERSTNER'S MEDIA INTERVIEW

Discussing the state of IBM and where the corporation is headed, CEO Gerstner in an IBM employee bulletin *THINK* interview said:

It comes back to win, execute, and team. Those are not slogans or even institutional values. They are personal commitments. They're not things of the head, they're things of the heart and the gut. They are behavioral, not intellectual. You do not get up every morning and salute them. You get up every morning and live them. We have completed, for the most part, the task of restructuring the institution. Our success now is going to be a function of personal behavior—the behavior of each and every one of us. We can't fix it with systems anymore.[1]

In spite of his claim "Those are not slogans or even institutional values," CEO Gerstner was stating IBM's values and defining what was important/unimportant, right/wrong, and good/bad for IBM. CEO Gerstner's statement is founded mostly on representative discourse processes, such as identifying, attributing, and evaluating, marked by the verbs "be" and "have." Through these representative processes he reveals his beliefs, attitudes, and emotions, which are very obviously about IBM's commitment to success.

In CEO Gerstner's statement, IBM's commitment to success is a configuration of knowledge (a concept) framed by two strategically positioned points of reference: the phrase "win, execute and team" in the first sentence and "Our success now" in the last but one sentence. These two points of reference are connected to the rest of the text through the lexical ties "those," "they," and "them," which make the text cohesive and predispose stakeholders to find underlying meanings and relations mutually accessible and relevant. Defining IBM's commitment to success, CEO Gerstner called upon the American Dream—a system of beliefs in individualism, achievement, the free-enterprise system, and freedom from controls. An institutionalized value of American culture, the American Dream legitimizes IBM's commitment to success.

Once legitimized, IBM's commitment to success became a capital which CEO Gerstner could use to secure "positions of possibility." CEO Gerstner's frequent and combinatorial use of the personal pronouns "we" and "I" and the possessive adjective "our," which signify relationships between himself, IBM and IBM's stakeholders, suggests CEO Gerstner to have employed his interview to use IBM's commitment to success as social capital. In other words, CEO Gerstner employed his interview to legitimize both his position as IBM's CEO and the underlying social structure of that position.

IBM'S MISSION STATEMENT

A commitment to success is also a (legitimized) idea fundamental to IBM's mission statement:

At IBM, we strive to lead in the creation, development and manufacture of the industry's most advanced information technologies, including computer systems, software, networking systems, storage devices and microelectronics. We translate these advanced technologies into value for our customers through our professional solutions and services businesses worldwide.[2]

This statement employs exclusively productive discourse processes marked by the verbs "strive," "create," and "translate" and the nouns "creation," "development," and "manufacture." Just as the social value *success* legitimized IBM's commitment to success in CEO Gerstner's interview, so too does it legitimize IBM's commitment to success in the corporation's mission statement.

A mission statement, it is known, is linked to corporate culture as both an impetus to and a reflection of a corporation's cultural values. Cultures, Schein (1985) has suggested in his model of levels of culture and their interaction, are manifested on three levels: artifacts and creations, values, and basic assumptions. Artifacts and creations (e.g., IBM's mission statement as a document) are visible. Values (verbalized in IBM's mission statement through productive discourse processes) are testable. Basic assumptions (in IBM's mission statement, that which gives legitimacy to IBM's cultural values, e.g., the American Dream) are invisible, preconscious, and taken for granted. Thus, IBM's mission statement, we believe, was used as symbolic capital to legitimize the corporation's culture. The mission statement's inclusive "we" defines all employees as responsible for that culture.

IBM'S ANNUAL REPORT

An example of IBM employing its commitment to success as cultural capital to legitimize its expertise is found on the first page of the corporation's 1999 annual report:

We're not changing our name. Just everything else.
And we're not the only ones.
Millions of enterprises aren't waiting for a revolution.
And they aren't just watching one either.
The revolution has arrived.
With stunning speed, it has swept all of us into a new
kind of economy and a new kind of society.
A world of new mindsets and new ambitions, to be sure.
But also a world where time-honored assets—customer
relationships, smart people, deft strategy—still matter.
This is the world of e-business.
It is a world where everyone looks both new and familiar.
Where any company and every company is a dot-com.
e-business is here. We're never going back.[3]

Through a rhetorical play of "rheme," or previously unknown, highly informative content [We're not changing. . . . Millions of. . . . With stunning speed. . . . It is a world . . .], and "theme," or known, low informative content [And we're not the only ones. The revolution has arrived. This is the world of e-business. e-business is here. We're never going back.], IBM defines its understanding of achieving success within the context of e-business. Just as CEO Gerstner's interview and IBM's mission statement work, so too does IBM's corporate annual report.

The rhetorical statement of a refusal to change IBM's name and a promise to honor traditional IBM values (customer relationships, smart people, deft strategy) is another idea: tradition, constitutive to IBM's corporate ideology. Like CEO Gerstner's statement, IBM's annual report is marked by representative discourse processes that express identity and connectedness.

IBM'S CORPORATE MEDIA ADVERTISEMENT

Finally, through an activity-centered semiotic discourse process foregrounding behavior, IBM's 1999 global corporate media advertisement for "IBM Global Services": "People who think. People who do. People who get it." provides an example of the use of IBM's commitment to success as economic capital to legitimize the purchase of IBM's products.[4] Standing for IBM, the word "people" suggests IBM to be the entity to which the process refers. A repetition of the phrase "people who" in three sequential constructions creates immense coherence.

CONCLUSION

Each of the above four CPD communicative events is an example of IBM institutionalizing, legitimizing, capitalizing, and inculcating its ideology founded on the idea of IBM's commitment to success. Employed as capital, IBM's ideology secures the corporation "positions of possibility." In CEO Gerstner's interview, IBM's commitment to success legitimizes IBM's corporate management to manage social groups within IBM that have different interests and different claims on IBM's resources. In IBM's mission statement, IBM's commitment to success legitimizes the corporation's values and corporate culture. In IBM's annual report, IBM's commitment to success legitimizes the corporation's expertise. And in IBM's corporate media advertisement, IBM's commitment to success legitimizes the consumer's decision to buy IBM's products and services.

NOTES

1. *THINK*, IBM Corporate Communications, 1998, 64/1, p. 6.
2. www.ibm.com.
3. IBM 1999 Annual Report.
4. *Harvard Business Review*, March–April 1999, p. 45.

PART III

Corporate Management

6

The Corporate Management Discourse Community

Use of the term "discourse community" testifies to the increasingly common assumption that discourse operates within conventions defined by communities, be they academic disciplines or social groups. The pedagogies associated with writing across the curriculum and academic English now use the notion of "discourse communities" to signify a cluster of ideas: that language use in a group is a form of social behavior, that discourse is a means of maintaining and extending the group's knowledge and of initiating new members into the group, and that discourse is epistemic or constitutive of the group's knowledge.

—*B. Herzberg (1986, 1)*

DEFINING THE CORPORATE MANAGEMENT DISCOURSE COMMUNITY

Constructing ideologies to practice power through consent, corporate power holders constitute what we refer to as a corporate management discourse community (CMDC). A discourse community should not be mistaken for a speech community, which shares knowledge of a specific language. While speech communities inherit their members "by birth, accident or adoption" (Swales 1991, 24), discourse communities recruit their members through specific forms of knowledge. A discourse community functions as a "center of a set of ideas" (Herzberg 1986, 1) and links discourse producers, discourse consumers, discourse, and social context in their natural interaction (cf. also Rafoth 1988; Swales 1991).

The CMDC belongs to a wider corporate habitat consisting of a macroenvironment encompassing a task environment that contains industries to which corporations belong. The macroenvironment is made up of political, economic, technological, demographic, governmental, international, and social/cultural components that affect corporations (cf. Wiener 1988, 534–545; Bateman and Zeithaml 1993, 60–71). The task environment incorporates customers, suppliers, and organizations with which corporations indirectly interact. Industries contain groups of directly competing corporations. At the center of a corporation is corporate management led by the CEO, to whom the authority held by the corporation's board of directors is given.

COMMON OBJECTIVES

Each member of the CMDC shares control over social, symbolic, cultural, and economic resources of interest to other CMDC members. A CMDC member's interest in resources under the control of another CMDC member leads both members to engage in actions that involve each other. Thus, CMDC members' aim toward maximizing the realization of their individual interests gives the CMDC a systemic character visible in CMDC members' objectives:

1. Practicing power through consent.
2. Creating wealth.
3. Establishing intercommunication among CMDC members. After all, it was corporate communication, and not an inevitable evolutionary force, that enabled the leadership of key corporations to expound new forms of organization and introduce change in the focus from manufacturing to marketing and finance (cf. Fligstein 1990).
4. Developing mechanisms to provide information and feedback among CMDC members. An example of such a mechanism is executive education, which is designed to provide a supportive learning environment and promote the exchange of information, ideas, and experiences.
5. Maintaining an optimal level of CMDC members (not too few, not too many) possessing discoursal expertise and adequate forms of literacy (cf. Swales 1991). For the purpose of maintaining the CMDC, discourse rules have to be mastered by all novices.

CMDC members' objectives become effective after the emergence of consensus among stakeholders, which assigns CMDC members the right to control stakeholders' actions and behaviors. To meet those objectives, CMDC members (re)define a corporation's discourse through discoursal practices. An example of a discoursal practice (re)defining a corporation's discourse is CPD.

CONCLUSION

As a social system, the CMDC promotes the regulation of discourse in corporations. An evidence of that process is CPD. Meeting the increasing demands of regulation, CPD takes on the role of defining CMDC members' social behavior. Gradually, CPD specifies what is right and what is wrong. Telling CMDC members how to relate their beliefs and desires to their behavioral output, CPD functions as a practical sagacity and stands for what the eighteenth-century Italian philosopher Giambattista Vico has referred to as a "criterion of practical judgment." Eventually, it is CPD, not the corporation or the CMDC, that defines stakeholders' understandings of a corporation and the CMDC. With time, corporate management—the creator of the corporate world—is made an epiphenomenon of that world.

7

A Disclosure of Power

The individual is no doubt the fictitious atom of an "ideological" representation of society; but he is also a reality fabricated by this specific technology of power that I have called "discipline." We must cease once and for
all to describe the effects of power in negative terms: it "excludes," it
"represses," it "censors," it "abstracts," it "masks," it "conceals." In fact,
power produces; it produces reality; it produces domains of objects and
rituals of truth. The individual and the knowledge that may be gained of
him belong to this production.

—*M. Foucault (1991, 194)*

VOICES FULL OF MONEY

Directly responsible for the strategic architecture of the multibillion-dollar
corporation, a key agent of global change, and a colossal locus of social
power,[1] the CEO is the superstar of the corporate world. She or he is also roy-
ally paid. In 1982 the average U.S. CEO earned 42 times more than an average
U.S. worker. In 2002 that ratio had grown to 282 to one. In 2003 Apple CEO
Steve Jobs was paid a total compensation of over $70 million, Danaher CEO
Larry Culp received a pay package worth $53 million, and MBNA CEO Chuck
Cawley made $52.1 million (Boyle and Tkaczyk 2004).

Admittedly, though, the CEO is not the corporation's only millionaire. It is
only fair to say that there are an increasing number of millionaires among
nonexecutive employees. About 30 percent of Microsoft's 31,000 employees
are millionaires. At Citigroup some 150 employees are worth more than $50
million, and some 1,000 employees make over $1 million in cash every year
(Wetlaufer 2000, 54).

The CEO's fame, however, has its price. The CEO is trapped in an acceleration of time: she or he is given less and less time to remain innovative, creative, and efficient, to embrace both magic-bullet– and kaizen-style progress, and to convince stakeholders that she or he has got "the right stuff" (Dauphinais and Price 1999, 19). CEOs are being hired and fired, or, as worded by Bennis and O'Toole (2000), "churned," at an unprecedented rate. The dismissal of a CEO is a quick killing. It never takes more than a week: "Nobody is more powerful than a chief executive, right up until the end. Then, suddenly, at the end, she or he has no power at all" (Thank you . . . 1999, 77). Henry Ford II, nicknamed Hank the Deuce, needed only five words—"I just don't like you"—to fire his much-celebrated CEO, Lee Iacocca.

Nevertheless, the CEO's landing, to be sure, is always a soft one. Upon leaving J. P. Morgan Chase, CEO William Harrison—in spite of the company's serious commercial-lending losses in 2001—received a special $10 million bonus for managing the company's merger in 2000. (An expense by . . . 2002, 12). To exit Honeywell International, CEO Michael Bonsignore was given a $9-million-plus-various-perks-including-executive-travel "golden parachute." And Richard McGinn, former chairman and CEO of Lucent Technologies, eased his pain of parting with a payoff worth $13 million for three years service (Money for nothing? 2001, 51). Still, there are signs that executive-pay practices may be undergoing a change: GlaxoSmithKline shareholders' vote lin 2003 against their firm's executive-pay plans may be the beginning of the end of "golden parachutes, golden handshakes, golden bungees and other happinesses" (Have fat cats . . . 2003).

EXECUTIVE POWER

The media, as we have just shown, love to disclose the CEO's power through money. The reason for this is a simple one. Nothing from the corporate world arouses so much public interest as the CEO's perks, bonuses, stock options, severance pay, and the like. Telling audiences how much the CEO makes, the media meet their general communicative purpose of entertaining, and their specific communicative purpose of informing.

Within the CEO media interview, however, the CEO's disclosure of power is subject to the genre's general communicative purpose of enabling the practice of power through consent. Take, for example, a *Harvard Business Review* interview "Organizing for Empowerment" with AES[2] Chairman Roger Sant and CEO Dennis Bakke (Wetlaufer 1999, 110–123) in which Sant and Bakke founded their ideology on a commitment to *empowerment*.[3] Although one would expect the idea of empowerment—implying, at least in part, a transfer of power in an organization from management to other employees—to induce the interviewees to "hide" their executive power, this is not the case. In their interview text-world model, both Chairman Sant and CEO Bakke disclose all of their executive power: power of position, reward power, coercive power, referent power, and expert power (cf. French and Raven 1959), as well as their community power and digital power (cf. Fox 2003).

Power of Position

The corporate manager's power of position rests on a social agreement that corporate management has the right and authority to direct the behavior of others. Stating

I made the decision about how many regional groups we would have and who would lead them.[4]

CEO Bakke disclosed his power of position. He did this using a dispositive discourse process marked by the personal pronoun "I" accompanied by the verb "made," in which CEO Bakke was an agent affecting a target: "regional groups."

Reward Power

Reward power is a corporate manager's control over the reward system within the corporation, which entitles corporate management to reward employees perceived as cooperative through attention, praise, access to resources, and material inducements (cf. Gouldner 1960; Kotter 1979). Corporate managers use reward power to create reciprocity, which generates a reaffirmation and reinforcement of allegiance and loyalty. Saying

When you pay someone a salary and make them eligible for bonuses and stock ownership, you are saying, "Our assumptions about you are no different from those we have about the plant leader. You can and should bring your brainpower and soul—your whole person—to work." In effect the company is saying, "You're a part of this organization; you have the same worth as everyone else."[5]

Chairman Sant disclosed his reward power. He did this through a semiotic, message-centered discourse process marked by the verb "say" and direct quote which foregrounds the communication (within the text-world model). Functioning as the "most unmediated text-centered instance" (Beaugrande 1997, p. 230), the direct quote enabled Chairman Sant to avoid explicit reference to his personal beliefs, attitudes, and emotions. "You" was used in two capacities: as an indefinite pronoun and as a personal pronoun. As an indefinite pronoun [you pay . . . you are saying], "you" claimed to solidarity while not being authoritative. "Vague and shifting in who it identifies" (Fairclough 1995, 181), the indefinite "you" enabled Chairman Sant to distance himself from his company's criteria of rewarding. As a personal pronoun [. . . You're part . . . ; you have the same worth . . .], "you" implied reciprocity. At the same time definite and indefinite, the text depersonalized and objectified Chairman Sant's reward power. Founded on a mutual accommodation of what each gives and gets, Chairman Sant's reward power claimed membership to a world shared by AES and its employees.

Coercive Power

Coercive power is a corporate manager's power to coerce employees perceived as uncooperative through a system of penalties (Gouldner 1960; Kotter 1979). Unlike reward power, which helps establish more permanent behavioral change, coercive power, at the best, results in compliance (Dickson et al. 1993, 145). Explaining

We demoted the individuals involved, and they took temporary pay cuts.[6]

Chairman Sant disclosed his coercive power. He did this using a dispositive discourse process marked by the verb "demote," in which he was an agent affecting a target: AES's employees. Interestingly, unlike CEO Bakke, Chairman Sant did not express his agentive role through the personal pronoun "I." He used instead the inclusive "we," which obscured his personal involvement in admonishing the penalty.

Referent Power

Referent power is based on the corporate manager's personal qualities and characteristics that appeal to others. Referent power invites approval and personal liking, stimulating imitation and loyalty. It is mediated through a capacity for empathy, moral reasoning, and charisma. Recounting

I often get e-mails or phone calls from people asking, How do you see this dilemma? What would you do in this situation? The questions are usually about fairness and integrity. They may sound like they're only about business, but they're not.[7]

Chairman Sant disclosed his referent power. He did this using a message-centered semiotic discourse process marked by the verb "ask" and two questions [How do you see this dilemma? What would you do in this situation?] that positioned him as a referent. Through the social values of "fairness and integrity," Chairman Sant interfaced AES and himself personally to societal terminal values that represent forms in which people like to experience their lives.[8] Chairman Sant's choice to use the personal pronoun "I" projected him as an individual possessing the capacity to structure social processes through personal actions.

Expert Power

Expert power is perhaps best defined as the act of a corporate manager sharing knowledge with employees to provide a "conceptual framework" that helps them understand their own professional experience (Nonaka 1998, 40). Expert power is an informal and "personal" source of power, which, by enhancing subordinates' motivation and inviting respect, constitutes a useful supplement to formal sources of power (position, control over rewards, control over punishments). But most important, expert power is fundamental to knowledge management, which is an organization's key source of competitive advantage. Only knowledge-creating companies, that is, those whose sole business is continuous innovation, Nonaka contends, can succeed (p. 22).

Knowledge, the French philosopher Michel Foucault claims in his book *Discipline and Punish* (1991), is never neutral; to possess knowledge means to possess power. According to Foucault, experts create the categories through which they define domains of factual knowledge and normalize judgments in others. Knowledge and expertise, Foucault explains, are a foundation of disciplinary power, based on surveillance of behavior, and integral to all social relationships. The enclosure of personnel in factories, hospitals, and prisons, and the regulation of behavior through timetables, examinations, and training, all serve to discipline and establish normalizing judgment, "one of the great instruments of power" in modern society. Indeed, almost two decades ago, Shrivastava (1986) argued about "orthodox strategic management" not being a "neutral, objective scientific discipline" but an ideology almost exclusively serving to "normalize the existing structures of American society and universalize the goals of its dominant elite." Davenport (1994) too has suggested that the disciplinary potential of knowledge often induces corporate management to treat knowledge as a source of power and money rather than a source of competitive advantage. Commenting

When I give speeches nowadays and ask the audience, "Why do businesses exist?" 75% of the people say the same thing, regardless of whether I am at Harvard Business School or a Christian college. They say, "To make money."[9]

CEO Bakke disclosed his expert power. He did this using an activity-centered semiotic discourse process marked by the verb "give," which foregrounded his behavior: giving speeches "at Harvard Business School or a Christian college." Disclosing his expertise, CEO Bakke attributed his position in AES's hierarchy primarily to his knowledge.

Community Power

Part and parcel of a corporate manager's power of position is community power: a corporate manager's power to relate corporate operations and policies to the social environment in ways that are mutually beneficial to both the corporation and society. Community power is an integrative notion that includes the individual, the corporation, the community, self-interest, and public good, all working together. Such an understanding of community power goes far beyond Milton Friedman's views on an organization's social responsibility as "using its resources and engaging in activities designed to increase its profits so long as it stays within the rules of the game, which is to say, engaging in open and free competition without deception or fraud" (1970, 33). Today, socially responsible community involvement is preventive and socially proactive, rather than restorative and socially reactive. Noting

To offset our carbon dioxide emissions in Connecticut, we funded the planting of 52 million trees in Guatemala . . . . to offset emissions from a plant in Hawaii, we gave a grant to preserve 144,000 acres of forest in Paraguay. In Pakistan . . . we've built four schools. We've built a school for 1,000 children in China.[10]

Chairman Sant disclosed his community power. He did this using productive discourse processes marked by the verbs "fund," "give," and "build," which showed him as an agent benefiting targets: communities.

A cornerstone of a corporate manager's community power is political power: a corporate management's ability to induce political structures to make concessions to management in the form of "an assortment of tax breaks, financial inducements, and public investments" (Reich 1991, 84). In common parlance, political power is the corporate manager's power of decision to invest in new processes essential for the economic future and welfare of regions and countries. As predicted by G. Wilson in his book *Business and Politics* (1985), corporate management is now politically more active and in this activity more visible and more successful than ever before. A linguistic demonstration of the growing importance of corporate management's political power is an augmenting glossary of terms, such as "lobbying," "corporate constituency programs," "coalition building," "advocacy advertising," "stonewalling," "strategic retreat," and many others used to describe how corporations manage the political environment.

Digital Power

An important constituent of expert power is what Bill Gates in his book *Business @ the Speed of Thought* (1999) refers to as digital power: the ability to develop a new digital infrastructure, to reinvent the way the organization works, and thus provide a competitive edge. Digital power identifies the CEO as a typical representative of a monochrone culture (Hall 1966) where time is segmented, precisely measured, painstakingly distributed (cf. McClelland 1963; Lawrence and Lorsch 1967; Rice 1978), and accelerated (Harvey 1989). Digital power highlights too a corporate manager's ability to challenge the future, which, Bill Gates exhorts, will be about mastering the digital universe. Recalling

So Flora put together an e-mail that detailed what she was planning to bid and why, and sent it to about 200 or 300 people within AES.[11]

CEO Bakke disclosed his digital power. He did this using an AES employee, Flora—an agent who affected an entity (200–300 people within AES) by e-mail—as evidence of AES's digital infrastructure. Flora's agentive role was realized through a dispositive discourse process marked by the verb "send."

CONCLUSION

Chairman Sant and CEO Bakke's disclosure of executive power in their media interview was an intentional and strategic display of traditional authority (community power), charismatic authority (referent power, expert power, and digital power), and rational-legal authority (power of position, reward power, and coercive power), which, we have said, are bases of legitimization. Chairman Sant and CEO Bakke knew that for most people power has a "positive valence" (cf. Ng and Bradac 1993, 14), and that messages delivered by individuals perceived as powerful are typically evaluated more beneficially than messages delivered by individuals perceived as powerless. Chairman Sant and CEO Bakke also knew that speakers perceived as powerful are accorded a higher social status and greater professional competence (cf. Bradac and Wisegarver 1984; Gibbons et al. 1991). Such individuals are commonly associated to dynamism—a power dimension rated through aggression, activity, and strength (Bradac and Mulac 1984)—which in Western culture is a much desired quality of a leader. Finally, Chairman Sant and CEO Bakke knew only too well that power goes to those "who are seen as having a right to it" (Cohen et al. 1992, 324) and that their disclosure of power would be essential to stakeholders' perception of their autonomy and ability to select social roles and enact commitments. Knowing all this, Chairman Sant and CEO Bakke strategically disclosed their executive power, and, in doing so, legitimized themselves and their ideology founded on the idea of AES's commitment to empowerment.

NOTES

1. A myriad of aphorisms refer to how the power of CEOs, magnified through the zealous efforts of subordinates, affects employees, ranging from the trite "When he sneezes, we all catch colds," to the more colorful "When he says 'Go to the bathroom,' we all get the shits" (Jackall 1996, 101).

2. Applied Energy Services.

3. Empowerment—the delegation of responsibility to employees—is generally accepted to actively involve employees in organizational changes (Stevens 1993), imbue them with a feeling of autonomy and importance, and enhance their loyalty toward management (Conger and Kanungo 1988). Skeptics (or cynics?) claim, however, that empowerment is, in fact, rarely practiced and that most talk about empowerment is simply rhetoric (cf. Legge 1995; Argyris 1998). Legge, for example, has argued that employees' commitment behind increased productivity in the 1980s in the U.K. was behavioral rather than attitudinal. Changes such as low levels of labor turnover and absenteeism were more a reflection of fear of job loss than a commitment to corporate values (p. 206).

4. *Harvard Business Review*, January–February 1999, p. 120.

5. *Harvard Business Review*, January–February 1999, p. 117.

6. *Harvard Business Review*, January–February 1999, p. 119.

7. *Harvard Business Review*, January–February 1999, p. 118.

8. Other terminal values would be: world at peace, family security, freedom, equality, self-respect, happiness, wisdom, national security, competence, friendship, accomplishment, inner harmony, comfortable life, mature love, world of beauty, pleasure, social recognition, and an exciting life (Rokeach 1979).

9. *Harvard Business Review*, January–February 1999, p. 120.

10. *Harvard Business Review*, January–February 1999, p 121.

11. *Harvard Business Review*, January–February 1999, p. 118.

8

A Disclosure
of Leadership

In the beginning was the word or, more accurately, the logos. And in the beginning, "logos" meant story, reason, rationale, conception, discourse, thought. Thus all forms of human expression and communication—from epic to architecture, from biblical narrative to statuary—came within its purview.

—*W. R. Fisher (1987, 5)*

MANUFACTURING ACQUIESCENCE

When in a moment of crisis, Ross Perot, founder of EDS, said: "Inventories can be managed, but people must be led" (Cohen et al. 1992, 4), he expressed an idea that has pervaded management throughout the entire second half of the twentieth century: Leadership is definitely the most important aspect of management.

The leader, it is known, is realized through her/his followers: members of the organization who, ideally, are loyal, enthusiastic, and at the same time think with their own heads (cf. Kelley 1988). To accumulate a body of followers, a leader has to create a belief in her or his ability to lead. A leader, as Harry Truman once said, has to "get men to do what they don't want to do and like it."

To create a belief in his ability to lead, Pepsi President and CEO Craig Weatherup, in a *Harvard Business Review* roundtable "Leveraging Processes for Strategic Advantage" (Garvin 1995, 84), told of how he used a "burning platform" anecdote to "set the stage" before presenting "detailed data" on the financial, market, and organizational pains Pepsi was facing:

A few years ago there was a fire on a North Sea oil rig. Because the rigs were 150 feet high, the workers had been instructed not to jump but to wait for help, now matter how bad things got. Despite the injunction, one worker jumped—and survived. Asked later to explain his actions, he said that he had looked behind, seen an approaching wall of fire, then looked down and seen the icy sea below. His rationale? "I chose probable death over certain death." Only eleven others survived the fire, out of several hundred workers.[1]

For CEO Weatherup's audience in the interview text-world model, that is, for Pepsi's employees, the "logos" of CEO Weatherup's anecdote (and the way he used it to manufacture acquiescence within Pepsi) was a disclosure of his leadership. For CEO Weatherup's audience in the real world, that is, for the readers of his media interview the "logos" of disclosing leadership through a story was a disclosure of CEO Weatherup's leadership. CEO Weatherup's use of a message-centered semiotic discourse process (marked by direct quotes), that presented the anecdote's content as unmediated, that is, as perfectly identical to the original communication, helped make the anecdote believable. Viewed from a language-ideology-power perspective, CEO Weatherup's disclosure of leadership, both in the text-world model and in the real world, represented a charismatic base of authority upon which he legitimized himself and his ideology founded on a commitment to transform Pepsi.

TRANSFORMATIONAL LEADERSHIP

Over the past century understandings of leadership qualities have changed dramatically. Traditionally, the manager was considered a typical representative of a "process orientation" who believed his duty was to get the job done. His objective was the status quo, which commanded a typical "If it ain't broke, don't fix it" attitude (Zaleznik 1992, 131). The inevitable result was mediocrity. Leadership, on the other hand, was assumed to be based on a mystical belief in the natural predisposition of the individual: only great people deserve the drama of power. Leaders were those who had a vision, and their attitude was: "When it ain't broke may be the only time you can fix it." Today, most definitions of a leader emphasize personal characteristics. A leader should possess intelligence, inner motivation, drive, and human skills and demonstrate social maturity. She or he inspires and uses her or his power of authority to delegate additional responsibilities, to intellectually stimulate managers, and to create awareness on issues and possible solutions (Deluga 1990). A leader instills trust, gives hope, and leads others toward a goal. A leader aims to create a new, immeasurable quality that is not always rationally definable. Bennis (1996) puts it, leadership is the "encounter of a leader, followers and a dream."

Reaching beyond employees' rational work-for-money exchange motive, today's leader is transformational. Whereas the former transactional leader used his legitimate power to order, reward, and punish, offering no fervor and no thrill, the transformational leader creates a vision of the future and an environment that motivates the employee to subordinate personal interests to those of the organization. Whereas the transactional leader expected that setting goals, coordinating, supporting, and, if necessary, criticizing would automatically result in satisfaction and high productivity, the transformational leader charismatically projects trust into his followers—giving them individualized attention and stimulating their intellect—which results in affection, commitment, and high-quality performance. Briefly, transformational leadership rests upon what Bennis and Nanus (1985) have referred to as the "Wallenda factor": a leader's unwavering self-confidence. (Karl Wallenda was a famous circus artist who fell to his death while performing his high-wire walk. According to Wallenda's widow, it was on that walkt that for the first time ever he had been afraid of falling. In all his successful walks, he had been absolutely sure he would succeed.)

MR. WELCH'S AND CEO FIORINA'S MEDIA INTERVIEWS

To further show how a CEO discloses her or his leadership in the CEO media interview text-world model, we look at the interviews of two world-famous transformational leaders: Jack Welch, former chairman and CEO of General Electric,[2] and Carleton S. Fiorina, CEO of Hewlett-Packard.

A Commitment to Globalization

In a *Harvard Business Review* interview, "Jack on Jack" (Collingwood and Coutu 2002, 93), Jack Welch recounted an experience following his return from India:

I'd just been to India, where I'd gotten a very good presentation from the people at an R&D lab . . . . Two days later, at our officers meeting, one of our top R&D guys says to me, "You got a lot of bull from those people. Their work isn't that good." So I say, "If I'm getting bull, it's partly your fault." Now, I love this guy—he's one of the top two or three R&D guys within the company. Extremely self-confident. But if we're truly a global company, this talk about "here" and "there" has got to end.[3]

Positioned "within" the interview text world, the anecdote relates to an event involving Mr. Welch as an entity performing the action of reprimanding one of his R&D guys. To tell his anecdote, Mr. Welch, just as CEO Weatherup, relied upon a message-centered semiotic discourse process (marked by direct quotes) to present the anecdote's content as perfectly identical to the original communication between himself and his "top R&D guy." In the same way CEO Weatherup's anecdote disclosed a personal characteristic of CEO Weatherup—his rhetorical skill—so too does Mr. Welch's anecdote disclose a personal characteristic of Mr. Welch: his belief in a free and open "global" society comprised of reasonable individuals who in judgments and conduct can be influenced by argumentation, and who are committed to the values of truth, freedom, reason, and justice.

A Commitment to a Merger

In a *BusinessWeek* interview, "Carly's Last Stand?" (Burrows 2001, 63–70), Carly Fiorina described and evaluated a state in a battle with the David & Lucile Packard Foundation, which opposed Hewlett-Packard's proposed merger with Compaq. Asked what she would do to overcome shareholders' negative feelings toward the deal, she replied

We've got a long way to go on this vote. We haven't filed a proxy yet. We don't have regulatory approval yet. We have at least another quarter's worth of results from both companies. It ain't over till its over.[4]

and made it very clear to her audience that she intended to succeed. Through her "It ain't over till it's over," CEO Fiorina expressed her unwavering belief in the HP–Compaq merger (and herself as its architect). At that moment, even CEO Fiorina's most ardent opponents had to acknowledge her leadership; a leadership that was to be crucial in securing those three percent stakeholder votes that on May 7, 2002 enabled Hewlett-Packard and Compaq to merge into the new HP. CEO Fiorina's "It ain't over till it's over" is a volitional discourse process which conveys, without her having to resort to the imperative and her power of position, CEO Fiorina's wish of not wanting the merger to fail.

CONCLUSION

In their media interviews, CEO Weatherup, Mr. Welch, and CEO Fiorina invented. Not in today's sense of the word, but in a Ciceronian sense of *invenire*, meaning the capacity to make the right decision on what to say. Inventing, CEO Weatherup, Mr. Welch, and CEO Fiorina resorted to the rhetorical procedure of heuresis: the use of one's knowledge to put together that which is appropriate to a message. While CEO Weatherup and Mr. Welch recalled past experiences, CEO Fiorina described and evaluated a present circumstance in her life (the merger). To realize their heuresis, CEO Weatherupe, Mr. Welch, and CEO Fiorina chose to rely on certain discourse processes. Whereas CEO Weatherup and Mr. Welch used semiotic discourse processes, CEO Fiorina used a volitional discourse process.

The right message, of course, requires taxis: the planning of discourse construction. Through the medium of writing, CEO Weatherup, Mr. Welch, and CEO Fiorina were able to carefully plan their discourse. The medium of writing also allowed them to more carefully select lexis: appropriate and expressive forms of language, for example, "I chose probable death over certain death," "This talk about 'here' and 'there' has got to end," and "It ain't over till it's over." Finally, although heuresis, taxis, and lexis have been referred to individually, they should not be thought of as stages in a process. Rather, as CEO Weatherup, Mr. Welch, and CEO Fiorina demonstrated in their interviews, heuresis, taxis, and lexis are organically connected through discourse.

NOTES

1. *Harvard Business Review*, September-October, 1995, p. 84.

2. During that time the corporation's market capitalization grew from $13 billion to over $400 billion (Collingwood and Coutu 2002, 88).

3. *Harvard Business Review*, February 2002, p. 93.

4. *BusinessWeek*, December 24, 2001, p. 68.

9

A Disclosure
of Social Position

And the class itself possesses a function, that of maintaining that part of
the total culture of the society which pertains to that class. We have to try
to keep in mind, that in a healthy society this maintenance of a particular
level of culture is to the benefit, not merely of the class which maintains it,
but of the society as a whole. Awareness of this fact will prevent us from
supposing that the culture of a "higher" class is something superfluous to
society as a whole, or to the majority, and from supposing that it is something which ought to be shared equally by all other classes.

—*T. S. Eliot (1962, 35)*

THE CEO'S SOCIAL POSITION

An established system of beliefs often used by the CEO to legitimize herself or
himself and her or his ideology is her or his social position. To explain how the
CEO legitimizes herself or himself through a social position, we refer to a *Harvard Business Review* interview with Franco Bernabé, CEO of the Italian corporation Eni. Briefly, the interview is about CEO Bernabé's role in Eni's transition "from a political quagmire into a clean, market driven business" (Hill and Wetlaufer 1998, 82). In the following extract CEO Bernabé recalls a crucial moment:

Because nothing would have changed. I believed the government wanted a real
change. I had the legal authority to do it, by the way. But normally you don't do
something like that without lengthy consultations with the corporate staff and, of
course, with the chairman. But if I had gone through that process, we would have

ended up with a compromise. I didn't want compromise—I wanted to have my objectives reached. So I sent the directive that I was in charge. It was really a shock to the chairman and everyone else.[1]

In this text CEO Bernabé is an agent [. . . So I sent the directive that I was in charge. . . .] affecting a target entity: Eni's chairman and everyone else. Issuing the directive that he was in charge, CEO Bernabé manifested his "power over," or rather, his new position in a social configuration of the corporation, to exert "power to," that is, to attain personal and collective goals. Exerting "power to," CEO Bernabé redefined social relations within Eni and, in doing so, disclosed his (new) social position as CEO. At the same time, that position confirmed CEO Bernabé's membership in a particular social class and his participation in particular social networks.

SOCIAL CLASS AND SOCIAL STATUS

Social class is an economically based concept that refers to "any group of people (who have the same) typical chance for a supply of goods, external living conditions, and personal life experiences, insofar as this chance is determined by the . . . power . . . to dispose of goods or skills for the sake of income" (Weber 1970, 181–182). Throughout history, the intersection of social classes and nations has been essential to developing "collective powers," which enabled societies to efficiently mobilize human capacities. The result was an extraordinary social density, providing the means for members of all social classes to actively participate in society (Mann 1993, 14).

It was the Danish anthropologist, Thomas Højrup (1983), who provided a first interactional analysis of the corporate manager's social position as a source of power. According to Højrup, the corporate manager belongs to a subgroup of professionally qualified wage-earners with power of control, which is one of the three subgroups constituting society (the other two subgroups being the self-employed, for example, fishermen, farmers, and shopkeepers, and wage earners without power of control). Each of these subgroups is characterized by a specific life mode founded on the subgroup's ideological orientation toward work, leisure, and family. The main objective of the corporate manager's subgroup is vertical mobility. Professional expertise (and, as we shall see, membership in social networks) enables members of this subgroup to progress through the social hierarchy, obtain control over others, exercise more and more power, and, ultimately, escape the control of others.

Up to the mid-1990s, the CEO was considered to be a member of the upper-middle class (e.g., Gilbert and Kahl 1982; Coleman 1983). Marking the emergence of global system theory, the 1990s redefined the CEO's class membership (e.g., Sklair 1995; Robinson 1996; Dicken 1998). Today, the CEO is treated as the founder and the chief member of the transnational capitalist class: a segment of world bourgeoisie representing transnational capital. She or he is the mainstay of the new "gentrifiers" (Butler 1995, 191): creators of the global cities of London, New York, and Tokyo—corporate "command and control" centers for transnational corporations. Other members of the transnational capitalist class are owners of transnational companies, globalizing bureaucrats and politicians, globalizing professionals, and consumerist elites (merchants and media) (Sklair 2000).

Gradually, the transnational capitalist class is becoming a global ruling class, aligning its economical interests with other social interests, for example, political and cultural, and assuming control of the "emergent transnational state apparatus and of global decision-making" (Robinson and Harris 2000, 2). The transnational capitalist class, Robinson and Harris further argue, manages "globalized circuits of accumulation which give it an objective class existence and identity spatially and politically in the global system above any local territories and polities."

The transnational capitalist class is pursuing "a class project of capitalist globalization" and becoming a "class-in-itself and for-itself" (p. 8). Transnational class socialization is manifested in the existence of world class universities, transnational think tanks, and bourgeois foundations such as the Harvard School of International Business and the Ford and Carnegie Foundations (p. 12). The CEO's membership in the transnational capitalist class makes her or him a member of the global power elite controlling the global market and, through this, the whole planet. It is a well-known fact, for instance, that CEOs of the top thousand transnational corporations constitute the core of the World Economic Forum (WEF), the leading planning body of the transnational corporations (p. 12).

Although there is a strong link between social class and social status, they do not mean the same thing. The concept "social status" has its roots in the sociological perspective of Max Weber, who studied the importance of social status in the capitalistic world. According to Weber, new bases of social status had developed in modern industrial capitalism, created by the changes of society related to the process of consumption, rather than that of production. It is lifestyle that plays a decisive role in status honor, meaning that "status groups are the specific bearers of all 'conventions'" (1970, 181–182). While class represents the economic dimension of social stratification, status constitutes a prestige dimension. The CEO's social status is based on her or his profession, financial circumstances (derived from income and ownership over property), residential area, lifestyle, public engagement, ancestry, and membership in associations. Similarly to other members of the transnational capitalist class, the CEO has typically graduated from an elite business school, is a consumer of luxury goods and services, and is increasingly inclined to residential segregation, living in "gated communities" secured by armed guards and electronic surveillance (Sklair 2000).

Functioning as a social variable, social class significantly influences the way a person uses language (Hudson 1998, 184). However, as all other social variables, for example, gender, race, and age, social class affects a person's speech only to the extent that it represents a social group with which a speaker wishes to identify herself or himself. Accordingly, the sociolinguistic variables (phonetic, phonological, morphological, lexical, and syntactic) typically found in a CEO's speech will depend on the degree to which the CEO belongs to the social class and social network with which she or he wishes to be identified. Nevertheless, social class remains the most widely used social variable in sociolinguistic and descriptive research into English, in the sense that results obtained on other variables, for example, gender, are usually interpreted in terms of social class or social prestige (Milroy and Milroy 1997, 55).

SOCIAL NETWORKS

Although the concepts of social class and social status can be used to explain a great deal of the CEO's social behavior, they cannot be used to explain how the CEO acts meaningfully as an individual to establish personal linkages to other people. For this, it is necessary to refer to the concept of social network: "a mechanism both for exchanging goods and services, and for imposing obligations and conferring corresponding rights upon its members" (Milroy 1989, 47).

Explained in simple terms, a social network is a network of messages, passing along social network links, that "can be seen as transactions, governed by the principle that the value gained by an individual in a transaction is equal to or greater than, the cost" (Milroy 1989, 45–46). Thus, while the concept of social class focuses on social hierarchy and inequality of wealth and power distribution, social network focuses on solidarity relations established by an individual (Milroy and Milroy 1997, 60–61). However, a social network does not really replace social class. Rather, small-scale networks of individuals' daily lives are a consequence of and coexist with larger-scale socioeconomic circumstances which determine relationships of power at the institutional level (Barnes 1954; Lomnitz 1977; Bright 1997). The concept of social networks has been well researched and given properties such as density, centrality, and reachability (e.g, Barnes 1954; Mitchell 1969; Boissevain and Mitchell 1973; Boissevain 1974; Scott 1988; Newman 2003; Marsden 2002; Kilduff and Tsai 2003). It has been calculated, for example, that an average American has a social circle of about 290 people (Killworth et al. 1990; Bernard et al. 1991; Newman 2003).

Individuals, of course, will try very hard, and probably go to extremes, to preserve their most important network relationships (Kapferer 1969). Depending on their structural characteristics, social networks are of either a low density (Figure 9.1) or a high density (Figure 9.2).[2]

Members of a low-density network are linked to each other by uniplex ties, that is, in one capacity, sharing membership in only one formal/informal social group. Members of a high-density network are linked to each other by multiplex ties, that is, in more than one capacity, sharing membership in more than one formal/informal social group.

In pursuit of their careers, CEOs are socially and geographically extremely mobile, which induces them to join both low-density and high-

Figure 9.1
A Low-Density Social Network

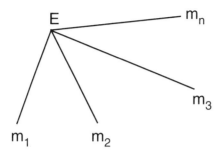

E = ego, individual at the focus of the network
m = other members of the network

density networks and form both loose-knit and close-knit network ties. Loose-knit network ties encourage the flow of knowledge and influence travel. Close-knit network ties serve coalitions and personal networks through which the CEO controls the corporation. Joining many low- and high-density networks, the CEO constructs a social hypernetwork, in which she or he resides (Figure 9.3).

In a hypernetwork the CEO is directly connected to other members of top management, the board of directors, and influential members of the community outside the corporation. This is the CEO's first-order network zone, representing a typical example of a cluster consisting of a network segment

Figure 9.2
A High-Density Social Network

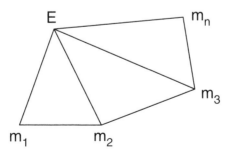

E = ego, individual at the focus of the network
m = other members of the network

Figure 9.3
The CEO's Hypernetwork

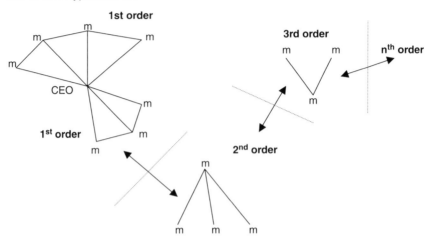

m = other members of the network

marked by a higher density than the rest of the network. The capacity of a cluster to enforce its communicative norms on members is very strong (Labov 1972), although, as argued by Gumperz (1992), the cluster members share "communicative preferences" rather than categorical rules. The corporate management discourse community is a typical network cluster.

Individuals indirectly connected to the CEO, for instance, a corporation's middle and lower management, form a second-order network zone. Last, persons who only rarely come into contact with the CEO form n^{th}-order zones. Compared to the first order (inner) zone, the other (outer) zones are less dense, generally marked by uniplex ties, and less subject to the supervision and control of a peer group.

Viewed from the perspective of social network theory, CEO Bernabé's power is not something that is owned by CEO Bernabé personally; it is something residing in a newly established network of social relations within Eni. For CEO Bernabé, the value [. . . I didn't want compromise—I wanted to have my objectives reached. . . . I believed the government wanted a real change. . . .] to be gained from opposing the old network and creating a new one was clearly greater than the risk [. . . . But normally you don't do something like that without lengthy consultations with the corporate staff and, of course, with the chairman. . . .]. Breaking up Eni's old (high-density) network, whose members shared interests in maintaining a status quo, was Franco Bernabé's first task as CEO. Stopping the reproduction of the old social order, CEO Bernabé was able to create a new social network and initiate a new corporate ideology.

CONCLUSION

Disclosing his social position as a CEO, as a member of a transnational cap-italist class, and as a node in a social hypernetwork, which was a node in a global enterprise network, CEO Bernabé used the authority of that position to legitimize his ideology founded on his commitment to transform Eni. CEO Bernabé was able to do this because a CEO's social position is a part of a sys-tem of beliefs in which class structure is viewed as beneficial to society as a whole. Indeed, as a member of the transnational capitalist class, CEO Bernabé was in the position not only to preserve the culture of that class, but also to fortify the culture of a society to which that class belongs. Transforming Eni, he showed the transnational capitalist class to be indispensable to the culture of his society. Thus, CEO Bernabé not only legitimized his own ideology, he legitimized too the ideology of a society based on a system of classes that pos-sess unequal levels of power and, ultimately, responsibility.

NOTES

1. *Harvard Business Review*, July-August 1998, p. 90.
2. The density of a network D may be calculated using the formula $D = \dfrac{100Nm\%}{N}$, where Nm is the total number of lengths and N is the total num-ber of possible links (Milrag 1989, 50).

PART IV

Media of CPD

10

Writing

The need for writing in modern literate societies—societies marked by pervasive print media—is much more extensive than is generally realized. When one examines the everyday world, one finds people engaged in many varieties of writing, some of which may be overlooked as being routine, or commonplace, or unimportant. These varieties, however, all represent the ability to control the written medium of language to some extent. It is fair to say that most people, on a typical day, practice some forms of writing.

—*W. Grabe and R. B. Kaplan (1997, 3)*

A PREFERRED MEDIUM

Writing is much more than just a medium of CPD. It, for a number of reasons, is the preferred medium of CPD. Making CPD permanent and available, writing, "a kind of language use with its own material practices" (Mukerji 1995, 149), gives CPD a documentary value. Through the medium of writing, a CPD communicative event becomes an artifact and, like other corporate artifacts, provides physical evidence of the corporation. Through writing, ideas contained in a CPD communicative event are taken beyond the event itself and linked to the entirety of a corporation's discourse.

Assuring the discretionary production and consumption of a CPD communicative event—from perfunctory to detailed—writing abstracts and decontextualizes CPD: it distances the writer from the reader in time and space. Through the medium of writing, a distinction between reading a CPD communicative event as information (as related to the event's propositional content) and reading it as interpretation (as related to the event's personal and interpersonal content) is made possible (cf. Ong 1986, 39).

Enabling a large amount of propositional content to be carefully and economically packaged, writing prevents the fragmentation of a CPD communicative event, often found, for example, in spoken interaction. Through the medium of writing a CPD communicative event is given precision. Without that precision, the many genres of CPD would not be possible.

Finally, and perhaps most important, as a traditional marker of social prestige (cf. Hudson 1998, 32), writing gives both the producer (a corporation) of a CPD communicative event and the receiver (stakeholders) of a CPD communicative event an increased awareness of the social context of their interaction (relations of power), of the importance of a community of writers (the corporate management discourse community), and of an exclusive language of that community (CPD).

LITERACY

Writing enables and generates literacy: an operational control over various reading and writing abilities. Throughout the history of mankind, literacy has been an important social, symbolic, cultural, and economic capital. From the very beginnings of writing, more than 6,000 years ago, scribal specialists, who recorded events and transactions and rendered them orally available to the masses, were greatly respected by society. Similarly, much of the power of religious orders was attributed to the "mystical properties" of reading and writing.

Although the Greek city-states and the Roman empire witnessed an upsurge of literacy, notably for political and commercial purposes, contrary to popular belief, the Greek and Roman masses were widely illiterate.

During the Middle Ages, literacy was generally consigned to religious structures. The development of literacy for nonreligious purposes started in the eighth century, and for business purposes in the tenth century. Up to the eleventh century, Western Europe, Stock (1983, 18) has argued, could have returned to an oral civilization. But by 1100 writing had become sufficiently institutionalized as to be "irreversible. . . . the die was cast."

Arguably, literacy is the most significant single step in the history of mankind. For the first time people were able to store and access great amounts of knowledge. But just as important was the role of literacy as a means of social emancipation. Literacy liberated mankind from the grips of myth, allowed drawing the line between the natural and the supernatural, helped develop critical skepticism toward previous systems of knowledge and beliefs, and enabled democracy and democratic institutions in today's sense (Goody and Watt 1963).

People's needs and desires to become literate made literacy a natural guardian of social order and social structures. In their book *Literacy, Schooling and Revolution*, Lankshear and Lawler (1987) explain how the "pursuit, attainment, and practice of proper forms of literacy was a vital galvanizing element within the active role played by working folk in making themselves a class" (p. 81).

Insomuch as literacy serves as a means to create social cohesion, it serves too as a means to create social division. In any society and in any era, prestigious forms of literacy—a precondition to a person's social and professional success—have been defined by the ruling class. As Lankshear and Lawler further explain:

Within social life, the working class had a well-defined station to observe and maintain. Relations of deference, acceptance of authority, and willingness to be controlled by one's betters, were culturally enforced. These relations extended to education as well. Whether or not the poor received education, what they received, and under what conditions, were details that were largely outside the power of the working class to determine. (p. 83)

From the mid-nineteenth century onward, with the introduction of compulsory education, literacy was systematically employed as a vehicle of power through consent. Used by power holders to instruct the masses how to work more efficiently, literacy helped to reproduce and reinforce existing social structures. For the selected few at the top, of course, nothing changed; they continued to use literacy as a source of social mobility and wealth accumulation.

Following World War II, functional literacy—an individual's ability to engage in activities in which literacy is required for her or his effective functioning in a community, and which enable her or him to continue reading, writing, and calculating for her or his own and the community's benefit— became a key educational objective of all developed countries. Because today the role of functional literacy is, essentially, to show people "how to work within a system from the perspective of people in power" (Delgado-Gaitan 1990, 2), it entails "more sophisticated ('smart'), abstract, symbolic-logical capacities" (Lankshear 1998, 3) than those needed in the past.

Contemporary society, though, should not be assumed to be wholly literate. Far from it. Presently, there are some 860 million illiterate adults in the world, of which two-thirds are women. UNESCO forecasts that by 2015 there will be some 800 million illiterate adults worldwide (Vision quest 2003).

A LEARNED SKILL

Historically, writing is preceded by speech. As old as mankind, speech is partly biologically determined and naturally acquired. Such is the immense importance of speech to mankind, that it has often been treated as a gift of a divine being. For example, in the Book of Genesis one of the first things Adam had to do was to name the acts of creation: "And out of the ground the Lord God formed every beast of the field, and every fowl of the air; and brought *them* unto Adam to see what he would call them: and whatsoever Adam called every living creature, that *was* the name thereof" (2.19).

Writing, on the other hand, is culturally transmitted and learned. From the very beginnings of literacy, writing has been accorded more importance than spoken practice. The more literate people became, the more importance they attributed to writing. Writing, therefore, has been traditionally regarded as the true form of language, while speech has been considered to be "unstable, degenerate and not worthy of study" (Biber 1991, 5). This is not to say that literacy should be regarded as founded solely on writing. On the contrary, reacting to the generally accepted assumption about the superiority of writing, early twentieth-century linguists identified speech as the primary form of language and writing as its derivative. However, It was not until the 1990s that Hymes's (1972) ideas of speech and writing as different, independent, and each in its own way contributing to the concept of communicative competence were widely accepted.[1] Today writing is simply seen as an expression of an individual's need to be integrated into discourse communities.

The skill of writing was first developed in ancient Mesopotamia, where it was motivated by the practical need to keep records of administrative, economic, and legal transactions. Typical documents dating from that time include "deeds of sale and purchase, contracts concerning loans, adoption, marriage, wills, ledgers and memoranda of merchants, as well as census and tax returns" (Coulmas 1989: 73). A famous monument witnessing Babylonian literacy is the Code of Hammurabi,[2] written in the Babylonian cuneiform (a wedge-shaped writing system) and inscribed on a 2.25-meter-high basalt column found in Iraq at the beginning of the twentieth century and now kept in the Louvre.

With time, the Babylonian cuneiform was taken over by the Egyptians, who evolved it into a hieroglyphic system. In the second millennium B.C., between Sinai and Syria, more simplified ways of writing, based on the cuneiform and hieroglyphic systems, started to develop. Around 1100 B.C., one such way developed into the Phoenician alphabet. By 800 B.C., the Greeks had developed that alphabet into their own, from which all subsequent European alphabets are derived.

Mesopotamia gave mankind not only the skill of writing, but many of its specific applications. The Sumerians, for example, were the first to use writing for the transmission of information across space and time. The "Enmerkar Epic" tells of the ruler of Erech who in the first quarter of the third millennium B.C. used a clay tablet letter to supplement the oral communication of a messenger. By the middle of the third millennium B.C., the Sumerians were also using writing for Wisdom literature: a literary genre dispensing general knowledge in the form of advice (Saggs 1999, 352).

The continually changing demands of public and political life throughout history have placed an emphasis on writing conceptualized as technology and founded on a set of skills based on "training, instruction, practice, experience, and purpose" (Grabe and Kaplan 1997, 6). Treating writing as technology helps us understand why the development of writing skills requires much effort and practice. At the same time, thinking of writing as a learned skill explains why some people never develop more sophisticated writing skills.

While writing and speech are complementary, there is no interchangeability between them. Writing, therefore, cannot be treated as "visual speech symbolism" (Sapir 1921, 19–20), or "derivative" of speech (Fillmore 1981, 153). Writing is chosen over speaking simply because the situational context dictates it to be so.

COMPOSING

A delimitative factor of writing is composing: a process of combining syntactic units into compact and coherent larger structures (Grabe and Kaplan 1997, 4–5). Over the last forty years, an increasing awareness of the fundamental importance of composing skills has motivated a large body of research into writing. Exploring the history of approaches to writing, Faigley (1986) suggested approximately four stages of development: the expressive, the cognitive, the social, and the discourse community stage. Each of these stages provided new ideas and insights while responding to issues identified by the previous stage. Based on Faigley's division, Grabe and Kaplan (1997, 88–112) suggested three major approaches to writing: the expressive approach, the cognitive approach, and a social-context approach.

The expressive approach viewed writing as an organic process, mainly aimed at the expression of the self. It was based on the assumption that an author possesses all the necessary creative resources for effective writing and is merely looking for an opportunity for expression. Despite its two great weaknesses—a disregard for the world model and the social context of writing, and an absence of a coherent theoretical foundation—the expressive approach was useful in that it served as a prelude to other approaches to writing.

Motivated by advances in cognitive psychology, the cognitive approach started in the early 1970s. One of the many cognitive models of writing is Flower and Hayes's (1977, 1984) model built on three basic premises underlying composition:

- composing is interactive
- composing is goal directed
- expert writers compose differently from novice writers

Lacking an explanation of how text is constructed, Flower and Hayes's model was criticized as methodologically unsound and vague. Their protocol analysis, a number of researchers argued, could not be either a primary or the only source of evidence for constructing a theory of the writing process. Still, the great merit of Flower and Hayes's model was in their having put a whole new range of issues up for public debate. In doing so, Flower and Hayes opened up research on writing to "more explicit and testable hypotheses . . . and more carefully defined research methods" (Grabe and Kaplan 1997, 93).

Another cognitive model of written composition is Beaugrande's (1984). Drawing from research on memory, attention, and reading, Beaugrande's model provides a detailed and well-argued description of what expert writers do. Critical of Beaugrande's model, Grabe and Kaplan (1997, 94) maintain it to be a "descriptive global model" and not an operational model making "specific falsifiable predictions."

At the beginning of the 1980s, a social-context approach toward writing emerged. Arguing that writing gains meaning only within a social context, this approach gave rise to a number of different perspectives on the writing process: ethnographic, sociolinguistic, sociosemiotic, and a discourse community perspective. A significant contribution of the ethnographic perspective is considered to be in its emphasis on the importance of observing reality and collecting real data in real social contexts. Using a social-context approach to research writing in primary education, Graves (1984) and Calkins (1986), for example, detected a major mismatch between learners' motives (children's wish to write) and institutional action (writing as used for testing, busywork, and disciplinary purposes). This mismatch, so it seems, has a counterproductive effect on the development of writing skills. Although criticized as to the depth and validity of its conclusions, a social-context approach toward writing has had important positive effects on the teaching of writing in U.S. elementary schools.

Arguably, the most important contribution toward understanding writing as a process was made by Halliday (1978) in his social-semiotic approach to literacy. As the whole language serves a socio-functional purpose, reading and writing, Hallday argues, are just extensions of the "functional potential of language" (p. 57). Questioning the match between writing as taught in schools and the real social needs of learners, Halliday has stressed too the possible negative effects of the formal education process upon children's motives to write.

KNOWLEDGE TELLING AND
KNOWLEDGE TRANSFORMING

Composing can be broadly divided into two major types of writing: knowledge telling (as in, for example, personal diaries, personal letters, business letters, lesson plans, sermons, newsletter items) and knowledge transforming (as in, for example, fiction). While knowledge telling is the sort of writing that to a large extent is known to the message producer, knowledge transforming is the "sort of writing for which no blue-print is readily available" (Grabe and Kaplan 1997, 5). According to Grabe and Kaplan, not every act of writing requires composing. Typical examples of writing without composing would be a shopping list, a note to a milkman, a questionnaire, a tax form, and a driver's license application form. All of these examples of writing are marked by an absence of syntactic units that can form larger structures.

If, however, text is accepted as a communicative event "wherein linguistic, cognitive and social actions converge," then, all texts have to be viewed as involving at least some degree of composition. Even creating a shopping list involves a knowledge of words, a choice of words, and relating those words to the real world. Furthermore, knowledge telling cannot really be disassociated from knowledge transforming. Since a relationship between the message producer and the audience is created by all types of writing, all writing involves both knowledge telling and knowledge transforming. As Halliday (1978) explained, every use of language incorporates at least three functions: the ideational, which is related to the selection of facts; the textual, which is related to the presentation of facts; and the interpersonal, which marks role relationships. A shopping list, for example, fulfills its ideational function by telling knowledge (stating the items to be bought), its textual function by listing, and its interpersonal function by marking buyer-related information outside the list (visible in the choice and sequence of items on the list). The unity of these three functions—ideational, textual, and interpersonal—makes any type of writing, even a simple shopping list, an act of knowledge transformation involving the matching of various segments of information and the choice of rhetorical options and constraints (Bereiter and Scardamalia 1987).

PATTERNS OF KNOWLEDGE

When composing, people typically use frames, schemata, and scripts—cognitive configurations, patterns, and routines through which they rationalize their cognitive resources.

Frame

A frame is a configuration of commonsense knowledge pertinent to a communicative event involving propositional content, but not the order of that content (Beaugrande and Dressler 1981, 90). A CPD communicative event's frame roughly corresponds to the CPD communicative event's specific communicative purpose.

Schema

A schema involves a global pattern of "events and states in ordered sequences linked by time, proximity and causality" (p. 90) to fit with the rearrangement of information. A schema relates a communicative event's content to the event's function and shows how, when, why, and for whom the communicative event was produced. Typical schemata are:

- narration (an event-process–related presentation, organizing connectedness through temporal and causal circumstances)
- recounting (a specific event–related presentation)
- description (a specific object–related presentation)
- reports (a general object–related presentation)
- instruction (a mode–related presentation)
- procedure (a general event–related presentation)

- explanation (a statement of reasons for a particular event or a situation)
- exposition (a complex sequence of multiple explanations)
- argument (a set of statements in support of beliefs, attitudes, and actions)

In the past, these schemata have been referred to as types of factual writing (Martin 1989), factual genres (Derewianka 1990), and viewpoints (Beaugrande 1997). They were also used to define genres. Labov and Waletzky (1967), for example, saw a genre as a schematic structure in which stages (either obligatory or obligatory + optional) occur in a fixed or at least partially fixed order. Similarly, van Leeuwen (1987), in his content-based account of media genres, described a *genre* as staged through different schemata such as narration, description, and exposition, which are concerned with the global motivation and approach of a discourse. A functional definition of a genre based on communicative purposes, as adopted in this book, not only solves the problems of previous structural definitions, but conveniently detaches schemata from the definition of a genre.

Within a CPD communicative event, various schemata are necessarily combined. Certain CPD communicative events do, though, prefer certain schemata. For example, while Shell's statement of objectives was primarily descriptive, Chairman Sant and CEO Bakke's media interview was primarily narrative. A CPD communicative event relying mostly on an instruction schema are corporate business guidelines:

Neither you nor any member of your family may solicit or accept from a supplier or customer money or a gift that could influence or could reasonably give the appearance of influencing IBM's business relationship with that supplier or customer. . . . If you have any doubts about a particular situation, you should consult your manager.[3]

Through the instruction schema of this extract employees are told what they are permitted or not permitted to do in hypothetical situations. While "Neither you nor . . . may " expresses prohibition, "could" is used to imply a possibility. The if-clause gives the text an overtone of tentativeness, nicely balancing the authority of "you." The use of "may" and the if-clause both increase the text's level of formality, which strongly supports the communicative event's specific communicative purpose of defining relations between a corporation and its employees.

Script

A script involves a pre-established routine defining a communicative event's situation and participants, and specifying participants' roles and their expected actions (cf. Schank and Abelson 1977) in the communicative event. A script sets the communicative event's social situation (Beaugrande and Dressler 1981, 90). Possessing knowledge of a particular script, a person can quite competently control a communicative event.

A CPD communicative event for which a corporate manager's familiarity with pre-established routines is especially important is the CEO media interview. The corporate manager's knowledge of structures underlying the CEO media interview script allows her or him to make the correct social moves. Through a series of questions the interviewer tries to elicit as much information as possible from the interviewee about her or him and her or his company. Selectively answering and commenting on questions, the corporate manager presents herself or himself and her or his company in the most favorable light. A CEO's familiarity with the CEO media interview script eliminates the need for her or him to think about the "whys" of the (now routine) situation.

Habitualization

Frames, schemata, and scripts are important because they provide the means for people to rationalize their cognitive resources. Referring to the existing frames, schemata, and scripts of a CPD genre, a corporation's management reduces its need for causal reasoning and for working out anew routine details of the content and form of a CPD communicative event. Indeed, if it were not for the names of companies and products, CPD communicative events within a particular CPD genre would be almost interchangeable.

Frames, schemata, and scripts are evidence of what Berger and Luckmann have referred to as "habitualization" (1991, 70–72), whereby meanings involved in people's actions become embedded as routines in those actions and available for their future action. Habitualization, Berger and Luckmann further explain, frees individuals from the burden of unnecessary decision-making providing a "psychological relief that has its basis in man's undirected instinctual structure" (p. 71). Relieving the tensions that result from undirected drives, habitualization provides a stable background that opens up a "foreground for deliberation and innovation." When a typification of habitualized actions (e.g., a CPD communicative event) becomes reciprocal and shared by all concerned (e.g., stakeholders and corporations), processes of habitualization result in institutionalization.

INSTITUTIONAL ISOMORPHISM

An example of processes of habitualization within corporations is what DiMaggio and Powell (1983) have named "institutional isomorphism": the inclination of corporations to copy instrumental practices from one another. DiMaggio and Powell distinguish between three types of institutional isomorphism: coercive, mimetic, and normative. Coercive isomorphism stems from social pressures exerted upon an organization by other organizations and by expectations of society. Mimetic isomorphism is a corporation's response to uncertainty, which, as DiMaggio and Powell argue, encourages imitation. When technologies are poorly understood, when organization's goals are ambiguous, or when the environment is uncertain, organizations tend to copy other organizations. The advantage of imitating those perceived to be more legitimate or successful is considerable: it supplies a good solution at little expense. Last, normative isomorphism is related to professionalization. An organization's legitimacy rests on a cognitive base produced by university-educated specialists who form networks that span organizations and enable a rapid diffusion of new knowledge. Modern executive education has created a pool of almost interchangeable individuals who occupy managerial positions and possess a similarity of orientation and disposition that may outweigh cultural variations that could otherwise be decisive for organizational behavior.

CONCLUSION

In its written form, CPD is a statement of a corporation's presence in society, the corporation's relationship with society, and the corporation's influence on society. The medium of writing turns CPD into an artifact, it abstracts and decontextualizes CPD, enables the careful packaging of CPD, and bestows social power on CPD. As an artifact, CPD acts as a representation for people in organizations, shapes their behavior, positions them in a social context, and helps ensure the reproduction of social circumstances that made that behavior possible.

Writing is also the medium through which processes of habitualized actions in a corporation, such as CPD communicative events, are typified and made reciprocal. Inasmuch as CPD communicative events are fundamental to the institutionalization and legitimization of a corporation's ideology, so too is writing.

Because the preferred medium of CPD is writing, the discoursal competence required of a corporate manager will be manifested mostly through the written form involving composing for both knowledge telling and knowledge transforming. To effectively tell and transform knowledge, a corporate manager has to be familiar with various patterns of knowledge, such as frame, schema, and script, typical to CPD, through which she or he is able to rationalize cognitive resources and habitualize her or his actions.

NOTES

1. Hymes was one of the first authors to define communicative competence as society-embedded: as a skill that includes knowledge of all the appropriate ways of using language, and that a speaker/listener requires to operate as a full member of a language community.

2. The Code of Hammurabi lists 282 laws assuring justice for the weak (Oates 1986, 75).

3. www.ibm.com/business_guidelines, 4.8.2.

11

Mass Media and CPD

In a *mass*, (1) far fewer people express opinions than receive them; for the community of publics becomes an abstract collection of individuals who receive impressions from the mass media. (2) The communications that prevail are so organized that it is difficult or impossible for the individual to answer back immediately or with any effect. (3) The realization of opinion in action is controlled by authorities who organize and control the channels of such action. (4) The mass has no autonomy from institutions; on the contrary, agents of authorized institutions penetrate this mass, reducing any autonomy it may have in the formation of opinion by discussion.

—C. W. Mills (1956, 304)

MASS MEDIA

To be sure, the interviews of Chairman Sant and CEO Bakke, CEO Weathrup, Mr. Welch, CEO Fiorina, and CEO Bernabé would not have been as they were without the "cosy cooperation" (cf. Thompson 1996, 140) of *Harvard Business Review* and *BusinessWeek*, founded on a willingness to collaborate with "purveyors of news." Indeed, the accommodating mood of mass media is crucial to a CEO's and a corporation's legitimization.

The Beginnings of Mass Media

The beginnings of mass media date back to the second half of the fifteenth century, when Gutenberg's techniques of printing began to spread throughout Europe (for a comprehensive account of the influence of media upon the development of modern societies, see Thompson 1996, 44–80). In late medieval and early modern Europe, the printing industry played an important role in the development of the capitalist economy. Based on principles of commodity production, printing gave rise to a new center of power greatly independent of the Church and the state. For the first time, the power of the Church was endangered by the symbolic power of printing and the growing number of printers, publishers, and enormous quantities of printed materials. Throughout the fifteenth and the first half of the sixteenth century, the Church, in collaboration with secular authorities, established a system of censorship, forbidding the printing of books that did not have ecclesiastical authorization.

In 1559 the Church compiled an "index librorum prohibitorum": a list of banned books, which remained in effect until the mid-nineteenth century. As many other cases of prohibition in the history of mankind, this prohibition too increased the desire for "forbidden fruit," which created a black market: books banned in one area were published in others and smuggled to readers.

Perhaps the most impressive proof of the symbolic power of printing is the role it played in the Reformation. It has been estimated that Luther's "Theses," posted on the door of the Augustinian church at Wittenberg on 31 October 1517, were distributed throughout Germany within two weeks and throughout Europe within a month (Thompson 1996, 57).

The convergence of capitalism, the printing industry and the diversity of languages in the late fifteenth and sixteenth centuries led to the emergence of "imagined communities," which were to become the bases for formation of nation-states (Anderson 1991, cited in Thompson 1996). As books were increasingly published in various vernaculars, readers became aware of belonging to a community of readers with whom they were linked through the medium of print and the use of common language. Today, in a similar way, the convergence of globalization, Internet and English as *lingua franca* is creating cyberspace: a "globally networked, computer-sustained, computer-accessed, and computer-generated, multidimensional set of overlapping 'virtual communities'" (Urry 2000, 71).

The Social Status of Mass Media

Controlled by social groups and individuals who possess various forms of social power, mass media tend to adopt a cooperative attitude toward the powerful and a restrictive attitude toward the powerless (Fairclough 1999b, 51; Thompson 1996, 140). Generally, access to mass media is limited to "identifiable individuals with known views and, ideally, well-known public figures who occupy some 'official' or semi-official position" (Halloran et al. 1970). In other words, a person's access to the media discourse is a confirmation of her or his "publicly acknowledged status and authority" (Fairclough 1999b, 64). The stricter the constraint on an individual's access to a particular medium, the greater the common perception of that medium as ascribing more importance to the public than to the private and as presenting facts, claims, and positions rather than personal feelings and circumstances (cf. Inglis 1996; Fairclough 1999a). Simply, that constraint defines the social status of a mass medium.

The social status of a mass medium is a statement that "characterizes not what is given in sentences and propositions, but the very fact that they are given, and the way in which they are given" (Foucault 2002, 124). The statement "cannot be hidden," but it is "not visible either. . . . It requires a certain change of viewpoint and attitude to be recognized and examined in itself." For example, placing their corporate advertisements in *National Geographic*, advertisers strategically use the social status of this esteemed publication with 114 years tradition and over a million circulation to institutionalize and legitimize their ideologies.

As all other discourse, media discourse is a "discourse of power," driven by groups' and individuals' will to power (cf. Foucault 1980, 1991). Mass media's claim to truth is simply a claim to power. Reproducing existing patterns of power distribution in society, mass media support ideologies of the dominant bloc. It is those relations of power in society, Enzensberger (1970) has argued, that, in fact, limit the full exploitation of media technological potential.

Herman and Chomsky's "Propaganda Model"

The relationship between mass media and the dominant bloc, or rather, the mutuality of their interests, has been described by Herman and Chomsky in their "propaganda model" (referred to in Chapter 1). The elite mass media, Herman and Chomsky have argued, are not just used by leading social actors to manufacture consent; they act as an ideological apparatus protecting and promoting the class interests of these actors and assuring their hegemony. According to Herman and Chomsky, five interrelated "filters" cause mass media to play a "propaganda role": (1) the ownership structure of dominant mass-media firms, (2) advertising as a primary income source of mass media, (3) the reliance of mass media on sources of information provided by centers of social power, (4) "flak," meaning social pressure put on journalists or editors who tend to be critical of the dominant bloc, and (5) the ideology of anti-communism. These five filters, Herman and Chomsky contend, represent loci of social power and induce mass media to support that power.

While Herman and Chomsky's model has often been dismissed as a "conspiracy theory" and criticized for its decidedly deterministic view of mass media, the fact remains that in today's society mass media tend to support centers of power. They do this indirectly, through covert rather than over censorship. The media visibility of centers of power, as Thompson suggests (1996, 140), is based on two points: a strictly constrained access to mass media, and the "self-censorship of news organizations which have something to gain from adopting a conciliatory stance."

RATIONALIZATION, COMMODIFICATION, AND SPECTACULARIZATION

Mass media have made CPD a part of the wider social processes of rationalization, commodification, and spectacularization. Rationalization constructs society as efficient, calculable, predictable, and controllable through nonhuman rather than human technology (cf. Ritzer 2000, 438). CPD's efficiency is achieved through media-generated availability and accessibility of CPD. Like a shopping mall, which, as Ritzer put it, is a highly effective "selling/buying machine," mass media provide a location for corporations to "sell" their ideologies and for stakeholders to "buy" those ideologies. CPD's calculability is attained in media-generated beliefs about corporations as providers of satisfaction. For customers, satisfaction is provided through innovation; for employees, through a superior work environment; for shareholders, through profit; and for communities, through social responsibility. CPD's predictability derives from the practice of corporations to standardize their CPD through CPD genres, communicative events, and language. Finally, CPD's controllability is founded on mass media removing the physical element from CPD by enabling corporations to control space and time.

Commodification and spectacularization construct society based on image to stimulate consumption (Debord 1994). The commodification of CPD is rooted in the unity of three "speaker roles" (cf. Goffman 1981): the role of mass media as a "principal," representing a viewpoint; the role of mass media as an "author," generating form for content; and the role of mass media as an "animator," delivering a message. The media discourse producer's full freedom to take on these roles and to assume full control of an audience is derived primarily from the spatial (and once temporal) disjunction between the media discourse producer and the media discourse consumer (cf. van Dijk 1988; Fairclough 1995).

INTERNET

The obvious example of a mass medium rationalizing CPD is the Internet: an interactive and sociable universe that offers corporations the possibility of not only linguistic but also extra-linguistic messages, interactive speech acts, and animated conversations (cf. Stafford 1994). The Internet integrates "thousands of networks of people, machines, programmes, texts and images in which quasi-subjects and quasi-objects are mixed together in new hybrid forms" (Urry 2000, 40). Allowing the continuous virtual witnessing[1] of corporations by everyone everywhere, the Internet has turned corporations into "digital nomads" (Makimoto and Manners 1997): commuters who use cyberspace to create mobile and instantaneous ideologies. But above all, Internet has returned written communication to the core of the corporation.

THE HP MERGER INTERNET NEWS SITE

The informality and lack of inhibition generally typical for cyberspace (cf. Reid 1995) encourage corporations to innovate their CPD. The HP merger Internet news site, created to elicit stakeholders' support for the HP-Compaq merger (referred to in Chapter 8), is such an example. This merger was special not only in its size—involving two "$40 billion behemoths" (Burrows 2001,

63—but also in the underlying power struggles between two parties: the pro-merger group orchestrated by HP CEO Carly Fiorina and the anti-merger group led by the HP's largest shareholder, the Packard foundation.

The HP merger Internet news site offered stakeholders, potential stakeholders, general public, and accidental viewers a multitude of merger-related messages: statements of merger benefits, press releases, letters to stakeholders, letters from members of senior management on merger benefits, and letters from members of senior management addressed to powerful opponents of the merger. The HP merger news site promised that the new HP would become the market leader, would double its services business, and would achieve annual cost savings of $2.5 billion. Positioning the HP-Compaq merger in cyberspace, the HP merger news site placed it on the public stage, turned it into public knowledge, and made it widely accessible and open for public debate. The following CPD communicative event was taken from the HP merger Internet news site:

Why support this merger?

By merging with Compaq, the new HP will become the market leader in servers, storage, management software, printing and imaging, and PCs, improving our ability to offer the end-to-end solutions customers demand. We will double our profitable and growing services business, enhance our R&D efforts, and extend our customer reach in 160 countries. We will achieve annual cost savings of $2.5 billion, adding $5 to $9 in present value to each HP share; and increase earnings per share by 13% during the first year following the merger. By improving profitability in enterprise computing systems, in PCs and access devices, and in IT services, we will have the financial strength to extend our successful imaging and printing franchise into new multi-billion dollar categories like digital imaging and digital publishing. All of this, of course, requires that we execute well; and we will. Indeed, those who suggest that the challenges ahead are beyond us greatly underestimate the people of the new HP. The closer you look, the more you will see that the merger of HP and Compaq is the single best way to strengthen our businesses and improve our market position, deliver more of what our customers need, enhance opportunities for our employees, and increase the value of your investment.[2]

"Why support this merger?" can be seen as performing three communicative actions: locutionary, illocutionary, and perlocutionary (cf. Austin 1962). Each of these actions links the event to its audience in a specific way.

The event's locution constates (declares, asserts, confirms) the merger, that is, makes it a part of stakeholders' world model. The event's ideational content, for example [160 countries, savings of $2.5 billion, increase earnings per share by 13%], is evidence of that action.

The events illocution relates to action performed by the event. According to Searle (1976), there are five basic types of illocutionary actions: representative, directive, commissive, expressive, and declarative. In a representative action the speaker is committed (in varying degrees) to the truth of a proposition. In a directive action the speaker tries to induce the hearer to do something. In a commissive action the speaker is committed to a certain course of action. In an expressive action the speaker expresses an attitude about the state of affairs. And in a declarative action the speaker alters the status of an object or situation. The highly frequent use of "will" projects "Why support this merger?" as a commissive action, an act of promise committed to the success of the merger.

Finally, the event's perlocutionary action relates to the event's actual effect upon its audience, which may or may not coincide with the illocutionary force of an event. The realization of the HP-Compaq merger shows the perlocutionary effect of "Why support this merger?" as having successfully matched its illocutionary force.

A communicative event's perlocutionary-illocutionary match is subject to constraints known as "felicity conditions"[3] (Searle 1976), which require the message producer to possess authority, show respect for conventions of a message, and assure audiences of her or his sincerity. "Why support this merger?" satisfied all of these three conditions. Like other HP-Compaq merger-related communicative events, it was carried by the legitimacy of Carly Fiorina as HP's CEO. Respect for discoursal conventions was achieved through the choice of the story format: a symbolic interpretation of the merger, which provided a meaning and a sequence for the audience. The story begins with reasons for the merger; it develops through a chain of events and actions, reaches a climax in the David and Lucile Packard Foundation's move to oppose the deal, and ends with the HP-Compaq merger. Finally, sincerity was manifested in the wealth of arguments offered to back up HP's promises.

COMPULSORY VISIBILITY

"Why support this merger?" is also an example of how the unprecedented development of mass media has fundamentally changed the way and rules by which CPD has to be managed. A corporation's visibility has become "compulsory" (Thompson 1996, 137): it is an imperative to which a corporation is forced to submit. Accordingly, corporations have become subject to "global scrutiny": a regime of visibility, involving vast and distant audiences and carrying the potential of great risk, but also great rewards (p. 148). It is compulsory visibility that made William Cooper Procter ("Do what is right") of Procter & Gamble, and John Akers ("Just say no") of IBM, and Carly Fiorina ("It ain't over till it's over") of Hewlett-Packard legends of corporate management.

EXTENDED MEDIAZATION

Another product of the massivity of media is "extended mediazation" (Thompson 1996, 110): a high degree of self-referentiality within the media. Self-referentiality results from the habit of authors to refer to other media messages, creating a network of references related to the same message, in order to legitimize their original message. For example, interfacing its "News":

"We pride ourselves in delivering consistent financial performance while fulfilling the dreams of our customers," said Jeffrey L. Bleustine, chairman and chief executive officer of Harley-Davidson, Inc. "For the fourteenth consecutive year, Harley-Davidson's dedicated employees, dealers, and suppliers have once again made this possible."[4]

with its mission statement:

We fulfill dreams through the experience of motorcycling, by providing to motorcyclists and to the general public an expanding line of motorcycles and branded products and services in selected market segments.[5]

Harley-Davidson created three dialogues. The first was a dialogue between "News" and CEO Bleustein's statement. The second was a dialogue between CEO Bleustein's statement and the corporation's mission statement. Clearly, CEO Bleustein assumed his audience's familiarity with Harley-Davidson's mission statement. A consequence of these two dialogues is a third dialogue: between "News" and the mission statement. This third dialogue is reinforced through the use of the direct quote, which renders Harley-Davidson's ideology—a commitment to fulfill the dreams of its customers—in its original form. The use of indirect speech would have subordinated the message, rather than incorporating it (which was the effect of the direct quote) and thus lessened the audience's attention. Facts would have been the same, but the effect would have been different. Through the direct quote, CEO Bleustine is foregrounded and Harley-Davidson's corporate news ostensibly related to the real world. Mutually supportive, Harley-Davidson's dialogues help to legitimize each other.

HP too relied on extended mediazation, via the Internet, television, and print, to legitimize its new corporate ideology: a commitment to invent. The cumulative effect was a new HP CPD, as for example, "Our promise to customers":

Invent. It's a simple word, but it carries rich significance. That's why "invent" appears under every HP logo. We are a company whose own inventive spirit—in research, in technology, products, in services, in business models, in the way we work—fuels the inventive capability of our customers. Our brand is about celebrating the inventive spirit—and the idea that the right technology can help people achieve remarkable things.[6]

The "promise" was made available by the Internet to the entire planet on the very day of the HP-Compaq merger.

CPD'S AUDIENCE

Central to mass media are audiences. All the main characteristics of mass communication—massivity, heterogeneity, temporal and spatial distance, public accessibility, onesidedness, and impersonality—are audience-related (Bell 1991, 85–95). CPD, as any other form of mediatized public discourse, reaches various audience segments: addressees (target audience), auditors (persons known and ratified as participants, but not addressed), overhearers (known to be there but not ratified), and eavesdroppers (not known to be there and not ratified). CPD's audience is both highly homogeneous and highly diverse. While homogeneity is presupposed in all of these audience segments' allegiance to the global economy, diversity is manifested in a variety of these audience segments' cultures, lifestyles, and attitudes.

Because of audience diversity in cultures, lifestyles, and attitudes, a corporation can never be perfectly sure whether an audience will be friendly or hostile, aware or unaware of circumstances, arguments, and counterarguments, and willing (or able) to understand a message in the same spirit in which it was intended. To elicit feedback, corporations invite stakeholders to submit their views on issues relevant to the corporation. For example, in Shell's 2000 report "People, Planet, and Profits" some 40 stakeholders' letters are reproduced under the title "You Told Shell." Whether praising

I admire your transparency in all your dealings. I think it is a good way of rebuilding the trust of the public in your company.[7]

or criticizing:

Why would Shell, an oil and gas company, be marketing alternative energy? I am sceptical about your motives.[8]

these letters are evidence of Shell respecting the "polling culture" of contemporary society.

Stakeholders' letters to Shell are simultaneously actuating and responsive. They are actuating by negotiating and renegotiating relationships with audiences, creating new images and expectations. They are responsive by confirming relationships with audiences and meeting audiences' predefined expectations (e.g., importance attributed to global information exchange, cultural diversity, sustainability, critical discourse awareness, etc.), which make up the global society. In sum, stakeholders' letters to Shell help to legitimize the corporation and its ideology.

CONCLUSION

Mass media are distinctly benevolent toward CPD. Apart from being a source of income for the mass media through, for instance, corporate media advertisements, CPD promotes the ideology of the dominant bloc, of which mass media are very much a part. Mass media define too CPD's audience which—being global—is increasingly inclined to view participation in CPD, both in terms of sending information and responding to it, as a key duty of their global citizenship.

Through mass media, CPD participates in the wider social processes of rationalization, commodification, and spectacularization of society. Thus,

CPD takes on three strategic roles: of a medium of virtual witnessing, of a medium of compulsory visibility, and of a medium of extended mediazation.

As a medium of virtual witnessing, a corporation's CPD replaces the corporation. In this sense, in a culture where "what you see is what you get," a corporation's CPD becomes self-legitimizing. As a medium of compulsory visibility, a corporation's CPD constitutes legitimate evidence of a corporation's social responsibility, accountability, and transparency. It functions as stakeholders' normalizing judgment to represent a set of norms stakeholders expect corporations to satisfy. As a medium of extended mediazation, a corporation's CPD becomes a network of references, which has to be managed on the basis of intelligence about that network. Strategically employed, a network of references gives a corporation the potential to productively generate, process, and apply its CPD.

NOTES

1. The syntagma "virtual witnessing" was created by Shapin and Shaffer (1985) to mean a process of accessing scientific evidence through perusal of scientific text (rather than, for example, witnessing an experiment itself).

2. www.votetheHPWay.com, March, 2002.

3. In Habermas's theory of social evolution (1975), "validity claims": comprehensibility, correctness, sincerity, and authority.

4. www. harley-davidson.com/company/news, January 18, 2000.

5. www.harley-davidson.com.

6. www.thenew.hp.com, June 13, 2002.

7. The Shell Report "People, Planet and Profits," 2000, p. 5.

8. Ibid., p. 29.

PART V

Quantitative Analysis

12

Five CPD Default Genres

The essential characteristics of corpus-based analysis are:
- it is empirical, analyzing the actual patterns of use in natural texts;
- it utilizes a large and principled collection of natural texts, known as a "corpus," as the basis for analysis;
- it makes extensive use of computers for analysis, using both automatic and interactive techniques;
- it depends on both quantitative and qualitative analytical techniques.

Taken together, these characteristics result in a scope and reliability of analysis not otherwise possible.

—*D. Biber, S. Conrad, and R. Reppen (1998, 4)*

CREATING A CORPUS

So far, we have explored individual CPD communicative events. We now turn to CPD genres: classes of CPD communicative events. To do this we need to generalize, which necessitates the analysis of a text corpus: a principled body of naturally occurring linguistic data, or rather, natural texts, enabling the identification of central and typical language features (cf. Leech 1991; Sinclair 1991; Biber et al. 1998). To assure the "generalizability" of results of a corpus analysis, a corpus has to be representative of the language segment under research. Corpus representativeness—the applicability of findings based on corpus contents to a larger hypothetical corpus—is still an open question in corpus linguistics. The representativeness of a text corpus, Leech (1991) has argued, tends to be assumed on the basis of its size rather than confirmed through a mathematical model. The problematic nature of corpus representativeness has also been underscored by Biber and colleagues (1998, 246). A researcher, they claim, is never fully aware of the extent of variation in languages or of all relevant contextual variables that need to be covered by the corpus. The need for corpus representativeness raises two key issues: corpus sampling techniques and corpus size.

Corpus Sampling Techniques

Because a text corpus is often assumed to be a reflection of a corpus domain (subject matter), sampling techniques are expected to assure a concentration of domain-specific words. However, neither the corpus domain nor domain-related sampling can guarantee an expected lexical profile. Ure (1971), for example, tells an amusing story of a text corpus recorded in a kitchen where a group of people were frying potatoes and talking about what they were doing. For those not acquainted with the situation, the recording was a mystery, as neither potatoes nor frying was lexically represented in the corpus. Ure's story points to the huge importance of both situational context and an appropriate interpretation of quantitative data.

Corpus Size

Another significant determinant of text corpus representativeness is corpus size expressed in terms of total number of words, total number of text samples, and total number of words within each text sample. A corpus has to be sufficiently large to include enough data to give a proper perspective on research goals and establish commonalities while disregarding individual variations. Any surplus text will significantly add to the amount of work involved and, possibly, drown relevant data in a mass of superfluous material.

In the earlier machine-readable text corpora,[1] such as the Brown, Lancaster-Oslo-Bergen (LOB) corpus, and the Survey of English Usage corpus (SEU), the number of words in a text corpus was customarily rounded off to one million words. This practice was further extended to the number of text samples in the corpus and the number of words in each text sample. Even now, in discussions on text corpus size an insecurity is felt, probably caused by the lack of empirical investigations into both corpus and text sample size. Nevertheless, two rules are respected when compiling a text corpus. For general-language and lexicographic studies, very large text corpora, consisting of millions of words, are essential (cf. Sinclair 1991; Biber et al. 1998). For a domain-specific text corpus, such as the corpus used in this analysis, the criterion "the more the merrier" does not necessarily apply.

Commenting on corpus-based analysis of linguistic variation, Biber (1990, cited in Biber and Finegan 1991; also Biber 1991) has shown how ten 1,000-word samples are quite representative of a genre and its use of certain grammatical features such as nouns, first- and third-person pronouns, past-tense markers, prepositions, and passives. The representativeness of small

(20–30,000 words), specialized text corpora that possess all the characteristics and relations found in larger corpora has also been convincingly demonstrated by Yang (1986, 93–103) and Greenbaum (1991, 83–91). The applicability of small text corpora is a plausible outcome of the characteristics of languages for specific purposes: predictable topics, specific distribution of syntactic structures, and specialized vocabulary.

COMPUTATIONAL TEXT ANALYSIS

Analysis of a text corpus assumes the use of computational text analysis (CTA). CTA has been used in many diverse fields, such as archaeology and psychology, in the study of linguistic variation (Biber 1991; Greenbaum 1991; Biber et al. 1998), lexicography (Landau 1989), analyses of stylistic properties of texts and genres (Biber and Finegan 1991; Crystal 1991a), and dialectology (Ihalainen 1991). (On the application of CTA in corpus linguistics cf. Aijmer and Altenberg 1991; Biber et al. 1998; Stubbs 2001.)

Apart from its obvious velocity, the computer offers a new quality to corpus-based studies. It actually makes possible what in the old pre-computer days was unthinkable. Data bases, which are indispensable for establishing reliable patterns of use, are simply too large to be dealt with by hand. Besides, as Biber and colleagues (1998) point out, a computer does not get tired and does not change its mind, which guarantees a stable and consequent analysis. Standard products of CTA are frequency lists, alphabetical lists, text concordances, and basic numerical parameters.

Frequency Lists

A frequency list shows absolute (and relative) frequencies of all "types" (different word forms) in a text corpus. Frequency lists can have a descending sort order (the word occurring the most appears first) and an ascending sort order (the word occurring the least appears first). Since CTA treats members (e.g., write, writes, writing, wrote, written) of a lemma (e.g., write) as different words, frequency lists are lemmatized by adding together the frequencies for all word forms of the lemma.

The vocabulary of English is generally divided into two categories: function (grammatical) words and content (lexical) words. This division, though, is not perfectly discrete, as all function words have at least some content. Function words (auxiliary verbs, modal verbs, pronouns, prepositions, determiners, conjunctions) have sparse meanings, adapt easily to their environment, and relate content words to each other. Function words occupy the top ranks of any frequency list. The ten most frequent words of the LOB (Lancaster-Oslo-Bergen) corpus, for example, are: "the," "of," "and," "to," "a," "in," "that," "is," "was," and "it" (Stubbs 2001, 126). The fifteen most frequent (inevitably, function) words of any English text account for about 25 percent of the text (cf. Landau 1989; Crystal 1991b).

Content words (nouns, adjectives, adverbs, main verbs) carry meanings, created and maintained by the use of language in millions of iterative actions. Unlike function words, they have stable meanings, adapt weakly to their environment, and do the meaning work in a text. In isolation, many words would be ambiguous, but then, a word hardly ever occurs in isolation. Invariably, a word is used in context, either physical (e.g., a road sign) or linguistic (e.g., an utterance), which, because both types of context belong to people's world model, eliminates potential ambiguity. It is generally accepted, therefore, that the meaning of a word is contained in its sense, or rather in "what is permanent about its relation to the world" (Hudson 1998, 80). Most words, however, have more than one meaning. How does one know, for example, which out of some thirty meanings of "time" have been used in the following two examples?

> It buys you *time* to incubate an idea . . .
> But every *time* we initiate a change . . .

To exactly determine the two meanings of "time," two steps are necessary: first, a reference to one's world knowledge, which contains all the meanings of "time"; second, a reference to the linguistic context ("buys" and "every"), which delimits possible meanings of "time." Cross-referencing world knowledge with linguistic context enables one to determine the meaning of "time" in "It buys you *time* to incubate an idea . . . " to be a length of time necessary for something, and the meaning of "time" in "But every *time* we initiate a change . . . " to be a specific occasion when something happens.

Content words occupy the middle and lower ranks of any frequency list. About 50 percent of all types on a frequency list belong to the hapax: words of frequency one.

Alphabetical Lists

Alphabetical lists show types in either alphabetical order or backward alphabetical order (right to left) with their frequencies of occurrence. Typically used for locating lexical items and checking data, alphabetical lists can also be employed as objects of study to formulate hypotheses and check assumptions (cf. Kjellmer 1984).

Text Concordance

Text concordance (also known as KWIC: KeyWord in Context) shows occurrences of all "tokens" (all words in a text) within their natural context (Table 12.1).

Providing quick access to individual lexical items (here the personal pronoun "I") and patterns of their co-occurrence with other words (the verbs "have," "spend," "become," "see," and "learn"), text concordance complements and clarifies the frequency list data.

Table 12.1
An Extract from Corpus^{CPD} Concordance for "I"

000081	therefore **i** had to reflect on them all patientl
000087	eenager, when **i** spent a year there through the amer
000091	ped me because **i** had to resolve problems on my own -
000097	france, where **i** became a senior economist with the
000098	i look back, **i** see how critical that experience wa
000099	at the oecd, **i** learned to analyze problems, to ge

The first known text concordance was the Vulgate Bible concordance, produced by the Parisian Dominicans in the mid-twelfth century. English biblical concordances were created in the mid-thirteenth century. By the mid-nineteenth Century, the first Shakespeare concordances were being made available. In those days concordancing was done by hand and lasted for decades.

Basic Numerical Parameters

Basic numerical parameters are: type-token ratio, hapax ratio, lexical density, average sentence length, and average word length.

Type-token ratio (TTR) is the ratio (%) of different word forms to the total number of words in a text. TTR is a reliable indicator of semantic precision (which is a result of careful lexical choice) and density of information.

Hapax ratio (HR) is the ratio (%) of the number of hapax to the number of types. HR reveals the rhythm by which the vocabulary within a corpus is augmented—a phenomenon that "gives us a glimpse of the extent of the lexicon at work" (Muller 1969, 54). Like TTR, HR is an indicator of the principles behind lexical choice and, accordingly, density of information.

Lexical density (LD) is the ratio (%) of the number of content words to the number of tokens. LD indicates the corpus's lexical choice and density of information and reflects circumstances typical to the production of the discourse (cf. Ochs 1979).

Average sentence length (ASL) in words is a key parameter of text readability, indicating how difficult a text is to read. Over fifty procedures are available for predicting reading difficulty (Crystal 1991b, 252): the best known are the Fog Index, the Flesch Reading Ease Formula, and the Flesch-Kincaid Formula. All of these formulae, though, have one weakness: they are based on the assumption that text readability is a result of word/sentence length and disregard more important factors such as sentence complexity and a reader's knowledge and motivation.

Average word length (AWL) in orthographic letters is evidence of a text's density of information and exactness of meaning (Zipf 1949; Biber 1991). Typical for discourse with high informational focus, greater average word length indicates a careful integration of information and a precise lexical choice.

CORPUS[CPD]

In this chapter we focus on the five CPD default genres: the corporate mission statement genre (MS), the CEO media interview genre (MI), the corporate business guidelines genre (BG), the corporate media advertisement genre (MA), and the corporate annual report genre (AR). To explore these genres, we compiled five subcorpora[CPD], all of which are collections of complete documents representing CPD communicative events within the same class. There are definite advantages in compiling a complete-document corpus: the danger of fragmentation, which could be created through collecting cut-out samples, is eliminated, and the validity of sampling techniques stops being an issue (Sinclair 1991, 19). Together the five subcorpora[CPD] constitute corpus[CPD] (Table 12.2). Computational text analysis of corpus[CPD] was performed in TEXTPACK for Windows.[2]

CORPUS[CPD] BASIC NUMERICAL PARAMETERS

Values for corpus[CPD] basic numerical parameters are presented in Table 12.3. To provide a perspective on these values, values for the basic numerical parameters of Fox's management ergolect corpus (corpus[ME]), to which we have referred in Chapter 2, are included.

The values for both text corpora signal a careful lexical choice, lexical precision, and exactness of meaning. A combination of comparatively long words and a high TTR value is a reliable indicator of lexical specificity (cf. Biber 1991, 238), which is known to be subjectively linked to high-status social groups,

Table 12.2
Corpus[CPD]

Corpus[CPD]	Running words	Complete documents
Subcorpus[MS]	20,160	420
Subcorpus[MI]	54,227	10
Subcorpus[BG]	37,017	10
Subcorpus[MA]	21,336	150
Subcorpus[AR]	58,458	10
Total	191,198	600

Table 12.3
Values for Corpus^{CPD} and Corpus^{ME} Basic Numerical Parameters

Basic numerical parameters	Values for Corpus^{CPD}	Values for Corpus^{ME}
Tokens	191,198	78,875
Types	16,175	9,238
TTR	8.45%	11.71%
Hapax	7,893	4,584
Hapax ratio	48.80%	49.73%
Lexical density (LD)	65.15%	53.75%
Number of sentences	10,728	3,898
Average sentence length	17.82	20.23
Average word length	5.54	5.74

intellectual and professional competence, and self-control (Ng and Bradac 1993, 43).

The values for corpus^{CPD} are evidence too of the importance of CPD's propositional content. They indicate that content to be determinant (pre-planned), stable (predictable), and complex (varied). A comparison of corpus^{CPD} parameters with parameters obtained by Biber for 23 genres (1991, 246–269) shows CPD to quantitatively resemble academic prose, official documents, and professional letters, while different from personal letters, adventure fiction, and mystery fiction.

CORPUS^{CPD} FREQUENCY LISTS

The top fifty lemmas for subcorpora^{CPD} and corpus^{CPD} in descending order are presented in Table 12.4.

The Definite Article

Expectedly, the top ranks of Table 12.4 are dominated by function words. The most frequent lemma in all subcorpora^{CPD}—with the exception of "we" in subcorpus^{MS} and "be" in subcorpus^{BG}—is the definite article. The average relative frequency of "the" for corpus^{CPD} is 3.9 percent, which, compared to some other written text corpora, is rather low. For example, the average relative frequency of "the" in the LOB corpus is 6.8 percent (Stubbs 2001, 126), and in corpus^{ME} 5.9 percent (Fox 1999b). The lower average relative frequency of

Table 12.4
Subcorpora^{CPD} and Corpus^{CPD} Top Fifty Lemmas

Rank	Subcorpus^{MS}	Subcorpus^{MI}	Subcorpus^{BG}	Subcorpus^{MA}	Subcorpus^{AR}	Corpus^{CPD}
1	we	the	be	the	the	the
2	and	I/me/my/mine	company names	you	and	be
3	the	to	to	to	of	to
4	to	we/us/our(s)	you/your	of	in	and
5	in	and	or	and	we	we
6	of	a	of	we	to	of
7	a	be	the	a	be	a
8	be	of	a	be	a	in
9	company names	in	and	in	by	you
10	company	have	in	with	on	have
11	customers	you/your(s)	not	it	company names	that
12	with	that	with	that	for	it
13	for	they/them/their(s)	for	can	have	for
14	good	it	that	company names	that	company names
15	service	for	may	more	this	I
16	world	do	it	for	company	with
17	people	people	any	have	operation	or
18	provide	but	as	no	data	not
19	responsible	with	competitors	or	production	do
20	will	not/no	information	they	reduce	people
21	community	company	if	when	with	on
22	on	at	other	at	year	they
23	quality	on	supplier	world	as	will
24	product	more	employee	on	from	as
25	value	will	business	what	business	company
26	work	can	have	business	environmental	much
27	high	as	such	people	group	but

Table 12.4 (continued)

Rank	Subcorpus^{MS}	Subcorpus^{MI}	Subcorpus^{BG}	Subcorpus^{MA}	Subcorpus^{AR}	Corpus^{CPD}
28	shareholders	say	company	will	other	can
29	employees	so	products	financial	will	good
30	success	this	should	local	countries	at
31	citizen	company names	from	new	more	business
32	mission	or	on	this	include	by
33	create	when	include	so	use	when
34	commitment	he	management	all	they	from
35	ethical	make	conduct	but	competition	customer
36	leading	there	marketing	class	principle	information
37	life	about	provide	countries	at	very
38	innovative	all	relationships	create	which	products
39	though	want	accept	comfort	also	work
40	build	what	property	just	billion	change
41	communication	from	situations	life	local	time
42	conduct	time	confidential	other	performance	what
43	deliver	business	proprietary	than	economic	employees
44	group	if	industry	today	prices	say
45	personal	change	deal with	about	over	which
46	superior	who	authorized	around	such	who
47	use	by	assets	benefit	capital	want
48	believe	years	determinate	day	impact	such
49	encourage	how	value	even	sale	global
50	excellence	see	whether	global	systems	how

"the" in corpus^{CPD} is probably an element of what Leech (1971, 84) has referred to as "abbreviated grammar": a reduced set of rules, typical for the language of press and commercial advertising.

Personal Pronouns

A highly frequent group of function words in Table 12.4 are the personal pronouns: "we," "I," "you," and "they." Personal pronouns in subcorpora^{CPD}

not only represent people, but, as our analysis of CEO Gerstner's statement in Chapter 5 showed, serve too as ties that create textual cohesion. Take, for example, a *Harvard Business Review* UPS corporate advertisement "Community Internship Program":

"I hugged all of them goodbye, then one little girl ran back and whispered, 'come back, ok?'" Every year for the past thirty years, UPS has sent a growing number of managers on a unique sabbatical. They leave behind their families and day jobs to spend a month living in communities that need help. They build houses. Tend to the sick. Feed the hungry. Through the UPS Community Internship Program, they not only help their new communities, they help themselves. They broaden their perspectives. They learn. And in the end, it makes them better managers. Not to mention better people.[3]

Connecting the propositional content of the second sentence of the text—UPS managers' social engagement—to every subsequent sentence, the personal pronoun "they," its objective form "them," and the reflexive pronoun "themselves" function as lexical ties making the text cohesive. At the same time, sheer repetition gives the personal pronoun "they" a force of meaning that takes it beyond its referent, UPS managers.

The capacity of pronouns to imply meanings beyond their referents has been explored by several authors (e.g., Maitland and Wilson 1987; Wilson 1990). Using examples from public, notably political, discourse, these authors have shown how the pronominal system of English gives speakers strategic possibilities to encourage solidarity, publicly identify allies and enemies, and self-distance themselves from topics, participants, and responsibilities involved in the process of communication.

Analyzing the use of pronouns for self-distancing in the political speeches of former British Prime Minister Margaret Thatcher, Wilson (1990, 71) drew up a characteristic pronominal scale that reflects Mrs. Thatcher's idiosyncratic style in the projection of her political ideologies (Figure 12.1).

According to Wilson, Mrs. Thatcher associated the greatest distancing strength to the pronoun "those," which she used to refer to groups she considered to be potentially subversive. Similarly, CEO Gerstner associated the pronoun "those" to concepts (slogans, institutional values) that he wished to mark as negative. Wilson's analysis of Mrs. Thatcher's speeches (1991, 184, Appendix, Table A.2) shows her to have preferred the use of the pronoun "we" (relative frequency 3.09%) over "I" (relative frequency 0.56%). Probably,

Figure 12.1
Pronominal Scale of Self-distancing for Mrs. Thatcher

0	1	2	3	4	5	6	7	8	9
I	we	you (direct)	one	you (indefinite)	she	he	they	it	those

Mrs. Thatcher (as did CEO Gerstner) considered the use of "I" to be too authoritative.

Generally, though, the CEO, as subcorpus[MI] top fifty lemmas show, prefers the use of "I" (relative frequency 2.74%) to "we" (relative frequency 2.42%). Serving as a locus for the CEO's most important values, the personal pronoun "I" is fundamental to the CEO's ideology. "I," Mead has explained in his book *Mind, Self and Society* (1962), is a form typically used by members of highly developed societies (primitive societies are dominated by "me"). Through "I," social actors show their independence of external and internal controls. Through "I," a person asserts herself or himself and leads social changes.

While the pronouns "we" and "I" are the key pronouns of the corporate mission statement genre, the CEO media interview genre, and the corporate annual report genre, the key pronoun of the corporate business guidelines genre and the corporate media advertisement genre is "you." Whereas in the corporate business guidelines genre "you" is definite, in the corporate media advertisement genre it is indefinite. Typically collocating with "may" and "may not," the definite "you" of the corporate business guidelines genre is authoritative. Finally, the high frequencies of "they" and "he" in the CEO media interview genre and the high frequencies of "he" and "they" in the corporate media advertisement genre are a consequence of these genres' use of a narrative schema in which personal pronouns show actors participating in events.

Company Names

The first content word to appear in Table 12.4 is "company names" (rank 9 in subcorpus[MS], rank 31 in subcorpus[MI], rank 2 in subcorpus[BG], rank 14 in subcorpus[MA], rank 11 in subcorpus[AR]). And since over 50 percent of all mentions of the lemma "company" in all subcorpora are self-referential, their frequencies can be added to the frequencies of "company names." Why do corporations name so ubiquitously? Simply because naming is powerful. As Merleau-Ponty (1962) aptly put it, it is impossible to "do or say anything without its acquiring a name in history."

Corporations are well aware of the importance of a name. When, for example, in 1999 First Chicago became Bank One, Bank One launched a corporate media advertisement under the title "If We Call a Rock a Stone, Isn't It Still a Rock?":

Names are powerful things. For years First Chicago has been making a name for itself in international banking. Our name has become synonymous with international capabilities from trade services to FX and risk management. And now First Chicago has chosen yet another set of words to define itself: Bank One. Just as calling a rock by another name cannot change what it is, our new name can't change the heritage we've created for ourselves and our clients. We wouldn't want to even if we could. Instead, we intend to strengthen our identity by taking on some of the properties of our new name.[4]

Calling on the legitimizing power of the name First Chicago, Bank One explained to its stakeholders that, in spite of the bank's new name, First Chicago remains First Chicago. A corporation's name, Bank One knew, bears an identity and an institutional value that can displace other names, identities, and institutional values (cf. Oakes 1998, 12). A corporation's name, Bank One also knew, "implies the existence of a nomenclature, which in turn implies a designated social location" (Berger and Luckmann 1991, 152).

Key Words

Along with company names, a number of content words, for example, "people," "shareholders," "employees," "world," "global," "countries," "much," and "business," occur in the top fifty lemmas of all subcorpora[CPD]. The presence of these content words is an indication of their importance as key words of corporations, the corporate world, and CPD.

In every language and language variety, key words[5] offer insight into the most important values and processes of a particular era, culture, society, social groups, and professions. In this sense, vocabulary can be regarded as a key to history, culture, and society (Wierzbicka 1999). Key words gain their status within a given social context and lose their status with changed circumstances. Around 500 B.C.E. a key word of Old Greece was "polis"–the name for a city-state and the principal political unit, representing the sole focus of law, morality, and religion. A key word of sixteenth-century Russia was "oprichniki"–the name for the secret police force responsible to Tsar Ivan IV, "The Terrible," that removed civil liberties and depopulated much of central Russia. Similarly, a key word in the United States between 1920 and 1933 was "prohibition," a key word in Europe during World War II was "collaboration," and a key word in the Soviet Union between 1985 and 1991 was "perestroika." Each of these key words, at a particular time, embodied specific historical circumstances and a scale of social values. Today, with changed circumstances, they have lost their significance and no longer elicit emotions.

To provide a perspective on the corpus[CPD] key words that represent corporate management values for the 2000s, management values for the 1990s and the 1950s are given in Table 12.5.

The 1990s values are represented by the top five key words of Fox's (1999b) analysis of the social identity of management ergolect. The 1950s values are represented by the top five key words of Buchholz's (1978) study of belief systems across different categories of American workers in that period. Compared, these three groups of values show how over the past fifty years a dramatic change in corporate management has taken place. The 1950s were dominated by an organization-man pattern that valued status and ascension within the organizational hierarchy. The 1990s were dominated by an emphasis on work and management. The 2000s are dominated by a humanistic belief system operating within the global market and focusing on stakeholders and knowledge.

Table 12.5
The Changing Values of Corporate Management

Val		
1950s Driven	*1990s Driven*	*2000s Driven*
hierarchy	company	company names
respect for authority	work	people
corporate efficiency	manager	customers
team player	management	business
career	organization	information

Subcorpora[CP] Characteristic Lemmas

From rank 11 down in Table 12.4, lemmas (both function and content words) more characteristic to a subcorpus[CPD] begin to appear. These characteristic lemmas, for example "product" in subcorpus[MS], "change" in subcorpus[MI], and "may" in subcorpus[BG], reflect a CPD genre's specific communicative purpose and are to be expected.

The characteristic lemmas of subcorpus[MS] are almost all content words: "customers," "good," "service," "provide," "responsible," "community," "quality," "product," "value," "work," "high," "success," "mission," "create," "commitment," "ethical," "leading," "life," "innovative." We believe this lexical profile to be a consequence of the genre's use of a descriptive schema (a specific object-related presentation).

Many characteristic lemmas of subcorpus[MS] are adjectives (responsible, high, ethical, leading, innovative, personal, superior), whose role is to elaborate the genre's propositional content. Among the characteristic lemmas of other subcorpora[CPD] there are few, if any, adjectives: in subcorpus[MI] none, in subcorpus[BG] four (confidential, proprietary, authorized, determinate), in subcorpus[MA] four (financial, local, new , global), and in subcorpus[AR] three (environmental, local, economic). Adjectives in subcorpus[MI], we note, occupy lower frequencies than in other subcorpora and are, therefore, not shown in Table 12.4. Adjectives typical of the CEO media interview are "big," "high," "political," "good," "great," "important," "new," "strategic," "commercial," "critical," "complex," and "difficult."

Adjectives in English closely correspond with property concepts: concepts referring to properties, qualities, or characteristics of referents. In his research into the use of the adjective class in seventeen languages, Dixon (1977) suggests seven types of property concepts: dimension (big, little), physical property (hard, heavy), color, human propensity (happy, clever), age (new, old), value (good, bad), and speed (fast, slow). In her analysis of dominant concepts of management ergolect, Fox (1999b) widened Dixon's typology to include another property concept type: spatiality (local, global).

Categorizing the above adjectives as property concepts shows the corporate mission statement genre to be focused mainly on human propensity and value, the corporate business guidelines genre to be focused on human propensity, the corporate media advertisement genre and the corporate annual report genre to be focused on value and spatiality, and the CEO media interview genre to be focused almost exclusively on values.

Completely different from the characteristic lemmas of subcorpus^{MS}, the characteristic lemmas of subcorpus^{MI} are mainly function words: for example, the verb "do" (rank 16), the personal pronoun "he" (rank 34), and the relative pronoun "who" (rank 46). We believe this particular lexical profile to be a consequence of the genre's use of a narrative schema (an event-process-related presentation). Similarly, lemmas characteristic to subcorpus^{MA} are mostly function words. Like the CEO media interview genre, the corporate media advertisement genre uses a narrative schema. Finally, lemmas characteristic to subcorpus^{BG} and subcorpus^{AR} are specific in that they combine function and content words. Whereas corporate business guidelines typically use an instructive schema (a mode-related presentation), the corporate annual report relies mostly on a report schema (a general object-related presentation).

Hapax

The bottom of all subcorpora^{CPD} frequency lists is occupied by the hapax. Two distinctive groups of content words belong to the hapax: professionalisms and scientific terms. Although rich in meaning to members of the corporate management discourse community, professionalisms may not be perfectly clear to outsiders. Yet, professionalisms are the most striking linguistic confirmation of corporate management's internalization of the corporate world and constitute ready evidence that being a corporate manager not only entails acting as a corporate manager, but also speaking as a corporate manager.

Scientific terms, the second group of content words found in the hapax, are as much a part of CPD as they are of various orders of scientific discourse. Consider, for example, the Aventis *Harvard Business Review* corporate advertisement:

Life is a source of constant mystery. It's true for everyone, especially scientists trying to discover the nature of life itself. The decoding of the human genome will open up a completely new understanding of the actual processes of life and the causes of many illnesses. Aventis, a world-leading research-orientated pharmaceutical company will utilize these new findings for innovative pharmaceuticals, preventive vaccines and therapeutic proteins. After all, it is our long term objective not only to treat illnesses but to prevent them. So that people can lead healthier lives.[6]

In this text, the biotechnological terms such as "decoding of the human genome" and "therapeutic proteins" are placed in a frame of two general truths: life is a source of constant mystery, and scientists are continually trying to discover the nature of life. As these two terms constitute a puzzle for anyone but an expert in the field of biotechnology, obviously, their textual function is much more than ideational. These two terms perform other—personal, interpersonal, contextual, and, possibly, aesthetic—functions that give them a status of semiotic symbols. In effect, they serve to legitimize the corporation and its ideology founded on a promise of healthier lives.

CONCLUSION

Applying CTA to a corpus of five CPD default genres—the corporate mission statement, the CEO media interview, the corporate business guidelines, the corporate media advertisement, and the corporate annual report—we were able to explore CPD at the level of genres, which elevated our understanding of CPD beyond the level of individual CPD communicative events.

CPD can be conceptualized only through individual communicative events, which are linked to CPD through genres that represent classes of CPD communicative events. CPD, CPD genres, and CPD communicative events are brought together in a CPD continuum (Figure 12.2).

The CPD continuum is a virtual system stipulating the potential linguistic choices available to all corporations. An individual communicative event is a realization of some of those potential choices. A totality of communicative events constitutes CPD. Between the two ends of the CPD continuum, that is, between actual choices and potential choices, lie systems of stabilized linguistic choices: CPD genres.

The existence of a CPD continuum generates a matrix of combinations involving CPD communicative events, CPD genres, and CPD as a whole. Up to now, in this book we have explored two combinations: individual CPD communicative events in individual corporations and sets of CPD communicative events in a large number of corporations. There are, of course, many other explorable combinations involving relations between CPD communicative events, CPD genres, and CPD. It would be possible, for example, to explore all CPD communicative events for one corporation, or one class of CPD communicative events (a CPD genre) for a number of corporations.

Because there has been no systematic research into CPD, little is known about the CPD continuum. Each point along the continuum offers a perspective on CPD at a different level of abstraction. Analyzing individual communicative events, we explored the event end of the continuum. Analyzing corpus^{CPD}, we explored the CPD end of the continuum.

Figure 12.2
The CPD Continuum

CPD communicative events   CPD genres   CPD

NOTES

1. The first machine-readable text corpus was the Brown Corpus, compiled by W. N. Francis and H. Kučera at the beginning of the 1960s at Brown University, Providence, Rhode Island. The Brown Corpus contains one million words of American English texts, published in 1961. The British equivalent of the Brown Corpus is the LOB (Lancaster-Oslo-Bergen) Corpus, containing one million words of written British English, also published in 1961. Second-generation text corpora are the Birmingham Collection of English Texts (20 million words) and the Long-man/Lancaster English Language Corpus (30 million words). Third-generation text corpora are the British National Corpus (one hundred million words) and the Bank of English (over 450 million words), which continues to grow. The best-known spoken corpora are the IBM-Lancaster Spoken English Corpus (52,000 words), the London-Lund corpus (approximately 500,000 words), and the Corpus of Spoken American English compiled at the University of California at Santa Barbara (200,000 words).

2. TEXTPACK for Windows was developed in the Zentrum für Umfragen, Methoden und Analysen (ZUMA), Mannheim, Germany (Mohler & Züll 1998). TEXTPACK is a versatile program that includes features such as content analysis, literary and linguistic computational analysis, and special-purpose procedures such as categorizing, classifying and tagging.

3. *Harvard Business Review*, January-February 1999, p. 15.

4. *The Economist*, October 30, 1999, p. 14.

5. The study of key concepts within a historical context is part of structural and historical semantics and the theory of semantic fields. The theory of semantic fields was first introduced by Trier (1931), and further developed by the French linguist Matoré (1951), who placed a strong emphasis on social criteria. Investigating the vocabulary of various sectors of society, Matoré defined a key word as "a unit expressing a society . . . a person, a feeling, an idea which are alive in so far as society recognizes in them its ideal" (1953, 68). For a more recent research application of key concepts see Fox (2000), who suggested a model of semantic fields to research an understanding of the concept "managerial ethics" in post-communist countries.

6. *Harvard Business Review*, February 2002, pp. 2–3.

13

Five Corporate Web Pages

Thus by the end of the twentieth century the Internet is a metaphor for the social life as fluid. It involves thousands of networks, of people, machines, programmes, texts and images in which quasi-subjects and quasi-objects are mixed together in new hybrid forms. Ever-new computer networks and links proliferate in unplanned and mixed patterns. In such a fluid space it is not possible to determine identities once and for all, since a fluid world is a world of *mixtures*. Messages "find their way," rather like blood does through multiple capillaries.

—J. Urry (2000, 40–41)

THE CORPORATE WEB PAGE

According to Cahners In-Stat Group, a high-tech market research and consulting firm, corporations are expected to boost their spending on Internet technology and services from $49 billion in 2000 to $110 billion by 2004 (Internet Infrastructure . . . 2003). Referring to the value of the Internet for modern businesses, Kneko Burney, In-Stat's Director of eBusiness Infrastructure and Services, explains:

Larger firms see the Internet as a cost effective means to improve communication across groups: employees, the supply chain, customers, etc. and are likely to improve the intelligence and robustness of this communication. In contrast, smaller firms are still defining themselves online. Given this, their focus will likely be to simply build a relevant point of presence on the Web and use it effectively.

Immediately available to all of a corporation's stakeholders anywhere, the corporate Web page has become a corporation's principal default genre, with which it "roams" across national borders. The corporate Web page has both the general communicative purpose of constructing a corporation's ideology to enable the practice of power through consent and the specific communicative purpose of providing stakeholders with instant information on a corporation, such as its history, business activities, financial performance, commitment to social responsibility, employee recruitment and training policies, and so on.

Although corporate Web pages do include propositional content taken from other corporate genres, in particular the corporate mission statement genre and the corporate annual report genre, the Web page has not been referred to as a collection of these genres. A corporate genre, we recall, is defined exclusively on the basis of functional criteria (general and specific communicative purposes), not propositional content. As a part of the corporate Web page, content originating from other corporate genres is subject to the Web page's specific communicative purpose, not the specific communicative purposes of those genres.

SUBCORPORA^{WP}

In this chapter we use CTA of the corporate Web page to explore the ideologies of five corporations: Accor, Airbus, Altana, Ricoh, and Vodafone.

Accor is the European leader and one of the world's largest groups in travel, tourism, and, corporate services. The corporation employs 150,000 associates in 140 countries and has 3,800 hotels covering 90 countries. Accor's services—designed, developed, and managed by Accor to help people "facilitate life essentials," "enhance their well-being," and "increase their performance"—are used by 13 million people every day in 32 countries.

Airbus is a leading aircraft manufacturer that consistently captures around half of all orders for airliners with more than 100 seats. Established in 1970, the corporation is based in Toulouse in the southwest of France and employs some 46,000 people around the world. Airbus operates 16 development and manufacturing facilities in France, Germany, Spain, and the U.K. and has subsidiaries in the United States, China, and Japan. Airbus's mission is to "provide the aircraft best suited to the market's needs and to support these aircraft with the highest quality of service." In 2002, Airbus achieved a turnover of some 19.4 billion euros.

Altana specializes in four medical fields: therapeutics, in-vitro diagnostics, imaging, and self-medication. The company's core competence is anchored in gastrointestinal, respiratory, and heart diseases. Altana has over 7,000 employees and 30 subsidiaries and holding participations in Europe, North and South America, and Asia. The company's main offices are located in Konstanz, Germany. In 2002, Altana recorded sales of 2.6 billion euros.

Founded in 1936, Ricoh is one of the world's leading suppliers of office automation equipment, including copiers, facsimile machines, data processing systems, and related supplies. The company is also renowned for its state-of-the-art electronic devices and photographic equipment. Ricoh aims to create an environment in which "virtually anyone can achieve effortless processing and management of all available information, including images, photos, text and figures." Today Ricoh has around 75,000 employees in Japan, North America, Europe, Asia, and Oceania.

Vodafone launched its first network in 1985. It is now one of the world's largest mobile telecommunications network companies, sereving more than 112.5 million customers. Vodafone's vision is "to be the world's mobile communications leader enriching customers' lives, helping individuals, businesses and communities be more connected in a mobile world." Vodafone's values are a "passion for customers," a "passion for Vodafone's people," and a "passion for the world around Vodafone."

The research premise proposed is that the highly frequent content words of a corporation's downloaded Web page (subcorpus^{WP}) represent ideas (concepts, meanings, actions) constitutive to a corporation's ideology.

SUBCORPORA^{WP} BASIC NUMERICAL PARAMETERS

Values for subcorpora^{WP} (SC^{ACCOR}, SC^{AIRBUS}, SC^{ALTANA}, SC^{RICOH}, SC$^{VODA-FONE}$) basic numerical parameters are presented in Table 13.1.

Compared to values for subcorpora^{CPD} basic numerical parameters (Table 12.3), values for subcorpora^{WP} basic numerical parameters, particularly for the hapax ratio, are somewhat higher, which shows the corporate Web page's propositional content to be determinant, stable, and complex.

Table 13.1
Values for Subcorpora^{WP} Basic Numerical Parameters

Parameters	SC^{ACCOR}	SC^{AIRBUS}	SC^{ALTANA}	SC^{RICOH}	SC^{VODAFONE}
Tokens	8,816	6,788	9,585	7,112	10,218
Types	1,940	1,654	1,908	1,433	2,037
TTR	22.01%	24.38%	19.91%	20.15%	19.94%
Hapax	1,056	894	985	786	1,107
Hapax ratio	54.43%	54.05%	51.62%	54.85%	54.34%
Lexical density	51.09	60.81	60.54	56.56	51.47
Total sentences	385	271	376	272	441
ASL	22.96	25.14	25.56	26.24	23.22
AWL	5.39	5.51	5.44	5.77	5.44

SUBCORPORA^{WP} FREQUENCY LISTS

Subcorpora^{WP} top fifty lemmas are presented in Table 13.2.

Table 13.2
Subcorpora^{WP} Top Fifty Lemmas

Rank	SC^{ACCOR}	SC^{AIRBUS}	SC^{ALTANA}	SC^{RICOH}	SC^{VODAFONE}
1	the	the	the	The	the
2	of	and	of	and	and
3	and	us	be	in	to
4	in	of	and	of	of
5	be	to	to	to	in
6	to	a	in	ricoh	our
7	accor	in	a	a	we
8	a	be	for	environmental	be
9	hotel	airbus	altana	be	vodafone
10	for	a300	stock/shares	fiscal	for
11	with	for	with	group	group
12	on	as	company	by	customers
13	management	with	by	japan	have
14	services	by	option	system	with
15	have	from	as	product	on
16	board	it	or	for	business
17	its	more/most	board	as	mobile
18	by	its	our	goal	will
19	or	operate	this	at	as
20	travel	new	management	that	that
21	as	on	on	our	by
22	sales	first	year	management	employee
23	customers	which	may	on	services
24	year	have	plan	manufacturing	world
25	developmental	so	will	with	network
26	france	systems	have	use	uk
27	you	family	not	wet	his

Table 13.2 (continued)

Rank	SC^{ACCOR}	SC^{AIRBUS}	SC^{ALTANA}	SC^{RICOH}	$SC^{VODAFONE}$
28	company	at	other	business	company
29	at	air	which	impact	use
30	business	flight	group	have	which
31	group	company	plans	all	make
32	world	service	at	resource	more/most
33	growth	customer	authorization	its	global
34	from	than	price	accounting	provide
35	shareholders	training	we	subsidiaries	or
36	corporate	can	that	recycle	all
37	countries	all	pharma-	activities	base
38	responsible	this	employees	company	new
39	this	passenger	from	conservation	us
40	supervise	provide	new	global	its
41	tourism	on	business	information	million
42	your	that	no	sales	their
43	financial	time	conduct	results	community
44	new	year	meeting	copiers	good
45	that	world	annual	this	develop
46	international	market	research	compare	environment
47	which	airlines	sales	from	data
48	brand	commonality	supervising	marketing	first
49	information	fly-by-wire	under	end	people
50	economy	maintenance	german	production	from

All the subcorpora^{WP} frequency lists are similar in their top ranks: The most frequent word is "the" (average relative frequency 5.36%). Like the higher hapax ratio, the high average relative frequency of "the" (for corpus^{CPD}, 3.9%) suggests the corporate Web page genre to have a higher level of exactness of message content than other corporate genres.

Unlike the top ranks of subcorpora^{CPD} frequency lists, the top ranks of sub-corpora^{WP} frequency lists are not dominated by personal pronouns. The first content words in all subcorpora^{WP} frequency lists are company names (found in ranks 6 to 9). This is to be expected: naming legitimizes.

Table 13.3
An Extract from Subcorpus^{ACCOR} Concordance for "Customer"

000002	ly-tailored to **customer** preferences and budgets.
000159	gnition, high **customer** loyalty and little competiti
000176	area manager - **customer** relationship has been improv
000262	the quality of **customer** events on behalf of the enti
000266	en: detecting **customer** needs—team leadership—te

Below company names, subcorpora^{WP} top fifty lemmas begin to differ in their content words. Each of these content words, we recall, represents an idea fundamental to a corporation's ideology. For example, the concept "hotel" designates an idea constitutive to Accor's corporate ideology, "A300" (the name of Airbus's fastest selling family of aircraft) designates an idea constitutive to Airbus's ideology, "stock/shares" designates an idea constitutive to Altana's corporate ideology, "environmental" designates an idea constitutive to Ricoh's corporate ideology, and "customer" designates an idea constitutive to Vodafone's corporate ideology. However, the same content word can have a different meaning for a different company. For example, concordances for the content word "customer" in subcorpus^{ACCOR} (Table 13.3), subcorpus^{AIRBUS} (Table 13.4), and subcorpus^{VODAFONE} (Table 13.5) show Accor and Vodafone to use "customer" as a management activity word related to managerial activities, and Airbus to use "customer" as a company activity word related to basic business activities. Obviously, Accor's and Vodafone's perception of "customer" is different from that of Airbus. That difference is built into each company's Web page, that is, each company's corporate ideology.

Table 13.4
An Extract from Subcorpus^{AIRBUS} Concordance for "Customer"

000110	north america **customer** services, inc.
000116	e 1990 , while **customer** services representatives all
000117	casc / airbus **customer** services training & support
000118	d training and **customer** sup the 5 , 000 square metre
000120	industrial and **customer** service activities and is fu

Table 13.5
An Extract from Subcorpus^{VODAFONE} Concordance for "Customer"

000017	ighest quality **customer** care at vodafone group plc
000151	ng to business **customers** – implement our data strate
000152	ervices to our **customers** – improve our offering to b
000159	sition for our **customers**, mobility means immediacy
000162	eract with our **customers** in ways that will enrich th

Subcorpus^{ACCOR}

The top content words of subcorpus^{ACCOR}—"hotel" (rank 9), "management" (rank 13), "services" (rank 14), and "travel" (rank 20)—are quite visibly related to the company's basic business activities. Often collocating with these words, the adjective "new" (rank 44) (Table 13.6) serves a promotional function. The immediately following content words "board" (rank 16), "sales" (rank 22), "customers" (rank 23), "year" (rank 24), "development" (rank 25), "business" (rank 30), "growth" (rank 33), "shareholders" (rank 35), "responsible" (rank 38), and "financial" (rank 43) are management activity words. Their lower ranks suggest Accor's management activities to be somewhat less important to the company's corporate ideology. Finally, the content words "France" (rank 26), "countries" (rank 37), and "international" (rank 46) are similar in that they constitute a spatial reference important to Accor. To conclude, Accor's corporate ideology gives a priority to the ideas of Accor's business activities (represented by "hotel," "management," "services," and "travel"), Accor's Frenchness, and the newness of Accor's services.

Subcorpus^{AIRBUS}

The top content word of subcorpus^{AIRBUS} is a business activity word "A300" (rank 10). The large number of business activity words in subcor-

Table 13.6
An Extract from Subcorpus^{ACCOR} Concordance for "New"

000019	**new** markets in new countries , taking advantage of t
000092	**new** hotels and 250 restaurants are op
000093	254 **new** hotels , including 12 sofitel pro
000123	development of **new** partnerships, with air france,
000124	y 22% with 639 **new** properties , partly due to the ac

Table 13.7
An Extract from Subcorpus^{AIRBUS} Concordance for "More"

000202	o 100 per cent **more** freight than the largest competi
000204	nes to develop **more** non-stop ultra-long haul service
000206	ly accumulated **more** than 500 flight hours in 195 fli
000244	be current on **more** than one fly-by-wire aircraft ty
000245	hort-haul gets **more** take-off and landing opportuniti

pus^{AIRBUS}, for example, "operate" (rank 19), "systems" (rank 26), "family" (rank 27), "air" (rank 29), "flight" (rank 30), "service" (rank 32), "customer" (rank 33), "training" (rank 35), "passenger" (rank 39), "airlines" (rank 47), "commonality" (rank 48), "fly-by-wire" (rank 49), and "maintenance" (rank 50), shows Airbus's business activities to be fundamental to the company's corporate ideology.

The function of promoting business activities, which in subcorpus^{ACCOR} is done by the adjective "new," in subcorpus^{AIRBUS} is done by the comparative "more" (rank 17) (Table 13.7), the adjective "new" (rank 20) (Table 13.8), and the noun "world" (rank 45) (Table 13.9). To conclude, Airbus's corporate ideology gives a priority to the ideas of Airbus's business activities (represented by "aircraft"), copiousness (represented by "more"), and newness.

Subcorpus^{ALTANA}

The top content words of subcorpus^{ALTANA}, for example, "shares" (rank 10), "option" (rank 14), "board" (rank 17), "management" (rank 20), "year" (rank 22), "plan" (rank 24), "meeting" (rank 44), and "supervising" (rank 48), are nearly all management activity words. The highest-ranked business activity words are "pharma" (rank 37) and "research" (rank 46). The adjective "new" (rank 40) collocates mostly with business activity words (Table 13.10) but also with management activity words (Table 13.11).

Table 13.8
An Extract from Subcorpus^{AIRBUS} Concordance for "New"

000236	re of airbus' **new** generation of jetliners , develop
000243	ually for each **new** airbus a mixed fleet flying build
000247	lly, for each **new** airbus aircraft added to the flee
000248	equipped with **new** lcd (liquid crystal display) sc
000249	estment plan, **new** programmes and major i the shareh

Table 13.9
An Extract from Subcorpus[AIRBUS] **Concordance for "World"**

000070	he a300 , the **world's** first twin-engine , twin-ai
000083	600 , with the **world's** most voluminous cargo hold
000090	through to the **world's** largest aircraft , the 555t
000192	ufacturing the **world's** largest commercial airliner
000239	through to the **world's** largest aircraft , the 555t.

Table 13.10
An Extract from Subcorpus[ALTANA] **Concordance for "New"**

000290	agonists are a **new** class of acid suppressants differ
000310	in addition, **new** data from a second placebo contro
000325	development of **new** microbe- and cancer-fighting pha
000332	institute : a **new** genomics research center underway
000333	research into **new** therapy approaches for cancer via

Finally, the word "conduct" (rank 43), a word obviously related to management activities, typically collocates with the words "code," "ethical," and "transparent" (Table 13.12) which shows ethical behavior to be an important idea constitutive to Altana's ideology. In sum, Altana's corporate ideology gives a priority to the ideas of Altana's financial activities (represented by "stock" and "shares"), Altana's business activities (represented by "pharma" and "research"), and Altana's newness, Germanness, and ethic.

Table 13.11
An Extract from Subcorpus[ALTANA] **Concordance for "New"**

000135	orization by a **new** authorization .
000136	the launch of **new** stock option plans is intended de
000140	ey data of the **new** stock option plans are specified
000175	**new** stock option plans may be launche
000192	ing 2002 and a **new** authorization is to be approved.

Table 13.12
An Extract from Subcorpus^{ALTANA} Concordance for "Conduct"

000032	ul and ethical **conduct** and compliance with legal and
000033	nd transparent **conduct** in dealing with risks * profe
000085	th the code of **conduct** and appropriate controls a co
000087	f this code of **conduct** is being sent to each employe
000088	f this code of **conduct** will not be tolerated.

Subcorpus^{RICOH}

The top content word of subcorpus^{RICOH} is "environmental" (rank 8), with which many of the other content words, for example, "system" (rank 14), "management" (rank 22), "impact" (rank 29), "accounting" (rank 34), "conservation" (rank 39), "information" (rank 41), and "results" (rank 43), collocate (Table 13.13). Among the top content words of subcorpus^{RICOH} are also the spatial words "Japan" (rank 13) and "global" (rank 40). In sum, Ricoh's corporate ideology gives a priority to the ideas of Ricoh's business activities (represented by "environmental") and Ricoh's Japaneseness.

Subcorpus^{VODAFONE}

The top content word of subcorpus^{VODAFONE} is "customers" (rank 12), which is a management activity word. The quantifier "more" (rank 32) and the adjective "new" (rank 38) collocate mostly with business activity words (Table 13.14, Table 13.15). Evidently, Vodafone's corporate ideology gives a priority to the ideas of Vodafone's management activities (represented by "customers"), and business activities (represented by "services"), Vodafone's UKness and global orientation, Vodafone's copiousness (represented by "more"), and innovativeness (represented by "new").

Table 13.13
An Extract from Subcorpus^{RICOH} Concordance for "Environmental"

000186	will merge its **environmental** impact information syst
000186	ion system and **environmental** accounting information
000186	system into an **environmental** management information
000191	, databases on **environmental** results and their applican
000263	**environmental** conservation activities

Table 13.14
An Extract from Subcorpus^{VODAFONE} Concordance for "More"

000190	lives richer , **more** fulfilled and more connected .
000192	er quality and **more** value , faster than anyone else
000220	ection process **more** efficient , enabling both the ce
000220	communities be **more** connected in a mobile world .
000017	st quality and **more** reliable networks * leading-edge

Table 13.15
An Extract from Subcorpus^{VODAFONE} Concordance for "New"

000143	vices * global **new** products and services * brand dev
000158	ations include **new** text , picture and video messagin
000164	inent entry of **new** licensees in many of our markets
000164	ntroduction of **new** 3g technologies , we can expect t
000170	again , with a **new** generation of advanced mobile tec

CONCLUSION

Research into social communities has shown how, besides being organized around social variables such as social class, gender, and age, communities are organized too around social types: abstractions through which people generalize about individuals and groups. People use social typing to construct cognitive models of society and position themselves in that society. Unlike members of a social network who know each other, and, with more or less regularity, communicate to each other, individuals and groups constituting a social type need not know each other or interact at all.

People typically use social typing when encountering new and unknown individuals and groups. Providing "unobservable characteristics" on the basis of "observable characteristics," social typing helps people to plan their attitudes and behaviors (Hudson 1998, 237). Applied to stakeholders' perception of a corporation's ideology, the concept of social type invites a number of questions. How does, for instance, the social type "Frenchness," a concept that in the minds of most people stands for a specific lifestyle, affect stakeholders' attitudes and behaviors toward Accor's ideology? Positively or negatively? Probably positively, because most people perceive Frenchness as a desirable trait of a corporation involved in hotel and catering. Similarly, how does the social type "Japaneseness" affect Ricoh's stakeholders' attitudes and behaviors toward Ricoh's ideology? Again, probably positively, because most people perceive Japaneseness as a positive trait of a corporation that manufactures office automation equipment. Another question is whether corporations through their CPD create corporate social types whereby a particular business activity becomes attached to a corporation's ideology? For example, did Accor create a corporate social type, "Frenchness"? Did Ricoh create a corporate social type, "Japaneseness"? And, finally, a question that has to be asked is: If corporations do indeed create corporate social types, how do these types affect stakeholders' perception of corporations and their ideologies?

At the present time little is known about corporate social typing. Nevertheless, it is common sense to assume that stakeholders will rely on social typing when building cognitive models of corporations. Similarly, it is common sense to assume that corporations will rely on social typing to create synergy between themselves and stakeholders.

PART VI

Specific Research Perspectives

14

The Corporate Metaphor

> Far from being merely a matter of words, metaphor is a matter of thought—all kinds of thought: thought about emotion, about society, about human character, about language, and about the nature of life and death. It is indispensable not only to our imagination but also to our reason.
> —G. Lakoff and M. Turner (1989, xi)

THE WORKINGS OF A METAPHOR

When CEO Gerstner described his understanding of personal commitments as "not things of the head" but "things of the heart and the gut," he was metaphorizing. CEO Gerstner, as Aristotle would have put it, gave an entity (personal commitments) a name (head, heart, guts) that belongs to something else (the human body). We refer to this entity, that is, the topic of the metaphor, as the "tenor," and to "something else," the term applied metaphorically, as the "vehicle."[1] The features common to the tenor and the vehicle (here: human traits of reason, spirit, emotions, will, and courage), constitute the ground of the metaphor. The distance between the tenor and the vehicle forms the angle of the metaphorical image (Ullmann 1983, 213), which is considered to be a key factor of a metaphor's expressive quality.

CEO Gerstner's metaphors "the head," "the heart," and "the gut," which are based on a conventionalized representation of an entity as a part of the human body, belong to so-called anthropomorphic metaphors.[2] Because the human body is closely associated with everything people do, it naturally constitutes a semantic domain lexicalized in all languages and, as such, is a rich source of metaphor.

The clear and logically organized functional structure of the human body is linguistically regarded as a partonomy, consisting of "part of" relationships in which some parts are more important than others (Andersen 1978). Knowing this, CEO Gerstner made a strategic use of the intrinsic importance of the head, the heart, and the gut to the human body to underline the importance of personal commitments to IBM. Metaphorically referring to the head, the heart, and the gut, CEO Gerstner treated them as possessing specific meanings and as different from other parts of the body, yet related to them. Reaching for a conventional schema that associates the head, the heart, and the gut to the human traits of reason, spirit, emotions, will, and courage, CEO Gerstner, in a simple and friendly way, invited IBM stakeholders to map these traits onto their notion of personal commitments. For CEO Gerstner, those commitments were "behavioral, not intellectual."

The Metaphor Cognition Process

Every metaphor offers its own reality, which, to be accepted by an audience as truthful, has to be identified and interpreted. Identification of "the head," "the heart," and "the gut" as metaphors, not as parts of a human body, was enabled through CEO Gerstner's and IBM stakeholders' shared social knowledge. In the metaphor identification phase, all possible meanings of "the head," "the heart," and "the gut" were activated. For example, possible meanings of "the head" could have been: a part of the body that has eyes, mouth, and a brain in it, the top or most important end of something, or one's mind and mental abilities. Possible meanings of "the heart" could have been: an organ that pumps blood, a center for emotions, a symbol of kindness and generosity, or a place of the deepest and strongest feelings. Finally, possible meanings of "the gut" could have been: alimentary canal, intestines, stomach, or the will and courage to do something difficult.

Interpretation of "the head," "the heart," and "the gut" was founded on CEO Gerstner's and IBM stakeholders' agreement on the intended meanings of these metaphors. In the interpretation phase, the nonrelevant meanings (of "the head"—a part of the body, the top or most important end of something; of "the heart"—an organ, a center for emotions, a symbol of kindness and generosity; of "the gut"—alimentary canal, intestines, stomach) were deactivated.

Acceptance of the metaphors "the head," "the heart," and "the gut" was a product of their intended meanings (of "the head"—one's mind and mental abilities; of "the heart"—the deepest and strongest feelings; of "the gut"—the will and courage to do something difficult) raising their activation and spreading into the rest of the text.

A Knowledge-creation Device

Using metaphor, CEO Gerstner started a knowledge-creation process. "The head," "the heart," and "the gut" enabled stakeholders to integrate new knowledge (of personal commitments being founded not on reason, but on spirit, emotions, will, and courage) with their existing knowledge (their pre-metaphoric understanding of personal commitments). In this sense, CEO Gerstner's metaphors served as an interim communicational category between knowing and articulating. They were his initial step in making tacit knowledge explicit, and as such, probably highly effective in fostering IBM employees' commitment to creative processes.

The key evidence of the knowledge-purveying quality of the metaphors "the head," "the heart," and "the gut" is what Davidson (1991) has referred to as "nonparaphrasability." Paraphrasing "the head," "the heart," and "the gut" as mental abilities, things of emotions, and courage would have, admittedly, captured the metaphors' truth condition, but it is the metaphors themselves that conveyed more and different. In sum, CEO Gerstner used his metaphors as a knowledge-creating device to highlight similarities, reconcile conflicted meanings, put together dissimilar and distant things, ideas or areas of experience, make the unknown familiar, create rapport, provoke insights, stimulate learning, and negotiate meanings.

METAPHOR THROUGH TIMES

There is nothing extraordinary about CEO Gerstner's use of metaphor. Metaphor is typical to all human communication. Although people often believe metaphor to be the property of poetry, literary discourse, and rhetoric, metaphor is "pervasive in everyday life, not just in language but in thought and action" (Lakoff and Johnson 1980, 3).

The skilful use of metaphor has always attracted enormous admiration. For Aristotle, a command of metaphor was a mark of genius. However, metaphorical speech *per se* is not an evidence of a special talent. Any individual, regardless of her or his intelligence, level of formal education, and social class, possesses the ability to create and use metaphor to realize personal communicational objectives. Even great poets, Lakoff and Turner (1989, xi) explain, "use basically the same tools we use; what makes them different is their talent for using these tools, and their skill in using them."

An awareness of the significance of metaphor as a creative force that can alter the meaning of language, assigned it a prominent place in classical rhetoric. A part of the *septem artes liberales*[3] and an important curriculum subject, rhetoric in ancient days was considered a "gentlemanly ornament" and a "mark of breeding" (Nash 1992, 5). Indeed, many contemporary ideas about metaphor are embedded in classical culture. It is Aristotle's classification of metaphor, developed by subsequent writers, notably Quintilian, that has played a crucial part in the rhetorical tradition and was taken over into semantics (Ullmann 1983, 3).

An understanding of metaphor as a knowledge-creating device is not new. Examinations of fourth century B.C.E. writings of Aristotle have revealed his essentially cognitive view of metaphor as a discourse mechanism that brings two ideas in contact to produce a new understanding. Especially important, Aristotle related the use of metaphor to a social context (Cameron 1999, 9).

In the seventeenth and the eighteenth centuries, the cognitive aspect of metaphor was downplayed. Emphasis was placed more on linguistic and philosophical aspects. The linguistic understanding of metaphor is well captured in semantics, which views metaphor as an expressive device, an outlet for intense emotions, a filler for a word one can not think of, a factor of linguistic motivation, and a source of synonymy and polysemy (Ullmann 1983, 212–213).

In the late 1970s a major change in the understanding of metaphor took place. Metaphor started to be viewed as a pragmatic (rather than a linguistic) phenomenon, as a speech act, a tool to accomplish a goal, and an element of a communicative purpose.

Finally, in the 1980s, owing to Lakoff and Johnson's book *Metaphors We Live By* (1980), metaphor was reinstated as a primarily cognitive phenomenon: a part of everyday life, language, thought, and action. Our world knowledge, the "conceptual system in terms of which we both think and act" (p. 3), Lakoff and Johnson stated, is fundamentally metaphorical in nature.

Central to all interpretations of metaphor—whether linguistic, pragmatic, or cognitive—is the nature of relationship between a metaphor and reality. While traditional analysis treats metaphor as a condensed comparison, registering existing similarities (Esnault 1925), more recent studies (Weinrich 1968, 1976; Lakoff and Johnson 1980; Lakoff and Turner 1989; Cameron and Low 1999; Nogales 1999) underpin the role of metaphor in creating new similarities and affecting human behavior. Creating a new reality, a metaphor becomes a guide for future actions, which, of course, fit the metaphor. Thus, the power of a metaphor to make experience coherent is reinforced, and the metaphor itself becomes a "self-fulfilling prophecy" (Lakoff and Johnson 1980, 156).

THE ORGANIZATION AS METAPHOR

Through metaphor the increasing complexity of a contemporary organization can be communicated in simple, everyday terms. For instance, the metaphor "sleeping beauty" can stand for a takeover target company, "dinosaur" for a large old-fashioned company, and "national champion" for the country's primary supplier of a product. A common metaphorical representation of the organization is an orchestra, where different professionals "playing" different "instruments" perform different tasks. The conductor is the manager who plans the performance, selects those numbers the orchestra can best perform, presides at rehearsals, and does many other things to make the performance notable (Brown 1990).

Throughout the twentieth century, three dominant metaphorical perspectives on an organization have emerged: military/mechanical, biological, and cognitive (Kreitner and Kinicki 1992, 638–643). A military/mechanical perspective is based on Weber's ideas about bureaucracy, which, Weber claimed, is the only way of coping with the administrative requirements of an organization. From this perspective an organization is a precisely functioning machine, its environment is predictable, and its primary goal is maximum efficiency. A biological perspective compares an organization to the human body and stresses the importance of an organization's interaction with its environment. From this perspective an organization's primary goal is survival through adaptation to its environment. Finally, a cognitive perspective sees an organization as a human mind. From this perspective the organization is a meaning system that possesses mechanisms with which it interprets an increasingly ambiguous environment. A cognitive interpretation is a result of contemporary organizations treating growth-through-learning as their primary goal.

THE ORGANIZATION AND METAPHOR

During the past two decades, researchers and practitioners in the area of organizational studies have too focused on the roles metaphor plays in organizations. What was once considered a rhetorical figure and an embellishment of speech, is now increasingly researched from various perspectives: as a means of understanding the organization (Morgan 1980, 1986; Oswick and Montgomery 1999; Wood 2002), as an instrument of organizational development and change (Oswick and Grant 1996; Öztel and Hinz 2001), as a tool of managerial decision-making (Morgan 1986, 1993), and as an instrument of knowledge-creation (Nonaka 1998). Overall, there is a strong consensus among researchers and practitioners about the importance of metaphor within the corporate communication system. The positive contribution of metaphor to an organization, however, is a point of disagreement (Grant and Oswick 1996, 2–6).

A Supportive Perspective

For most authors analyzing the use of metaphor in organization, metaphor is a positive force. Metaphor entices "imaginization" (Morgan 1993): an interpretive process offering a variety of perspectives, interpretations, and reinterpretations of business situations. Provoking new insights and allowing for a multitude of perceptions, metaphor helps people in organizations to formulate "what they know but cannot yet say" (Nonaka 1998, 34). Merging distant and dissimilar areas of experience into a single image, metaphor generates a conflict, which starts a creative process. Attempting to define the insight offered by the metaphor, employees try to reconcile the conflicted meanings and thus take the first step in making tacit knowledge explicit.

Viewed from a supportive perspective, metaphor is "liberating": it combines language and thought and shapes and enhances one's appreciation of an organization's reality. A supportive perspective, Grant and Oswick (1996, 3–4) further explain, emphasizes three roles of metaphor in organization. First, metaphor changes an existing view of a particular issue in an organization and creates a parallel social reality. Second, metaphor facilitates the acquisition of knowledge and the understanding of new phenomena in an organization. Third, metaphor serves as an instrument of investigation in an organization to explain and diagnose problems, and create solutions.

An example of an exploration into the role of metaphor as a creator of knowledge in corporations is Stephens's (1994) case study on typical activities of a CIO (chief information officer). According to Stephens, the most important shared characteristics of a CIO's communication are a high level of empathy and a skilful use of metaphorical language. Empathy, Stephens suggests, improves the CIO's use of metaphor, which, in turn, increases the level of empathy. Linking metaphor and empathy, Stephens grasped well the immense importance of metaphor to a senior executive's pedagogical role in a corporation.

Another study that demonstrates the gains derived from linking metaphor to knowledge is Öztel and Hinz's (2001) consultancy project in Danish sugar factories, aimed at reducing accident rates. Consultants, Öztel and Hinz suggest, should use metaphor as a device of unconscious learning. They should offer stories rather than theories, and pictures rather than scientific explanations. Above all, they should "fuel" emotions rather than supply cause-effect analyses, make suggestions through acting characters rather than concepts, and appeal to people's inner wisdom rather than some abstract laws.

Finally, according to Morgan (1986), the metaphorical imagery typically employed by an organization is relatable to its management style and conceptions of conflict and power. The dominant metaphorical imagery of organizations, Morgan argues, suggests the existence of three types of organizations: unitaristic, pluralist, and radical. In a unitaristic organization, led by an autocratic CEO, where power is not an issue and emphasis is placed on unity, the dominant imagery is leadership, team, and right direction. Conflict is uncommon and caused by "troublemakers." In a pluralist organization, led by a democratic CEO, where power is the medium for conflict resolution and its balance may legitimately shift over time, the dominant imagery is coalition, allies, and opponents. Conflict can be stimulated and can facilitate resolving rather than suppressing differences. Last, in a "radical"[4] organization, society is viewed as comprising antagonistic class interests and as held together by both coercion and consent. Reflecting relations in society, radical organizations are marked by an unequal distribution of power, and the dominant imagery is fighting, warfare, and battleground.

A Critical Perspective

Not all researchers accept the reliability of metaphor (e.g., Tsoukas 1993; McCourt 1997) and metaphor analysis (e.g., Pinder and Bourgeois 1982; Linstead 1993; Palmer and Dunford 1996) as a means to obtain insights into an organization. Based on their research of the use of metaphor by employees of a large U.S. multinational, Oswick and Montgomery (1999, 14) have argued that metaphor often misleads and obscures. More specifically, metaphor, Oswick and Montgomery maintain, constrains processes of projection, reinforcing pre-existing ways of thinking and perceiving, rather than developing fresh insights and generating new ways.

Along with colloquialism, regionalisms, slang, and humor, metaphor is known to be a neuralgic point of cross-cultural business communication. For example, *The Tower of Business Babel* (1991), an investigation into English of international business carried out by the Parker Pen Company, has shown how even standard idioms (most of them metaphors) of the English language such as "keep one's shirt clean," "someone's marbles are loose," "skin the cat," and "run of the mill," can cause serious misunderstandings.

Another criticism of metaphor in organizations is that metaphor may constrain knowledge. Because metaphors lack clarity and precision, they, apparently, do not contribute to truth, and their "goodness of fit" is impossible to measure (Grant and Oswick 1996, 5). Also, metaphors can be confusing. Metaphors, it is argued, commonly appear as a result of contact between two scientific fields where scientists borrow concepts from one field and metaphorically apply those concepts to another field without having sufficient knowledge to do so. "Concealed in seductive figurative language," and almost impossible to "get rid of" (p. 4), metaphors are deceiving. Finally, metaphors, it is further argued, often serve as instruments of "ideological distortions" (p. 6). For example, the usual representation of organizations as organisms or mechanical entities can induce stakeholders to accept certain behaviors in organizations without questioning them. In turn, such acceptance can make stakeholders believe that organizations are uncontrollable. The effect is a "false consciousness" that protects organizations from all forms of critical evaluation (p. 6).

THE CEO'S METAPHOR

If the "metaphorical structure of the most fundamental concepts" in a culture is, as Lakoff and Johnson (1980, 22) suggest, coherent with the most fundamental values (beliefs, attitudes, and emotions) of that culture, then an analysis of metaphors used by the CEO as the creator of a corporation's culture should point to ideas fundamental to the ideology of the corporate world. The aim of this chapter is to discover those ideas.

A quantitative analysis of the CEO's metaphors in Subcorpus^{MI} shows the CEO to prefer metaphors based on the dominant vehicles: warfare, animal, sport, the human body, the family, religion, and Wild West (Table 14.1).

Warfare Metaphor

The CEO's favorite metaphor is a warfare metaphor that projects the CEO as an army leader, the CEO's followers as an army, and the corporate world as a battlefield:

Table 14.1
The CEO's Metaphor

Dominant Vehicles	Relative Frequency
Warfare	41.4%
Animal	22.2%
Sport	19.9%
The human body	8.0%
Other (the family, religion, Wild West)	8.5%

But if the CEO doesn't know what the front line looks like, how can he set the right policies, call up the right artillery or time the next advance?[5]

In Western culture, management is generally seen as engaged in war (Follett 1940; Harragen 1977; Cohen et al. 1992; Solomon 1992; Jackall 1996). The dominance of warfare images of the corporate environment has been attributed to various reasons. Solomon (1992), for example, has linked warfare metaphor to the identity crisis of corporate America. Thinking of business in terms of war, Solomon stresses, is wrong, as it corrupts the heroic philosophy of warfare. Guest (1990, 390), on the other hand, suggests warfare metaphor to be rooted in a "frontier mentality," with the chief aim of reflecting the CEO's readiness for conflict with a powerful, (un)known enemy.

Warfare metaphor fits a corporation's reality into a binary "good vs. evil" schema. The interests of the corporation (more specifically, the interests of the CEO and the dominant group) are always projected as good, while the interests of competitors and nondominant groups are implied to be evil and undermining the interests of the corporation and even society as a whole. Producing a binary assumption—the corporation is good, everyone else is evil—warfare metaphor induces stakeholders to approve the corporation's struggles for power and resources.

Animal Metaphor

Animal metaphorical imagery belongs to the oldest devices of literary style (Ullmann 1983, 215) and is fundamental to numerous important works of literature (from Aesop's fables to Orwell's *Animal Farm*). Whether understood as images of animal humans or human animals, animal metaphor offers various connotations: humorous, ironical, pejorative, and grotesque.

Animal metaphor is a favorite means for relating organizations to attributes of strength (strong vs. weak), size (big vs. small), and speed (fast vs. slow) (Keizer and Post 1996; Oswick and Montgomery 1999). This is possible because of metaphor's inherent ability to lend itself to the human habit of conceiving things as "having quintessential properties" (Lakoff and Turner 1989, 196). For example, in

We put in place a management team that lacked the standard business tools. They didn't know what cash flow was, they didn't understand much about marketing. But their ambition was incredible. You could feel their hunger to excel. . . . Each project was led by a champion—some from top management ranks, some from the other "hungry wolves."[6]

the metaphor "hungry wolves" relates corporate management to the quintessential properties of a wolf and, by extension, to the properties of any predator: resoluteness, fearlessness, and independence.[7] Focusing on the quintessential, animal metaphor functions as an effective and economical reference system in which participants are precisely located and associated with various attributes.

Sport Metaphor

Of all the CEO's metaphors, sport metaphor:

Guys, you're gonna go up to the plate with two strikes against you. . . . But you've got one huge advantage: your competition has minor-league pitchers.[8]

best portrays the CEO's competitive spirit and the CEO's need to be projected as a champion. The CEO's performance is her or his "track record," the CEO's followers are members of a "winning team," and the corporation and the corporate world represent a "playing field." Implicit in sport metaphor is the idea of fair play, which is a key value of global business. But most important, sport metaphor enables the CEO to present her or his personal and corporation's success as an outcome of studied commitment.

There is considerable similarity between sport metaphor and warfare metaphor. Both are based on a binary schema: warfare metaphor on a "good-evil" schema, and sport metaphor on a "win-lose" schema. Both are rooted in the cultural values of progress, achievement, success, and competitiveness. And like warfare metaphor, sport metaphor underlines (and fosters) the importance of instrumental cohesiveness: a sense of togetherness resulting from group members' beliefs that only through team effort can the common goal be achieved.

Anthropomorphic Metaphor

Anthropomorphic metaphor, we have noted, belongs to the most frequently used types of metaphor occurring in most languages and literary styles (Ullmann 1983, 214). Anthropomorphic metaphor refers to the human body itself, to parts of the human body (e.g., head, face, hand), and processes within the human body (e.g., breath, swallow, digest) (Deignan 1995, 1–17).

Discussing the extraordinarily high frequency of anthropomorphic metaphor, Giambattista Vico wrote: "In all languages, the greater part of expressions referring to inanimate objects are taken by transfer from the human body and its parts, from human senses and human passions. . . . Ignorant man makes himself into the yardstick of the universe" (cited in Ullmann 1983, 214). Vico's "yardstick" is itself a metaphor reflecting the natural tendency of humans to answer higher-order questions in terms of lower-order descriptions.

Like CEO Gerstner, Nestlé CEO Peter Brabeck in a *Harvard Business Review* interview relied on anthropomorphic metaphor:

There are certainly many companies out there that are very sexy, like a 20-year-old girl. Everyone wants to know all about them. We are not that. We don't want to be. Our company is more like a 40-year-old, someone who is strong and trim, and who can easily run 10 miles without being pushed or pulled.[9]

He too made use of the human body as a semantic domain that holds meanings to which he wished to relate his corporation. Comparing Nestlé to a "40-year-old" who is "strong and trim," CEO Brabeck made tacit knowledge (Nestlé's stamina) explicit.

Family Metaphor

Family metaphor embodies group unity and projects an image of the corporation as a compact whole:

This social cohesion is reflected in the poster of the Silicon Valley "family tree" and in frequent references to firms or individuals as "grandfathers" or "offspring."[10]

A fundamental social unit, a prototype social (primary and referent) group, and a key factor of socialization process, the family is a traditional symbol of harmony, love, altruism, and giving in all cultures. Like warfare metaphor and sport metaphor, family metaphor suggests socioemotional cohesiveness, but of a different kind. A family metaphor establishes a sense of togetherness resulting from an individual's emotional satisfaction found in associating with a group.[11]

Religious Metaphor

Religious metaphor embodies concepts, symbols, and stories that are globally shared, easily recognizable, and precisely defined. For example, in

At that meeting, we presented our policy bible, a 21-page book that communicates the essential principles by which we run the company.[12]

the common ground linking the tenor (company policy) to the vehicle (the Bible) is the importance of company policy to the organization. Reference to an unquestioned authority—the Bible—helps to legitimize the company's policy.

Researching human resource management, Keenoy and Anthony (1992) have drawn attention to the use of religious metaphor in the discourse of organizations which, they argue, suggests that managers possess an element of the supernatural, divine, and magical. Through the use of religious metaphor, human resource management, Keenoy and Anthony maintain, shifts perceptions of reality and manufactures "acquiescence in corporate values" (p. 239). Similarly to family metaphor, religious metaphor constitutes an important part of a collectively held vision of a social order in which the authority of fundamental social values is never questioned.

Wild West Metaphor

Wild West metaphors such as

- "bite the bullet": the brave behavior of executives under pressure (In the Wild West, gunfighters would bite the bullet during surgery to find relief from pain.)
- "hip shooter": an executive who acts on instincts rather than deliberation (In Wild West movies, gunmen never took careful aim.)
- "maverick": an executive who acts independently (The word "maverick" originally meant a stray animal without an owner's brand.)

glorify the ideal of individualism, a central value of contemporary American society and the American Dream. Historically, the ideal of individualism is at the very basis of concepts fostered by the romantic Old South, the romantic East with its celebration of the principles of capitalism, and the romantic West, which "captured the imagination of all America in folktale and legend" (Fisher 1987, 146).

Researching the meaning of individualism to middle-class Americans, Bellah and associates (1985) found their respondents to hold two predominant views on individualism: as "a belief in the inherent dignity and, indeed, the sacredness of the human person" and as "a belief that the individual has a primary reality whereas society is a second-order, derived or artificial construct." Briefly, America sees individualism (also self-reliance, efficiency, practicality and success) as a value "attendant on family, work, neighborhood, peace and freedom" (Fisher 1987, 151). The pragmatic advantage of using a dominant vehicle that embodies fundamental societal values such as individualism (or family), lies, as Fisher argues, in a speaker's character being perceived as constituted by these values and, as such, "immune to 'rational' criticism" (p. 146).

Interestingly, although Wild West metaphor is unquestionably grounded in an era of American history and, therefore, rightly expected to function as culturally specific, mass media and global "Coca-colonization" have made it culturally universal.

CONCLUSION

The role of metaphor in organizations has attracted intense research attention. Research into metaphor is either supportive and views metaphor as a positive force contributing to an organization, or critical and views metaphor as a negative mechanism potentially damaging the interests of an organization. While a supportive perspective interprets metaphor as a device that provokes new insights into an organization, facilitates acquisition of knowledge, and helps people understand the complexities of organizations, a critical perspective sees metaphor as misleading, obscuring, constraining knowledge, fixating pre-existing ways of thinking and perceiving, and preventing the development of new ideas.

Within CPD, metaphor holds neither a priori positive nor a priori negative value. Corporate metaphor, as all CPD, is simply a part of the language-ideology-power relationship in an organization.

A quantification of the CEO's metaphors shows them to be based on a number of dominant vehicles, each of which expresses the CEO's beliefs, attitudes, and behaviors. The CEO's favorite types of metaphor seem to be warfare metaphor that projects the CEO to be engaged in continuous combat, animal metaphor that projects the CEO as a predator, and sport metaphor that projects the CEO as a champion. Together, these types of metaphor define the corporate world as a battlefield and suggest the idea "management is war" to be fundamental to the ideology of that world.

NOTES

1. Although attempts have been made to replace "tenor" and "vehicle" with alternative terms, for example "primary subject" and "secondary subject" (Black 1979), tenor and vehicle conventionally remain in use.

2. Other major types of metaphors are animal metaphor, from abstract to concrete metaphor, and synaesthetic metaphor. Animal metaphor is based on the transfer of animal images, applied to people, plants, and things. From abstract to concrete metaphor relates to transferring abstract experiences into concrete terms. Synaesthetic metaphor is based on transposition from one sense to another, for example, sound to sight or touch to sound (Ullmann 1983, 214–218).

3. The seven skills—grammar, rhetoric, logic or dialectic, arithmetic, music, geometry, and astronomy—in Roman times proper to a free citizen.

4. Legge (1995, 33) suggests that this "radical" frame of reference is constructed by observers of management rather than "publicly claimed by managers themselves."

5. *Harvard Business Review*, March–April 1990, p. 38.

6. *Harvard Business Review*, March–April 1991, p. 103

7. The positive connotation of "hungry wolves" is typically eurocentric. In both European and American culture the wolf traditionally signifies individualism, loyalty, courage, and stamina. In Russian fairytales, for example, the wolf has the status of an auxiliary of a second order—a positive character who helps the hero by performing certain (limited) tasks—and is in the same category as wizards and spirits emerging from a ring (Propp 1971). In Chinese culture, on the other hand, the wolf is a synonym for cruelty, greed, and lechery (Engholm 1991, 230).

8. *Harvard Business Review*, July–August 2000, p. 100.

9. *Harvard Business Review*, February 2001, p. 114.

10. *Californian Management Review*, 3/90, p. 97.

11. "Beer busts" and "popcorn parties" (informal employees' meetings outside working hours) are evidence of corporate management's awareness of the importance of socioemotional cohesiveness.

12. *Harvard Business Review*, March-April 1991, p. 104.

15

Globalization

Transformations in self-identity and globalization . . . are the two poles of the dialectic of the local and the global in conditions of high modernity. Changes in intimate aspects of personal life . . . are directly tied to the establishment of social connections of very wide scope . . . for the first time in human history, "self" and "society" are interrelated in a global milieu.
—A. Giddens (1991, 32)

THE SHRINKING WORLD

In its corporate media advertisement "Never underestimate the importance of local knowledge," HSBC[1] institutionalizes a commitment to *globalization*—a "symbiotic and irreversible" (Urry 2000: 210) relationship between the local and the global—as an idea fundamental to its ideology:

To truly understand a country and its culture, you have to be part of it. That's why, at HSBC, we have local banks in more countries than anyone else. And all of our offices around the world are staffed by local people. It's their insight that allows us to recognize financial opportunities invisible to outsiders. But those opportunities don't just benefit our local customers. Innovations and ideas are shared throughout the HSBC network, so that everyone who banks with us can benefit. Think of it as local knowledge that just happens to span the globe.[2]

Through that idea HSBC asked its stakeholders to think of globalization as something more than just an irreversible and inevitable social process whereby national economies are converted into an integrated world economy and the production of goods and services transnationalized (Robinson and Harris 2000, 6). Within the context of HSBC's media advertisement, globalization is built on identifiable actors with defined roles and precise responsibilities. For HSBC, globalization means glocalization.

THE MEANING OF GLOBALIZATION

Globalization is a concept which has so permeated every aspect of life, from fast food to the Internet, that it can apply to everything and mean anything. What then is meant by globalization? In the literature, the term "globalization" has been defined from two broad perspectives: supportive of globalization and critical of globalization.

A Supportive Perspective

From a supportive perspective, globalization is seen as a golden age of cosmopolitanism, overcoming the political and economical limitations of nation-states (Urry 2000, 13). Globalization is a historical process that changes the organizing principles of social interactions and transactions through intercontinental or transregional networks (Held and McGrew 1998, 220). Mann (1993, 11), for example, emphasizes the unifying function of globalization of transforming a collection of ideological communities and nation-states into a "single power network" around which reverberate shock waves "casting down empires, transporting massive quantities of people, materials and messages." Torn between the need for global effectiveness and the need for local responsibility, nation-states, Castells (1997, 304) argues, have become just nodes of a broader power network, increasingly denationalized, mobilized, technologized, informationalized, and consumerized.

In a similar vein, Lankshear (1998) views globalization as a major transition from an agroindustrial to a postindustrial information/service economy. Linking distant and, inevitably, distinct parts of the world, globalization causes a shift "from more personal face-to-face communities to impersonal metropolitan and, even, virtual communities" (p. 3). Globalization has fragmented traditional notions of community and led to the decline of the nation-state which is no longer seen as being able to "deliver social and economic well-being" (Morgan 1990, 225). As membership in nation-states loses importance, membership in organizations gains importance. Wealth, income, and social standing, Morgan further explains, "are increasingly derived from being a member of, for example, IBM rather than being British or American."

For Giddens (1990, 78), globalization is about the spectacular conquest of space by time. Events and activities not only take place on a global scene, but are planned and coordinated globally. A product of the global compression of time and space is what Urry (2000, 126) has referred to as "instantaneous time": an understanding of time as "inconceivably brief instants which are wholly beyond human consciousness." The compression of time and space,

Urry contends, takes place through IT-induced global technology, transportation, media, and communication, that carry "ideas, people, images, monies and technologies to potentially everywhere" (p. 208).

Finally, Castells defines globalization as the "capacity to work as a unit in real time on a planetary scale" (1996, 92). The productivity and competitiveness of the global economy's actors, Castells suggests, depend upon their ability to generate, process, and apply knowledge-based information and include the cultural-institutional attributes of the whole system "in the diffusion and implementation of the new technological paradigm" (p. 91). Simply, the global economy works because it is "informational, not just information-based."

A Critical Perspective

From a critical perspective, globalization is viewed as supporting marginalization and exploitation, as a new mediaevalism in which powerful empires such as Microsoft, Coca-Cola, and McDonalds keep reconfiguring economies and cultures in their global interests (cf. Cerny 1997). The benefits of globalization, disapprovers of globalization stress, are mostly concentrated in the so-called Triad of North America, Western Europe, and Japan (cf. Weiss 1998, 176). Indeed, as Busch (2000, 38–39) reminds, world economic development is far from global; it is almost exclusively regional. Three-fourths of the world, for example, do not have access to a telephone (Mittelman 2000, 90–107). It is not surprising, therefore, that much of the world is excluded from the processes and benefits of globalization.

Polarization of the globe into "haves" and "have nots," disapprovers of globalization further stress, contradicts the very meaning of the word "global" and accentuates the "core-periphery" relationship: the "core" is defined as the locus of the owners of modes of production and the "periphery" as the producers. Within a capitalist mode of production, the "core" is dependent on the exploitation of the "periphery" (cf. Wallerstein 1987, 501–513). Thus, viewed from a critical perspective, globalization is far from a process in which financial markets, media, and pressure groups challenge traditional centers of power.

GLOBAL CITIZENSHIP

Probably the most important effect of globalization is the way it has redefined an understanding of citizenship, which can no longer be described in terms of rights and duties within the nation-state. Rather, a model of global citizenship is evolving within an increasingly deterritorialized notion of a person's universal rights (Soysal 1994, 3). The global society, it seems, is driven by at least six types of global citizens (Urry 2000, 172–173; cf. also Falk 1994; Robinson and Harris 2000):

- global capitalists who seek to unify the world around global corporate interests, which are increasingly denationalized

- global reformers who use large international organizations (for example, UNESCO, IMF, WHO), to moderate and regulate global capitalism
- global managers who seek to implement various forms of knowledge to reduce various hazards
- global networkers who set up and sustain social networks through travel
- "earth citizens" whose objective is to take responsibility for the planet
- global cosmopolitans who develop an ideology of openness toward "others."

Each of these roles, Urry (2000, 175) contends, is primarily about responsibilities: participating in the global information exchange, nurturing an openness toward cultural diversity, developing an ethical and sustainable way of life, joining in the global discourse, being socially accountable, and promoting public, collective, shared, and global rather than individual and national interests. Obviously, global citizenship entails much more than, as claimed by Stevenson (1997, 44), the ability to acquire goods in a global market or, as suggested by Meijer (1998, 239), expressing one's lifestyle and alignment with global values through consuming, for example, Coca-Cola. A global citizen has many duties and obligations toward the global community upon which the well-being of that community inevitably rests.

THE DISCOURSE OF GLOBALIZATION

Globalization is a concept that has emerged through the discourse of globalization witnessing an ongoing "global reconstitution" (Urry 2000, 162), promoting global values, transmitting changes in economic, political, and cultural relationships all over the globe, and both challenging and accepting local cultural practices and local knowledge. The discourse of globalization "took off" in 1989, a year marked by the fall of the Berlin Wall and the prodemocracy movement in China. The sheer intensity of the discourse of globalization—incessantly utilized by corporations, politicians, philosophers, sociologists, economists, and environmentalists—has institutionalized the name "global" and allowed it to replace, at least partly, the name "international."[3]

The discourse of globalization—through which the meaning of globalization is defined—is naturally a part of CPD, in particular the CPD of airline companies, for whom globalization is an idea fundamental to their ideologies. Airline companies not only state their absolute commitment to globalization: they, in fact, redefine the very meaning of globalization. For example, using its corporate media advertisement

Wouldn't it be nice to belong to an alliance that recognizes your status on eight of the world's finest airlines? Our alliance does just that, along with giving you access to more lounges. Smoother transfers. More ways to earn and redeem frequent flyer miles. And over a quarter of a million people to help every step of the way. Welcome to **one**world™.[4]

to list the corporation's attributes [. . . access to more lounges. Smoother transfers. More ways to earn and redeem frequent flyer miles. And over a quarter

of a million people to help every step of the way.] , **one**world endows globalization with a numinous power. So too does the airline company Sabena, for
which globalization means "no ticket to lose, no queues, no waits":

Have you flown Sabena lately? Then you've probably noticed the improvements
we've been making. And if it's been a while, you might be surprised at how our
latest e-travel ideas can simplify flying. Like e-ticket (no ticket to lose) and e-
check-in (no queues, no waits). Discover the ease of e-travelling on the net. Or the
next time you fly.[5]

And for US Airways, globalization represents a systematic upgrading of
comfort:

Upgraded comfort in every class. Welcome aboard US Airways' new, widebody
A330-300 Airbus. Whether you're flying First Class, Envoy Class (business) or
Economy, you'll find wider aisles, larger overhead bins, quieter cabins and
roomier seats complete with computer data port and laptop power. Or, relax with
a state-of-the-art, on demand personal entertainment system with a video monitor
at every seat. Thank you for flying with us on US Airways.[6]

while for Cathay Pacific globalization stands for effortlessness and efficiency:

To get somewhere in this world, there's no better airline to fly than Cathay Pacific.
Our home, Hong Kong, provides a natural hub through which you can effortlessly
and efficiently connect with all 4 corners of the globe via our award-winning international airport. So you'll feel as fresh when you arrive as you did when you took
off.[7]

Redefining the notion of "globalization," **one**world, Sabena, US Airways,
and Cathay Pacific each turned it into an archetype: a constantly recurring
motif, which is treated with great reverence and, as archetypes generally do,
having an awe-inspiring effect. The archetypical character of "globalization"
pushes its meaning beyond an economical, social, and political interpretation
to give it an almost religious quality.

THE GLOBAL NETWORK

Because globalization is a process undergoing continual social change, it
cannot be represented through content. One way of defining globalization is
to relate it to a set of interconnected design factors in terms of their being supportive or resistive to control (Beaugrande 1997, 93). Four factors decide
which means will serve which ends, or rather, which features of globalization
are essential to its perpetuation (p. 88): fluctuation vs. stability (the extent of
change within globalization), novelty vs. familiarity (the extent to which globalization confirms/disconfirms known facts), complexity vs. simplicity (the
intensity of interaction among participants in globalization), and determinacy

vs. indeterminacy (the clarity/nonclarity of decisions among competing alternatives in globalization processes). Presently, globalization is:

- Fluctuating: the world keeps changing at an increasing pace corresponding to the general acceleration of time.
- Novel: the world constantly witnesses unexpected and often shocking events.
- Complex: participants in the process of globalization are extremely varied in their cultural, political, and economic backgrounds.
- Indeterminate: continual social and scientific developments make it very difficult to envisage the future.

To meet the demands of fluctuation, novelty, complexity, and indeterminacy, capitalism is networking. All dominant social functions and processes are organized around networks. Expansive, dynamic, and innovative while not disruptive to the system, networks are pivotal to globalization (Castells 1996). A consequence of networking is a new organizational form: a network enterprise " whose system of means is constituted by the intersection of segments of autonomous systems of goals" (p. 171). A network enterprise is based on a horizontal rather than a vertical model, and on a formation of strategic alliances with other corporations.

As might be expected, corporations' ideologies are also networked. In a November 2002 *Harvard Business Review*, IBM used its corporate media advertisement titled "Saks turned it on" (against a photo of a line of Saks's garments), to network its corporate ideology—a commitment to success, to Saks's corporate ideology——a commitment to quality. Networked, IBM's ideology and Saks's ideology are made mutually supportive: each serves to legitimize the other.

CONCLUSION

The concept of globalization invites many understandings and interpretations. Whether approving or disapproving, all of these understandings and interpretations are similar in that they confirm the enormous economic, political, and social impact of globalization. Urged on by IT technologies, processes of globalization can only continue to intensify and affect society in unprecedented ways. The future development of globalization remains open to speculation. One thing, though, is certain: corporations, as cornerstones of global enterprise networking, are bound to play a decisive role in that development.

Because globalization is a process driven predominantly by Western social values, corporations should ask themselves whether their corporate ideologies work too for non-Western stakeholders. Are all people basically the same? Is, as a manager of a well-known advertising agency claimed (Barnet and Cavanagh 1994, 169), a headache, everywhere a headache—and an aspirin, everywhere an aspirin? Or is there more to it? Corporations should also ask themselves how globalization affects people. Does globalization create communities in which people know each other, or does globalization create communities in which people do not know each other? The answer to these questions, it seems, lies in new technologies, especially telecommunications and the Internet, that encourage the building of social relationships irrespective of spatial distances. In this respect, glocalization, which brings together the local and the global, creating and sustaining local communities within the global world, takes on a decisive role.

NOTES

1. The Hongkong and Shanghai Banking Corporation Limited.
2. *Harvard Business Review*, November 2002, p. 75.
3. The adjective "international" was coined in 1780 by the British philosopher Jeremy Bentham (1748–1832) who, while apologizing for his temerity in creating a new term, expressed his hope that the word would be "sufficiently analogous and intelligible" (Ullmann 1983, 139). Bentham probably never imagined that the word "international" would one day become an absolutely indispensable item of all discourse.
4. *National Geographic*, November 2000.
5. *National Geographic*, September 2000.
6. Ibid.
7. *National Geographic*, November 2000.

16

Gender

> It could well be that to speak like the powerless is not only typical of women because of the all-too-frequent powerless social position of many American women, but is also part of the cultural meaning of speaking "like a woman." Gender meanings draw on other social meanings; analyses that focus on sex in isolation from the social positions of women and men can thus tell us little about the meaning of "women's language" in society and culture.
>
> —*W. M. O'Barr and B. K. Atkins (1998, 386)*

"IT AIN'T OVER TILL IT'S OVER"

In Chapter 8 we explained how CEO Carly Fiorina, stating "It ain't over till it's over," disclosed her leadership, and, in doing so, legitimized herself and her ideology founded on the idea of a commitment to the HP-Compaq merger. There is nothing exceptional about CEO Fiorina's reply. It is perfectly consistent with the idea "management is war," fundamental to the ideology of the corporate world. What is exceptional, however, is CEO Fiorina's membership, as a female, in an almost exclusively male social group—the corporate management discourse community.

Having erased all personal and corporations' names from CEO Fiorina's interview, we asked 42 students of a postgraduate business course to describe the interviewed CEO in as many details as possible. The students described CEO Fiorina as powerful, competitive, decisive, assertive, self-assured—and male. Our students' assessments elicit a number of questions. Why was CEO Fiorina assigned a male gender? Is CPD a "male" language? Is

CEO Fiorina's perceived "maleness" a part of her ideology? How does CEO Fiorina's perceived "maleness" relate her to other corporate women and corporate men? And finally, how does CEO Fiorina's perceived "maleness" relate to CEO Fiorina?

LANGUAGE AND GENDER

The first influential study to correlate language and gender was Lakoff's article "Language and woman's place" (1973), soon followed by her book of the same title (1975). As a result of social inequality between genders,[1] women, Lakoff argued, have been taught to use "women's language,"[2] which is marked by a set of lexical, phonological, and syntactic-pragmatic traits. Typical for women, Lakoff contended, are elaborated vocabularies in the area of fashion and cooking, the use of imprecise intensifiers (e.g., divine, gorgeous), and the use of polite and euphemistic forms. Whereas men, Lakoff claimed, are encouraged by society to express their emotions and use "strong" expletives such as "damn" or "shit," women are forced to hide their emotions and taught to use "oh dear" or "fudge." The language imposed on little girls in their childhood, denying them the right to express themselves precisely and forcefully, Lakoff concluded, twenty years later is used as an argument to accuse them of not being able to express themselves precisely and forcefully. The overall result is that women appear "marginal to the serious concerns of life, which are preempted by men."

Although heavily criticized for founding her arguments on intuition, introspection, and casual observation, Lakoff's study ignited one of the most controversial topics of sociolinguistics: language and gender. Indeed, Lakoff's hypotheses were to represent a rewarding starting point for a number of important studies on language and gender. One such study was O'Barr and Atkins's analysis of the speech of male and female witnesses in American courtrooms, first published in 1980. The authors found that Lakoff's so-called "women's language" was neither typical of women nor limited to women. On the contrary, women of high social status, for example, expert witnesses, displayed speech patterns Lakoff had described as typically "male." On the other hand, men of low social status who held subordinate jobs or were unemployed used language features Lakoff had proposed to be typical for women. It would be more accurate, O'Barr and Atkins concluded, to refer to "women's language" as "powerless language," since such language tends to be associated with a low social status, irrespective of gender (1998).

Investigating male dominance in mixed interaction, Leet-Pellegrini (1980) also showed that what at first sight seemed to be a domination of gender was, in fact, a subtle combination of professional status and gender. And analyzing interruptions in mixed interaction, Beattie (1981) too confirmed differences in social status and social power to be accountable for "strong" and "weak" language. The quality of mixed interaction, Troemel-Ploetz (1998, 456) has emphasized, depends essentially on the power politics of female-male relationships: men are in possession of social control and, when they see fit, "recourse to violence."

An interesting perspective on female-male communication was provided by Deborah Tannen (1990) in her best seller *You Just Don't Understand*. According to Tannen, women and men are treated differently, talked to differently, and taught to talk differently from the moment they are born. Consequently, women and men grow up in different cultures and develop different expectations as to the role of their talk in relationships, which in mixed interaction leads to cultural misunderstanding.

Tannen's idea of cultural misunderstanding as the core of gender inequity has been denounced for serving the "male research perspective," "selling the status quo," and contributing to a mystification rather than an explanation of the language-gender relationship (Troemel-Ploetz 1998, 450). Tannen's "linguistically innocent stance," Troemel-Ploetz has argued, fails to inform the reader that gender inequity—essentially a political issue—is produced through a set of language options that both reflect and construct differences in status and power. Language options producing gender inequity, Benhabib (1997, 243) further elaborates, constitute, a discourse of "those who have won out and who have codified history as we know it." A perfect evidence of language being a codification of power, Wilson Nelson (1998) has suggested, is communication in predominantly female research teams. Because in such teams women are autonomous and therefore considered to be superior, male team members tend to adopt gynocentric models of communication.

Although the relation between language and gender has been subject to numerous hypotheses, a coherent theoretical frame has not yet been established. Language, research confirms, offers evidence of social status and social power, but not of gender (cf. Eckert and McConnell-Ginet 1998). So far, no linguistic feature has been unambiguously related to gender. No proof exists of language as either gender-dominated or an instrument of gender discrimination. Explorations into the language-gender relationship, it seems, have been more successful in terms of elaborating hypotheses than confirming them.

THE GENDER STEREOTYPE

If language does not function as an instrument of gender inequity, how can CPD be associated to gender? And if CPD is not related to gender, why was CEO Fiorina assigned a male gender? There are two probable reasons for this. First, most CEOs are men. And second, society still, stereotypically, perceives power, competitiveness, decisiveness, assertiveness, and self-assurance, which CEO Fiorina amply manifested, as male traits.

Throughout history men have been perceived as competent, competitive, and focused on material wealth accumulation. Accordingly, they have been taking on the assertive and powerful social roles of, for example, politicians, leaders, and managers. Women, on the other hand, have generally been viewed as less competent, more sensitive, and more expressive, concerned with care and the quality of family life. Women's traditional social roles were those of caring and self-sacrificing, such as nursing and teaching.

However, the gender stereotype "powerful man–powerless woman," is not a "universal of the social mind" (van Dijk 1998, 173). It is "specifically developed, learned, and reproduced in specific sociohistorical contexts, and among specific (dominant) groups." Rough and simplifying, the gender stereotype, as any other stereotype, guides people's understanding of social reality. As such it constitutes the highest level of code-marking, manifested in the characterization of groups and the assignment of groups' social importance (cf. Labov 1966).

Prejudices and stereotypes, it is also known, affect information processing (Bodenhausen and Wyer 1985; van Dijk 1996, 163–183), which is exactly what happened to our students. Influenced by the gender stereotype, they attributed a male gender to linguistic information that was gender-neutral. In other words, they made an inference on the basis of their world model, which had taught them to associate power with the male gender.

A typical consequence of the gender stereotype is a perceived difference in men's and women's attitudes toward profession. For men, profession and professional success have always been a source of self-esteem and an important factor of masculinity (Stiver 1991, 224). Woman, on the other hand, have been taught to put home and family first. Men had careers, women had jobs. Even today many women experience a conflict between their professional and private personalities, fearing their professional success may jeopardize their private life and vice versa. Statistics show such fears not to be unjustified. For example, in the U.S., 49 percent of ultra-achieving women (but only 19 percent of ultra-achieving men) are childless (Hewlett 2002, 68).

A recent study *Women Entrepreneurs: Out from under the Glass Ceiling* (Mattis 2004) reveals that women entrepreneurs—who are free from the restraints habitually imposed upon corporate women by corporations—are considerably more likely to have children than corporate women: 82 percent as compared to 64 percent (p. 157). Presently it is not quite clear, Coates (1998c, 297) warns, whether the conflict between private and professional life that women experience is just a temporary consequence of social transition from a male toward a heterogeneous workforce, or a problem that will constantly accompany women on their way to the top.

In corporate management, the gender stereotype has generated the tenet—admittedly, shared more among men than among women (Schein and Mueller 1992)—that men make better leaders. Corporate women have been perceived as "trespassing upon men's territory," as doing a "man's job," and as deviant (Gutek and Morasch 1982; Sheppard 1989). Accordingly, the key characteristics of a successful manager—assertiveness, self-assurance, ambition, and courage—have been regarded as typically male. Influenced by such beliefs, women managers, it has been noted, when describing themselves have tended to use "male" labels, such as "self-assured," "assertive," and "rational," while women in "female" professions, for example, nurses, used more "feminine" terms, such as "sympathetic," "deferent," and "loyal" (Powell and Butterfield 1979).

GENDER POLARIZATION

Historically, the gender stereotype is a consequence of the process of gender polarization. To maintain power, men have always limited membership to the social groups to which they belonged and discriminated against women. For millennia, men have been defining women in terms of male beliefs, practices, and ideologies. All deviations from such beliefs, practices, and ideologies were, of course, interpreted as deficiencies. Acting within a "power for oneself only" model that defines power through size, strength, and domination (Surrey 1991,165), men created, maintained, and controlled the hierarchical system of power. Over time, the male attitude toward social power became the norm and, therefore, a social advantage. The female attitude, which according to Surrey could be termed "power emerging from interaction," was perceived as a deviation from the norm and, therefore, a social disadvantage. Aware that such a balance of power can be maintained only through gender polarization, the dominant group (men) refused diversity and insisted on differences.

Gender polarization has led to a historical division of discourse. Whereas women were traditionally raised for private discourse focusing on the maintenance of private and family ties (Gilligan 1982; Wells 1979; Coates 1998a), men were brought up for public discourse, the essential part of which is the exchange of professional information. Both political speech and professional languages were created by male speakers for male professional and social needs. Thus, men have always been perceived as better equipped for interaction in the public sphere and professions. Women, on the other hand, were excluded from public—professional and political—life and denied access to power.

A century ago, Ruskin (1905) commented on the differences between men and women:

The man's power is active, progressive, defensive. He is eminently the doer, the creator, the discoverer, the defender. His intellect is for speculation and invention; his energy for adventure, for war, and for conquest (. . .) the woman's (. . .) intellect is (for) sweet ordering, arrangement, and decision. (. . .) By her office and place, she is protected from all danger and temptation. A man ought to know any language or science he learns thoroughly, while a woman ought to know the same or language or science only so far as may enable her to sympathize in her husband's pleasures.

He emphatically ascribed the culturally desirable characteristics "active, progressive, defensive," to the powerful social group (men), and the culturally irrelevant characteristics "sweet and protected" to the powerless social group (women). Refusing diversity and insisting on differences, Ruskin not only characterized two groups (men and women), but also assigned them different levels of social importance. In doing this, Ruskin justified an androcentric status quo and supported an ideology in the service of power. He could, of course, have accepted diversity, but this would have meant disputing the dominant ideology of that time.

In spite of the tremendous social progress made over these past hundred years, the gender stereotype still remains a part of the contemporary world model. For example, in a *Harvard Business Review* article a reputable social psychologist, describing the promotion-related struggle of a (prudently paranoid) middle manager, wrote: "then he realized that one of the female contenders started wearing power suits" (Kramer 2002, 65). Using the buzzword "power suit," the author not only confirmed the existence of the gender stereotype, he tacitly, although probably inadvertently, used the gender stereotype as a conceptual frame to develop and express his ideas.

Underlying gender polarization (and gender stereotype) is a strategy of oversimplification that uses statistical differences between two groups to indicate that certain characteristics are shared by all members of one group and no members of the other (Bing and Bergvall 1998, 503–504). Through oversimplification the average success of a group is used to constrain the individual. In a well-known court case, "EEOC v. Sears," in which the retail corporation Sears was sued for gender discrimination, Sears attributed the reasons for not hiring women in commission sales to "natural" differences between genders. Applying a strategy of oversimplification and presenting women as a homogeneous group that, being different, apparently did not want more lucrative jobs, Sears won the case.

A GENDER-NEUTRAL STYLE

Within the gender stereotype, CEO Fiorina's style of communication was referred to as "masculine." Could she have embraced a more "feminine" style? After all, in Western business practices, a "feminine" style of communication is gradually attaining legitimacy and has been proven to be more effective in reaching business agreements than the stereotypical macho style (Rosener 1990). While a masculine style of communication is more direct, confrontational, and self-promoting, a feminine style seems to be based on solidarity and a respect for collocutor's face. A negotiation strategy typical for women is "win/win," rather than "win/lose," which seems to be typical for men.

Still, it is only fair to state that in the same way a masculine style of communication uses gender as a strategy, so too does a feminine style. If a masculine style of communication supports male dominance in organizations, will not a feminine style of communication support female dominance? Is there an alternative to the "masculine-feminine" dichotomy within organizations? Advocating a gender-neutral "postmodern" approach to corporate communication, Weiss and Fisher (1998) envisage both corporate women and corporate men renouncing communication principles stereotypically considered "appropriate and natural" and turning toward culture, its strengths, its weaknesses, and, above all, "its need to be 'adapted' in other contexts" (p. 4).

THE GLASS CEILING AND GLASS WALLS

CEO Fiorina is one of the very few women to have broken the glass ceiling and glass walls of the corporate world. At the beginning of the 1990s there were between 0.5 percent and 6 percent women among CEOs of American transnationals (cf. Fierman 1990; Solomon 1990; Schwartz 1992). At the same time, over 50 percent of all university graduates, about 35 percent of all business school graduates and over one-third of all managers in the U.S. were women (Schwartz 1992, 108). A decade later, in 2002, women in Fortune 500 companies held 11.1 percent of board seats, represented 1.1 percent of inside directors (those drawn from top management of the company), and made 2.7 percent of top earners (the five most highly paid officers at Fortune 500 companies) (Break your boundaries 2002: 1) . Today, although women make up half of America's labor force, only two Fortune 500 companies have women CEOs or presidents. Ninety of those 500 companies do not have any women among their corporate officers (Gettings and Johnson 2004: 1).

There exists copious evidence, too (e.g., Carli 1999; Murrell 2001; Fels 2004; Mattis 2004; Winn 2004), as to the difficulties women experience entering top management and progressing in their careers. One consequence of the glass ceiling and glass walls is a wage gap. As a rule, the higher the professional level, the wider the gap. Motherhood, apparently, carries a wage penalty of 7 percent per child (Hewlett 2002, 70).

Some 15 years ago, top corporate women were earning up to 40 percent less than their male colleagues (cf. Opportunity 2000 1988; Kreitner and Kinicki 1992, 51; Bateman and Zeithaml 1993, 381). At the beginning of the 1990s, the average wage of a university-educated woman was approximately equal to the wage of a high school–educated man (Ivancevich et al. 1994, 328). At the beginning of the 2000s, women in the U.S. earn 78 percent of the male wage, in France 81 percent, in Sweden 84 percent, and in Australia 88 percent (Hewlett 2002, 69).

There have been attempts to interpret the female-male wage gap, not as a proof of discrimination, but rather as evidence of women's freedom of choice. According to Furchtgott-Roth (1999), equally qualified women and men earn approximately the same in the American workplace. The majority of men among today's highly paid professionals and executives, Furchtgott-Roth argues, is a consequence of the 1970s, when few women studied business and law and majored more in subjects commanding lower salaries. In those days, women earned about 5 percent of all law and business degrees, compared with today's 40 percent. Women, Furchtgott-Roth further argues, have a tendency to interrupt their careers, mainly for family reasons. In a business culture where tenure and experience are highly valued, interruptions simply have their price, which women have to pay.

Another denial of the existence of the glass ceiling is the testimony of Christine Stolba, a senior fellow of the Independent Women's Forum, made before the Committee on Government Reform (Testimony of Christine . . . 2002). According to Stolba, corporations prevent those who decide to devote more time to their personal lives (women) "from advancing at the same rate as those who devote more uninterrupted time to the workplace" (men).

In Europe, the position of women in corporate management does not seem to be any better. At the beginning of the 1990s, women represented about 2 percent of U.K. top management (Fischer et al. 1993). Some six years later, seven out of the top 200 managing directors in the U.K. were women (A world fit . . . 1999, 44). And even in enlightened Scandinavia, where the proportion of women in the labor market is continually growing—some 60 percent of all university students, most of the law students, most of the students in Lutheran seminaries, and four-fifths of all students at medical schools are women—comparatively few women reach the top. In Denmark too, women, although matching their share of the population in medicine and diplomacy, still seem to be underrepresented in business. For example, in the Copenhagen Business School MBA program only one-sixth of all students are women (Strindberg's nightmare 1996, 35).

AMBITIONS AND ASPIRATIONS

Unquestionably, the HP-Compaq merger is evidence of CEO Fiorina's immense ambition to succeed. It is also evidence of professional ambition as a decisive personal characteristic of a CEO. Because most CEOs, it is well known, are men, is CEO Fiorina, with her ambition, an exception to the rule? Put another way, is professional ambition a male trait? Definitely not. Research into individuals' professional ambitious and aspirations has shown no difference between women's and men's abilities and motivations: both women and men are ambitious and achievement oriented (Powell 1993; Brockbank and Traves 1996). As far as ambition goes, a corporate women's problem is not so much about not being ambitions. Rather, the problem is in a society which still treats women's professional ambition as a necessary evil, and is willing to condone women's professional success only if women can prove their having satisfied the needs of their families. Only after a woman has proven her capacity to be a "real woman," is she permitted to be professionally successful (Fels 2004).

Anyway, a meta-analytic review of gender and leader effectiveness has shown no difference in effectiveness in leadership unless the leadership role is gendered, that is, the leader is expected to be male or female (Eagly, Karau, and Makhijani 1995). In the case of a gendered leadership role, the more effective leader will be the one who corresponds to social role expectations. Numerous studies, projects, and investigations have confirmed female executives to perform on par with men, or even better. According to a recent study of Fortune 500 companies "The Bottom Line: Connecting Corporate Performance and Gender Diversity" by Catalyst, there is a clear link between gender diversity and financial performance. Independent of the industry, companies with the highest representation of women in top managerial positions have better financial performance (a 35 percent higher return on equity and a 34 percent higher return to shareholders) than companies with the lowest representation of women (The bottom line . . . 2004, 2).

GENDER DISCRIMINATION

If the scarcity of women in corporate management cannot be attributed to differences in ambitions and aspirations between corporate women and corporate men, what can it be attributed to? Is it possible that gender discrimination still exists within a modern corporation?

In the past, gender discrimination in organizations was easily detectable. As Meyerson and Fletcher (2000, 128) explain, "A respected female executive would lose a promotion to a male colleague with less experience, . . . or a talented female manager would find herself demoted after her maternity leave." Today, because all forms of discrimination are prohibited by law, gender discrimination in organizations, if practiced, will be invisible and concealed in the gender stereotype.

A number of reasons have been put forward to explain, and therefore confirm the existence of, gender discrimination in corporations. Because "female" traits in management are looked upon negatively, women managers, Broverman and colleagues (1972, 75) have suggested, can have more negative self-concepts than men. Consequently, women tend to be less secure regarding their professional performance. When discussing their profession, women, Wong and colleagues (1985) and Statham (1987) have shown, focus on image construction less intensively than men, emphasize the importance of their job for the organization and society less often than men, and ascribe their professional success to professional talents much less often than men. Evidently, a man's style of communication seems to better express characteristics highly valued in management, such as assertiveness and self-assurance. It is not surprising, therefore, Fierman (1990) has argued, that corporate women experience difficulties in finding mentors in organizations. Naturally, lacking powerful sponsors, corporate women get fewer high-visibility assignments. This, in turn, makes corporate women still less attractive to potential mentors and sponsors. Also highly damaging to a corporate woman's career, according to Hewlett (2002, 72), seems to be the popular myth about women who, interrupting their careers to start a family, are no longer "serious contenders." Finally, the unwillingness of women to negotiate for themselves and ask for what they want and need in the workplace, Babcock and colleagues (2003) emphasize, further contributes to gender inequity in corporations. It is, though, interesting to note that when women in organizations do become assertive, they are discouraged and often labeled as "bitchy" or "pushy" (p. 14).

Responding to limitations imposed upon them within corporations, corporate women react in a number of ways: they hit, run, or conform. Objecting, protesting, and suing, women hit. Over the past ten years, for example, monetary benefits paid out by employers charged with sexual harassment in U.S. EEOC (Equal Employment Opportunity Commission) proceedings have risen from $12.7 million in 1992 to $50.3 million in 2002 (Sexual harassment charges . . . 2003).

Realizing how their careers are being short-circuited, and unable to break the glass ceiling, many corporate women look for new challenges—they run, causing serious leaks to the "employee pipeline" which creates enormous costs to corporations (Mattis 2001: 4). More often, corporate women move into entrepreneurship (Fraker 1984; Hartman 1986; Tayler 1986; Bacas 1987; Hewlett 2002; Mattis 2004; Winn 2004), which, by allowing them to combine career and family, offers greater professional flexibility. At the end of 2002, out of all firms in the United States, 38 percent were owned by women (Break your boundaries 2002, 2).

Finally, women conform. Tacitly accepting the gender stereotype, women change their individual image and align with the "enemy." Why are corporate women willing to embrace an essentially hostile stereotype? The answer is a simple one: to realize professional ambitions on what is perceived as men's turf (Coates 1998c, 297; McElhinny 1998, 322). An attempt by a corporate woman to join the "old boys network" can, however, have an unforeseen outcome. In her book *They Can Kill You, but They Can't Eat You* (1994), the late Dawn Steel, for example, recounted how she climbed to a senior executive position at Paramount Pictures by becoming "one of the boys." With the arrival of a new president, her chummy membership in the "boys' club" changed. A few months later she was dismissed.

Corporate women could respond to limitations imposed upon them by disputing the gender stereotype. This, however, would impose a long-term obligation of changing their group image and, inevitably, hamper individual advancement (cf. Tajfel 1978, 1981). Besides, corporate women know that objecting to limitations imposed upon them in fundamentally androcentric organizations entails the risk of isolation and of becoming objects of animosity (Colgan and Ledwith 1996, 287). In a research on gender-equity issue selling in corporations (Ashford 1998), more than half of a group of 210 female MBA graduates declared themselves unwilling to sell. Raising the gender-equity issue, they claimed, would brand them as "whiners, aggressive, and rebels" and seriously damage both their image and credibility in organizations (p. 5).

DIVERSITY INITIATIVES

Still, whatever the difficulties corporate women do experience in the corporate world, the fact remains that corporations are becoming acutely aware of the importance of female professionals as a business resource and are increasingly addressing various gender-related issues, such as retaining women in organizations, committing to diversity, sponsoring women for senior executive positions, creating women-friendly work-life policies, and stimulating a gender-independent curriculum design for management education.

According to Meyerson and Fletcher (2000), corporations build diversity programs on three strategies. First, they encourage women to assimilate by adopting masculine attributes, such as assertiveness, male-style decision making—and golf. Second, corporations support specifically feminine needs and situations, for example, formal mentoring programs, alternative career tracks, flexible work arrangements, extended maternity leave, and nursing rooms. Third, to induce male managers to better appreciate typically feminine qualities, for example, a willingness to listen and cooperate, corporations emphasize differences between women and men. While these initiatives have definitely contributed to gender equity in organizations, they have their limitations. Dealing with symptoms rather than sources of inequity, they enable women "to play on an uneven playing field, but . . . do not flatten out the field itself" (p. 130).

A way out, Mattis has suggested (2001, 2), is for corporate diversity initiatives to focus less on "fixing women" and more on educating employers. The need for systemic solutions is also being voiced by corporate women themselves, who call for a change in career practices, workplace practices, and organizational culture (Hewlett 2002). To help high-achieving career women better balance their professional and private lives, corporations, corporate women have suggested, should introduce:

- a time bank of paid parenting leave that would allow for three months of paid leave, taken when needed, until the child turns 18
- restructured retirement plans in which penalties for career interruption would be limited
- career breaks allowing an (unpaid) leave of absence up to three years with the assurance of a job
- reduced-hour careers: creation of high-level jobs which would permit reduced hours, but still offer possibilities of promotion
- alumni status for former employees, which would help women who have left or are not active in their careers to stay in the loop. Former employees could be tapped for advice and guidance, and the company would continue to pay their dues and certification fees.

In truth, what is regarded as gender inequity in a corporation is just a fragment of a much wider issue: criteria of advancement. Most organizations, as middle and upper level women managers have often claimed, simply do not possess transparently defined criteria of advancement (Colgan and Ledwith 1996, 92), which inevitably encourages all forms of discrimination. Transparent criteria, on the other hand, would give everyone a chance. As Bing and Bergvall (1998, 503) have argued, the point is not that everyone is created equal, but that everyone should be allowed an equal opportunity. Within a corporation, that means equal access to resources and power. Needless to say, the key to equal opportunity is accountability: exactly defined and assigned on all levels, from the corporate top down to each individual employee.

AN ANDROGYNOUS WOMAN

CEO Fiorina's perceived maleness suggests her to have responded to limitations imposed by the gender stereotype through conformation. Disclosing her power, she assigned herself a characteristic of androgyny.

Overall, an androgynous model of behavior is advantageous to a corporate woman's professional identification and advancement (Kapalka and Lachenmeyer 1988; Gardner et al. 1994, 128). Ascribing their success, like men do, to their professional abilities and by projecting more self-assurance (Wong et al. 1985), androgynous women have a greater chance of professional advancement. Pragmatic reasons aside, corporate women are not really left with much choice, as processes of socialization in corporations offer only male models to rely on (Colgan and Ledwith 1996, 33).

According to a stream of research based on a gender role congruency hypothesis (Nieva and Gutek 1981; Haccoun, Haccoun, and Sallay 1978; Bradley 1980; Eagly, Makhijani, and Klonsky 1992), in the long run the androgynous model does more harm than good to corporate women. Since behavior congruent with a person's gender role tends to be rated more favorably than gender role–incongruent behavior, female managers acting masculine are evaluated as less effective, are not liked by peers, and are seen as more threatening than male bosses. A possible conclusion could be that female leaders who wish to be both effective and positively evaluated have to act both masculine *and* feminine, to give an impression of being both cool (to prove effectiveness) and warm (to be evaluated favorably). In their research on constraints of gender roles in organizations, Kawakami and White (2000) have shown, however, that female managers do not necessarily have to combine male *and* female traits and need not be cool *and* warm. The secret of positive evaluation, Kawakami and White contend, is *mindfulness*. If female leaders are at the same time mindful and cool, they will be rated favorably and perceived as effective.

The androgynous model, we believe, is a true Catch-22. To advance, corporate women have to go androgynous. On the other hand, the androgynous model reinforces the gender stereotype, which slows down corporate women's advancement on the corporate ladder. In the long run, adopting the androgynous model, women probably impede their advancement on the corporate ladder. It would nevertheless be a mistake to think of the androgynous model as a sign of a woman's weakness. Psychological androgyny, manifested in the ability of a woman to select the most appropriate way of verbal behavior out of a large repertoire of possibilities, is known to contribute to a woman's psychological balance. Experiments have confirmed androgynous women to be psychologically more stable than men (e.g., Elyan et al. 1978, 129). Indeed, the adroitness with which perceivedly androgynous women

CEOs accept "male" discourse and use it for their own goals could over time, as Colgan and Ledwith (1996, 282) have envisioned, endanger male supremacy in corporations. Under favorable circumstances, this might lead to the formation of groups of "wise women" (p. 283), an avant-garde of organizational changes, who will plead for visibility of gender-equity issues in corporations.

CONCLUSION

The gender issue in corporations affects CPD in at least two ways: ideationally and interpersonally.

At an ideational level, CPD is a medium through which corporate management can express their views on gender issues and include those views into a corporation's culture through, for example, diversity initiatives. Thus, CPD can function as a medium of approaching, discussing, explaining, and solving gender (in)equity in an organization.

At an interpersonal level, CPD is a medium through which corporate management practices power through consent. In the shadow of ideology and power, CEO Fiorina employed gender as a system of meanings and entitlements and as a social (not biological) category based on her professional choice, her social role, and her corporation's registered culture. Wishing to communicate in a socially influential way, CEO Fiorina publicly manifested her familiarity with the characterizing power of the gender stereotype and used the gender stereotype to disclose her social position and to legitimize herself and her ideology.

Because corporate management is predominantly male and because social power is still widely seen as a "male turf," CPD "naturally" embodies a social cognition of a male stereotype that genderizes a corporation's ideology. In contemporary society this is no longer acceptable.

Probably, a first step toward eliminating gender inequity from organizations will be purging CPD of the gender stereotype "powerful man/powerless woman." The assumption "men make better leaders" will have to be replaced by another assumption: "leader qualities are gender-independent." Such a leap forward is possible only if the tenet that key qualities of a good manager are assertiveness, self-assurance, and courage (traits believed to be typically male) is modified to include empathy, mutuality, and solidarity (traits believed to be typically female). In short, a contemporary gender-exclusive corporation will have to transform into a gender-inclusive corporation.

Of course, the essence of CPD will not change: CPD will always remain a "powerspeak." What will change, though, will be a balance of genders within the corporate management discourse community. Once the gender stereotype vanishes from society, socially desirable traits will no longer be gender-related. They will, though, remain power-related, because power will always be quintessential to a corporation. Only this time, power, and consequently CPD, will be gender neutral.

NOTES

1. The most obvious historical indication of gender inequity is masculine generics: the use of "he," "his," and "man" as sex-indefinite human referents. As a grammatical rule, masculine generics was installed in 1746 and as a legal usage in 1850 by a British Act of Parliament. It has been estimated that during a lifetime, a person will come into contact with the generic "he" over ten million times (MacKay 1980, cited in Ng 1996, 279). Today, masculine generic forms are being increasingly replaced with "she," "s/he," and "person/persons/people." In a study of masculine generics based on a 525,000 running word corpus taken from selected American publications, including daily newspapers and popular magazines, published between 1971 and 1979, Cooper (cf. 1989, 19–20) showed the use of masculine generic forms to have greatly declined. Within this period the rate of use of masculine generic forms fell from 12.3 to 4.3 per 5,000 words. The largest decline was found in the use of "man," for which the 1979 rate was just 16 percent of the 1971 rate.

2. In Lakoff's writings applied both to language typically used by women and to language used to describe women.

17

The CEO's
Media Interview

> When an individual plays a part he implicitly requests his observers to take seriously the impression that is fostered before them. They are asked to believe that the character they see actually possesses the attributes he appears to possess, that the task he performs will have the consequences that are implicitly claimed for it, and that, in general, matters are what they appear to be. In line with this, there is the popular view that the individual offers his performance and puts on his show "for the benefit of other people."
>
> —E. Goffman (1990, 28)

A CORPORATE DRAMA

To enable the CEO to legitimize herself or himself—through a disclosure of power, leadership, and social position—the CEO's media interview has metamorphosed into a play: a spoken or written performance that has a plot, uses language in action, and is performed on a stage by actors playing roles.[1] And true to Bernard Shaw's definition of good drama, the CEO's media interview also presents a conflict, which is what makes it so exciting. As Shaw put it, "The end may be reconciliation or destruction; or, as in life itself, there may be no end; but the conflict is indispensable: no conflict, no drama" (1946, vii). Take, for example, the extract from CEO Bernabé's interview discussed in Chapter 9. It was the presence of conflict—between CEO Bernabé and Eni's senior management team—that gave that interview its dramatic quality.

The stage upon which CEO Bernabé's interview is enacted, the prestigious publication *Harvard Business Review*, assigns the interview an appropriate level of importance. What the Old Vic is for a London theater play, the *Harvard Business Review* is for a CEO interview. The interviewers, or rather, the authors of the play, Linda Hill and Suzy Wetlaufer (1998) communicate to CEO Bernabé's audience primarily through the interview's "prologue" in which they state the setting and the angle of the interview, brief the audience on circumstances of the events referred to in the interview, comment on selected parts of the interview, and conclude: "Bernabé's idealism and patriotism have earned him widespread respect and are perhaps his greatest sources of power" (p. 84).

The plot of CEO Bernabé's interview, as can be surmised from the extract, is presented through a series of connected events, starting with the Italian government's decision to clean Eni of corruption, and ending with CEO Bernabé's victory over his opponents. CEO Bernabé is an agent [. . . So I sent the directive that I was in charge . . .] affecting a target entity: Eni's chairman and everyone else. The events are a part of the process of Eni's transition.

The lead role in CEO Bernabé's interview is played by CEO Bernabé himself, who is presented as a figure (the person he aspires to be), as a character (the person he is), and as a type (exemplifying characteristics of a CEO). For example, in spite of strong opposition within Eni, CEO Bernabé never once doubted his ability to effect changes. He too demonstrated his possession of the "Wallenda factor." Other *dramatis personae* in the interview include the Italian government, the chairman, corporate staff, and everyone else. All of them enact their roles indirectly via CEO Bernabé. To represent relationships between CEO Bernabé and other *personae*, we make use of Greimas' (1966) actantial model, developed for the analysis of content structure of folktales and myths. Greimas' model includes three pairs of actants: subject-object, helper-opponent, giver-receiver (Figure 17.1).

Placing the interview within Greimas' model shows CEO Bernabé as the subject, Eni's transformation as the object, CEO Bernabé's supporters as helpers, the chairman and everyone else as opponents, the Italian government as the giver, and stakeholders as receivers. Relationships between the actants (e.g., giver–subject–receiver, giver–subject–opponent, giver–object–receiver, and subject–object–giver) create CEO Bernabé as a figure, a character, and a type. CEO Bernabé is projected as a hero who, striving for an object (a new Eni), surmounts obstacles and defeats opponents.

Figure 17.1
An Actantial Representation of CEO Bernabé's Interview

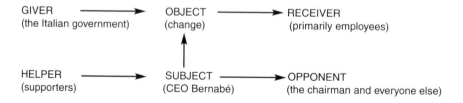

THE CEO'S ARGUMENT

As the role actor of the CEO media interview, the CEO has a special script, through which she or he expounds her or his argument. Behind every argument lies an urgent occasion: a reason for the argument. An argument may be forensic, designed to establish the truth or wrong of people's conduct and behavior. It may be epideictic, designed to bestow praise on someone. And it may be deliberative, designed to establish the credibility of someone's behavior. Designed to justify his actions, CEO Bernabé's argument is deliberative. An example of a CEO's argument that is forensic is CEO Gerstner's interview (in Chapter 5) in which he defines the validity of IBM's corporate values. An example of a CEO's argument that is epideictic is Chairman Sant and CEO Bakke's interview (in Chapter 7) in which they praise AES's employees.

Building an Argument

The CEO's argument is built upon four essential elements: claims, an audience, an exigency, and grounds. The CEO's claims make up her or his argument's syntagmatic structure and may be serial in that they follow each other or hierarchical in that each claim is defended. Through her or his claims, the CEO deals with important matters of probability and the nature of things. Generalizing and summarizing a collection of particular instances and experiences relevant to herself or himself, the CEO makes evaluative claims and propositional claims. Claiming "Because nothing would have changed," CEO Bernabé made an evaluation. An example of a propositional claim is CEO Gerstner's "It comes back to win, execute and team."

The CEO's audience has to be convinced. Addressing an antagonistic audience, CEO Bernabé attempted to lessen their disdain for his argument. Addressing a favorably inclined audience, CEO Bernabé tried to get them to accept his argument.

The CEO's exigency is her or his need to present her or his argument at a certain time, in a circumstance, or for a purpose. Saying "I wanted to have my objectives reached," CEO Bernabé expressed the need to present his argument. Similarly, saying "We can't fix it with systems anymore," CEO Gerstner expressed the need to present his argument, and saying "You can and should bring your brainpower and soul—your whole person—to work," Chairman Sant expressed the need to present his argument.

The CEO's grounds are the reasons she or he offers to support a claim. Reasons function as benefits offered by an argument. CEO Bernabé's benefits were his "objectives." CEO Gerstner's benefits were "win, execute and team." Chairman Sant's benefits were "You're part of this organization."

Defending a Claim

The CEO defends her or his claim through credibility, exactness, verification, and evaluation. To give credibility to her or his claim, the CEO offers a perspective on it. Saying "But normally you don't do something like that," CEO Bernabé provided a perspective that emphasized the unconventionality (and bravery) of his actions. Through using metaphors, CEO Gerstner provided a perspective that created knowledge. Through using message-centered semiotic discourse processes, Chairman Sant provided a perspective that foregrounded the process of communication itself.

To give exactness to her or his claim, the CEO often defines through description, or more exactly, through listing: a representation of instantiations in which stative predicates, for example "have" and "be," are used to formulate the definition. For example, in his interview, CEO Gerster used listing [Those are not slogans or even institutional values. They are personal commitments. They're not things of the head, they're things of the heart and the gut. They are behavioral, not intellectual.] to define the meaning of "win, execute, and team." Through a description schema, CEO Gerstner was able to delineate a situation he assumed would hold for an unspecified period of time and specify items (IBM values) he assumed to have stable identities. Arguing that personal commitments are "behavioral, not intellectual," CEO Gerstner defined a stage in the evolution of IBM.

To verify a claim, the CEO explains her or his motives behind that claim. The CEO does this by demonstrating the existence of a link between a cause and an effect. Saying "I didn't want compromise—I wanted to have my objectives reached," CEO Bernabé explained his motive behind his actions as a necessity of change to prevent, alter, and interfere with causal processes, and to bring about or prevent an effect. Saying "We can't fix it with systems anymore," CEO Gerstner explained his motive behind his actions as a necessity of sufficiency in whose presence an effect must occur.

Finally, to evaluate a claim, the CEO offers an assessment of its consequences. The good consequence of CEO Bernabé's claims was change. The good consequence of CEO Gerstner's claims was success. The good consequence of Chairman Sant's claims was empowerment.

THE CEO'S STORIES

Unquestionably, the CEO's favorite argument are the stories that she or he so willingly tells. The CEO's stories have a narrative schema and are linguistically characterized by a high frequency of personal pronouns, quotations, and the past tense. A good story is eternal. It is an evaluation that "pervades not only the processes whereby 'what happens' becomes part of one's experience, but also the processes whereby an experience is situated in the 'here and now,' the 'why,' and the 'to whom' of its telling" (Schiffrin 1994, 307). The best examples of stories are the Iliad and the Odyssey, the Bible, and fairy tales—narratives of life and death, love and hatred, war and peace, all of them testimonies of human experience.

The CEO's stories relate to the CEO's personal experiences, that she or he has decided to reveal. CEO Bernabé's story, for example, was about his experience in Eni's transition. Through stories, the CEO situates herself or himself within the interview. Stories provide the CEO with identifiable modes of implication, such as evaluation, explanation, and definition, which, however, as Fisher (1987, 48) explains, cannot be ultimately persuasive. Rather, these modes of implication function as argumentative forms—admittedly, important ones—used to express values that constitute good reasons for the acceptance of the CEO's arguments. Good reasons are socially and culturally determined. They warrant an accurate symbolization of the world, and capture "the experience of the world, simultaneously appealing to the various senses, to reason and emotion, to intellect and imagination, and to fact and value" (p. 75). Good reasons can take various individuated forms, such as "arguments, metaphors, myths, gestures and other means of creating communicative relationships" (p. 143). A good reason, used by both CEO Bernabé and CEO Gerstner, was the ideal of individualism [I didn't want compromise—I wanted to have my objectives reached.], [Our success now is going to be a function of personal behavior—the behavior of each and every one of us. We can't fix it with systems anymore.], achievable through effort, persistence, self-reliance, the free-enterprise system, and freedom from controls. Chairman Sant's good reason was empowerment.

CONCLUSION

Without a doubt, it was the fundamental motivational need for power and achievement that drove CEO Bernabé to obtain and exercise control over others and establish the new corporate ideology of Eni. The need for power gave CEO Bernabé the basic energy he required to initiate and sustain action and his capacity to translate intention into reality. The need for achievement propelled CEO Bernabé, after ten years of low profile at Eni, to seize power "more boldly than anyone may have expected" (Hill and Wetlaufer 1998, 84). Stating his right to command and to expect others to obey [So I sent the directive that I was in charge. It was really a shock to the chairman and everyone else.], CEO Bernabé publicly declared himself both as a member of a powerful group and as a powerful individual. In doing so, he and his group (Eni's new corporate management) became a norm against which other groups (Eni's previous corporate management) could be evaluated, and, when necessary, criticized or trivialized. Within his drama, CEO Bernabé "held the world . . . a stage where every man must play a part." Playing his part, CEO Bernabé legitimized himself and his ideology of transforming Eni.

NOTE

1. Occasionally, CEO media interviews are brought together in the form of a book, such as Dauphinais and Price's *Straight from the CEO* (1999).

18

Promotionalization of CPD

> . . . the spirit of modern consumerism is anything but materialistic. The idea that contemporary consumers have an insatiable desire to acquire objects represents a serious misunderstanding of the mechanism which impels people to want goods. Their basic motivation is the desire to experience in reality the pleasurable dramas which they have already enjoyed in imagination, and each "new" product is seen as offering a possibility of realizing this ambition.
>
> —*C. Campbell (1995, 89–90)*

THE PROMOTIONAL FUNCTION OF CPD

In a world that views consumption as the most desirable of all modes of behavior and a commodity in itself, it is not surprising that promotion has become "generalized" (Wernick 1991) as a communicative function of all discourses, including CPD. To promote themselves, or rather their goods and services, through which consumers consume corporations' ideologies, corporations have incorporated a number of communicative strategies originating in the discourse of advertising into CPD.

AESTHETICIZATION

In its 1999 annual report, Heineken stated:

"Bringing enjoyment to people's lives" is one of Heineken's core values. It goes beyond the supply of quality products. It also has to do with respect: respect for society, human emotions, and the offer of a relaxing and unforgettable experience. Being there, around the world, is important but is only treasured when one knows and respects local values, and manages to unite various cultures. Heineken pursues these goals in different ways, big and small. We have four thematic pages containing several examples to show you what we mean by this.[1]

Through that statement, Heineken transformed the simple act of drinking Heineken beer into a campaign for uniting cultures around the world. Giving Heineken beer a value unrelated to its basic function, Heineken aestheticized it. The corporation was able to do this because of the basic inequality of manufacturers and consumers in the sphere of circulation: a sphere where commodities are exchanged for money (Haug 1971). While the buyer wants the commodity to possess use value, the seller, whose only interest is to sell, is happy as long as the commodity appears to possess use value. The more aesthetically appealing a commodity, the faster it will sell.

Wishing to aestheticize its beer, Heineken had a number of options at hand: to aestheticize it through some inherent trait (e.g., color), through a trait closely connected to the beer (e.g., the shape of beer cans/bottles), or through a trait completely detached from the beer that appeals to stakeholders' emotional and sensual responses (e.g., uniting cultures). Choosing the third option, Heineken was able to extend the process of aestheticization beyond the product itself onto its corporate ideology founded on the idea of "bringing enjoyment to people's lives," which it defined and legitimized through the social value of "respect."

THE CORPORATION'S SLOGAN

Promotion is always founded on a promise. To state their promises, corporations use slogans—short, easily remembered, catch-phrases: "Consider it done" (UPS), "Dedication you can count on" (WestLB), "Forever New Frontiers" (Boeing), and "Innovation delivered" (Accenture). Usually a part of a corporate media advertisement, the corporate slogan is a signification for a more complex message. For example, in Hitachi's corporate media advertisement, "Global vision"

Hitachi's visionary technology is revealing nature's deepest secrets to the naked eye. Our versatile electron microscopes—indispensable tools in the nanotechnology revolution—have a multitude of uses in fields ranging from semiconductors to biotechnology. And our non-invasive Magnetic Resonance Imaging (IMR) systems provide medical professionals with fast, accurate diagnostic and surgical tools. Saving lives, or simply making life better, is the global vision at Hitachi.[2]

the accompanying slogan "Inspire the Next" catches its audience's attention not so much by what it says but more by what it implies.[3] It is precisely the slogan's brevity, simplicity, and lack of specificity that arouses. Conceptually related to the advertisement's "visionary technology," "nanotechnology revolution," and "global vision," the slogan "Inspire the Next" gives consistency to the advertisement. Articulating an insight, it induces disparate stakeholders to perceive the advertisement through the eyes of the corporation. Simply, "Inspire the Next" is Hitachi's irresistible promise, with which the corporation gives legitimacy to its ideology of "saving lives, or simply making life better."

The ideological use of slogan is not new. Throughout the history of mankind short catch-phrases have been used by social groups who wanted to institutionalize their ideologies. Flags, coats of arms, uniforms, and mottoes all witness the use of ideology in the service of power. Functionally, there is no difference between the Order of the Garter's motto, *honi soit qui mal y pense* (the shame be his who thinks ill of it), inscribed in the British coat of arms and today's corporate slogans. Both serve as "rallying calls" for stakeholders to close ranks in the attainment of common objectives. Both contain ideologies of their times. The ideology of the Order of the Garter is feudalism, a system in which loyalty to lords-superior—for which subjects were rewarded with land and protection—was the main purpose of life. The ideology of today's world is consumerism, a system in which the acquisition of commodities (for whatever reason) becomes the main purpose of life.

Contemporary audiences are easily seduced by slogans. As Redfern (1989, 115) has observed, slogans seem to be the only poetry, along with pop-song lyrics, an average Western person hears after elementary school. It would be wrong, however, to take for granted stakeholders' acceptance of corporate slogans and the promises they contain. On the contrary, the sheer proliferation of essentially similar slogans may invite suspicion. If a stakeholder is inclined to believe a corporate slogan, she or he will be motivated to accept its promise. If a stakeholder mistrusts a corporate slogan, she or he will be motivated not to accept its promise. If a stakeholder approves of the corporate world, she or he will be motivated to approve of the corporation's slogan. If a stakeholder disapproves of the corporate world, she or he will be motivated not to accept the corporation's slogan. If a stakeholder approves of the power of a corporation, she or he will be motivated to accept the corporation's slogan. If a stakeholder disapproves of that power, she or he will be motivated not to accept a corporation's slogan. Finally, a corporation's slogan has a material base (a medium), which too is subject to a stakeholder's approval/disapproval.

HYPERBOLIC LANGUAGE

Arguably, the most visible evidence of CPD's promotional function is found in mission statements that are pervaded by hyperbolic language, created through combinations of superlatives (e.g., most, best, greatest, finest, fastest), determiners (e.g., every, each, any), and verbs marking productive discourse processes (e.g. strive, increase, expand, maximize, create, achieve, optimize):

- superlatives
To be the world's best in chemicals and electronic imaging.[4]
To manage our customers' Finest Hour.[5]
McDonald's vision is to be the world's best quick service restaurant experience. Being the best means providing outstanding quality, service, cleanliness and value, so that we make every customer in every restaurant smile. To achieve our vision, we are focused on three worldwide strategies:
  - Be the best employer for our people in each community around the world
  - Deliver operational excellence to our customers in each of our restaurants, and
  - Achieve enduring profitable growth by expanding the brand and leveraging the strengths of the McDonald's system through innovation and technology.[6]

- determiners
To be America's best quick service restaurant chain. We will provide each guest great tasting, healthful, reasonably priced fish, seafood, and chicken in a fast, friendly manner on every visit.[7]
Microsoft's vision is to empower people through great software—any time, any place and on any device.[8]
To give unlimited opportunity to women.[9]

- verbs marking productive discourse processes
We strive to:
(1) increase volume,
(2) expand our share of nonalcoholic sales worldwide,
(3) maximize our long-term cash flows and
(4) create economic value added by improving economic profit.
We achieve these goals by strategically investing in the high-return beverage business and by optimizing our cost of capital through appropriate financial policies.[10]

The mission statement's hyperbolic language performs three functions. First, creating stakeholders' awareness of the corporation, it attracts their attention. Second, presupposing stakeholders' need for self-actualization[11]— the realization of stakeholders' unique potentials—it stimulates their interests and creates desires. Third, symbolizing a corporation's means to meet stakeholders' needs for self-actualization, hyperbolic language motivates action. Thus, Dell's use of hyperbolic language

Dell's mission is to be the most successful computer company in the world at delivering the best customer experience in markets we serve. In doing so, Dell will meet customer expectations of:
- Highest quality
- Leading technology
- Competitive pricing
- Individual and company accountability

- Best-in-class service and support
- Flexible customization capability
- Superior corporate citizenship
- Financial stability[12]

announcing "the best customer experience" is much more than a list of Dell's objectives: it is a promise that both stimulates and satisfies a customer's need for self-actualization through the "highest quality" and "leading technology." Knowing that even those few who have satisfied their highest-level needs will still be motivated to go on, for the need for self-actualization can never be entirely fulfilled, Dell links its corporate ideology to a never-ending cycle of human motivation.

COGNITIVE MODELS OF ADVERTISING

Wishing to more effectively persuade stakeholders, corporations have turned to sophisticated cognitive models of advertising. Such models, similarly to hyperbolic language, are based on the expectation of an audience's reaction evolving through three stages: a cognitive stage, in which awareness of the message is created and attention attracted; an affective stage, which results in interest for the message, preference, desire, yielding, and acceptance; and a behavioral stage, which leads to action. For example, on the day of the Hewlett-Packard and Compaq merger, the new HP issued a post-merger address, "We are ready":

Today, Hewlett-Packard and Compaq join together to form the new HP.
Eight months and a million hours of planning by our integration team have prepared us for this day.
Today, management teams are in place in every country in which we operate.
Today, three-year plans are finalized for all our products.
Today, eighty-thousand sales, services and support professionals are ready to address your needs.
Today, the new HP online store is open for business
Today, we thank our customers, partners, employees and shareowners for their continued trust and support.
Today, the new HP is ready.[13]

The aim of the address was to invite stakeholders' reaction on three levels: cognitive, affective, and behavioral. The address created awareness and attracted attention through the repetitive use of "today," a deictic expression, relating the corporation to a time and place. Positioning the new HP temporally, "today" helped the corporation to replace all previous ideologies of the "old" HP and Compaq with a new HP ideology. Positioning the new HP spatially [Today, management teams are in place in every country in which we operate.] , "today" anchored the new HP ideology on the global market. In both its temporal and its spatial function, "today" stood for something new, different, and promising.

Stakeholders' interests and desires were created through the selective use of the propositional content of the address [eight months and a million hours of planning, integration team, in every country, three-year plans . . . for all our products, eighty-thousand sales, services and support professionals, online store, continued trust and support] that reflected the impressive effort made by the two corporations to realize the merger deal. Thanking stakeholders for their "continued trust and support," the address not only immediately involved stakeholders in the inception of the new HP ideology, but also subtly confirmed the correctness of their approval of it.

Having created an awareness of a better HP, which in turn created new interests and desires, the address motivated stakeholders' action: to give their support to the new HP. Because the address was highly persuasive, the belief and attitude change it created, we assume, was of a permanent nature.

Cognitive models of advertising, as, for example, the one underlying HP's address, are based on balance theory, that was established by Fritz Heider (1958), one of the founders of social psychology. Balance theory explains why people need cognitive consistency, why they need to link ideas and concepts in a logical and consistent way, and why they have a general preference for balanced states rather than imbalanced ones. Used strategically, people's tendency toward cognitive consistency offers a basis on which persuasion can be built. Take, for example, Canon's *National Geographic* corporate advertisement "As Canon sees it," that shows a photograph of a magnificent Iberian lynx, accompanied by a text describing the lynx in minute detail:

An Iberian lynx sits quietly in the dry autumn grass, her tufted ears turned toward a potential intruder. Her two cubs are hidden in a thicket nearby, eating a newly caught rabbit, their staple prey. Born in the hollow of a large tree, the cubs soon move on to bushes where intertwined brambles and thick stalks provide refuge during the next weeks of their lives. The Iberian lynx once roamed throughout Spain and Portugal, but today only small and fragmented populations exist. Providing protection outside of reserves and ensuring suitable habitat with prey are vital to the future of the endangered Iberian lynx. As a global corporation committed to social and environmental concerns, we join in worldwide efforts to promote greater awareness of endangered species for the benefit of future generations.[14]

Using stakeholders' assumedly positive attitude toward the Iberian lynx as an endangered species, the advertisement aims to create stakeholders' positive attitude toward Canon. Within the frame of balance theory, Canon, the lynx, and stakeholders constitute cognitive elements which form a triangle of relationships (Figure 18.1).

Because people prefer a harmonious and balanced state among cognitive elements, Canon's (declared) and stakeholders' (assumed) positive attitude toward the Iberian lynx should create a cognitive balance. The first four sentences of the advertisement focus on reinforcing stakeholders' positive attitude toward the lynx. The last two sentences focus on Canon's role in the worldwide movement of protecting endangered species, which demonstrates

Figure 18.1
A Triangle of Relationships

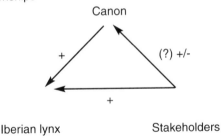

Canon

Iberian lynx   Stakeholders

Canon's positive attitude toward the lynx. Tending toward cognitive consistency, stakeholders, via an unconscious mental realization, create a positive attitude toward Canon and its ideology.

ADDRESSING REFERENCE GROUPS

Finally, corporations' continually increasing promotional efforts have led them to target CPD at stakeholders as reference groups, each of which has its own values, norms, and judgments. Consider, for example, Nalco's philosophy of operations, "Building value":

For customers
Nalco seeks to improve the profitability and process performance of our customers' operations and to assure a return on their investment with us. We are on-site problem-solvers and we bring technically innovative solutions to our customers' dynamic systems. Our goal is customer satisfaction in all that we do.

For employees
Our employees are the strength behind our customer focus. We strive to add value through our quality process and through an environment of opportunity, challenge, trust and reward so that employees may effectively satisfy our customers, contribute to our goals and enjoy personal growth and fulfilment. We will treat each other with respect and dignity. All employees should be able to work in an environment that is safe, healthy, free from discrimination and fair in all aspects of work, pay, benefits and career opportunities.

For shareholders
Nalco is committed to strategy of leadership, focusing on markets, strengths and financial goals that will build shareholder value and provide continuous growth. We expect to make a reasonable profit so that we can reward our shareholders and employees, invest in our future and enrich the communities in which we operate.

For communities
We will obey the law, act ethically and with integrity, be responsible with respect to the environment and be active and interested in civic and community affairs.

Safety, product stewardship and Responsible Care® are essential ingredients of our value-building commitment. Nalco employees are expected to uphold these commitments in all aspects of their work. We strive to conduct our business so that everyone who comes in contact with Nalco enjoys the same considerations and fair treatment.[15]

Addressing stakeholders individually as customers, employees, shareholders, and communities, Nalco provides all of these groups with psychological sustenance and a sense of belonging. Customers are addressed through profitability and innovativeness, employees through personal growth and fulfillment, shareholders through value and continuous growth, and communities through ethics and integrity.

CONCLUSION

The life course of postmodern society is highly destandardized: the range of acceptable behaviors has increased, and there is no longer a "regular" life pattern (Buchmann 1989). Contemporary stakeholders are "hedonists and dreamers" torn between the perfections of their dreams and the imperfections of reality, which gives rise to their "continual longing" and "inexhaustibility of wants" (Campbell 1995, 95). Believing themselves able to direct their own lives, stakeholders have become awkwardly unpredictable. Their demands on corporations are ceaselessly changing, and their approval of corporate ideologies may not have much to do with the objective merits of those ideologies.

To control and regulate such a volatile group, corporations have emphasized the promotional function of CPD, best seen in the use of communicational strategies typical to the discourse of advertising. Playing on contemporary society's need to consume, and the variety of reasons for consumption, CPD's promotional function appeals to stakeholders as consumers, to the ideology of consumerism, and to apparatuses of control of which consumers are a part.

NOTES

1. Heineken 1999 Annual Report.
2. *The Economist*, October 19, 2002, p. 40.
3. The inference of information in a slogan is achieved through an ellipsis, a process by which essential information is compacted and redundant information excluded.
4. www.kodak.com.
5. www.marconi.com.
6. www.mcdonalds.com.
7. www.ljohnsilvers.com.
8. www.microsoft.com.
9. www.marykay.com.
10. www.cocacola.com.

11. According to Maslow (1970), self-actualization is at the top of the hierarchy of human needs. The hierarchy starts with basic physiological needs (food, drink, shelter), followed by safety needs (security, freedom from fear), social needs (acceptance, affection, belonging), and self-esteem needs (achievement, approval, recognition).

12. www.dell.com.

13. www.thenew.hp.com, June 13, 2002.

14. *National Geographic*, December 2000.

15. www.ondeonalco.com.

PART VII

Postscript

19

Adjourning
the Exploration

One of the problems I can see in the pathway of development of management studies in the UK is that as people have been trained in hybrid areas like marketing, strategy and organizational behavior so they have progressively become more and more disengaged from the social science disciplines such as sociology, anthropology, economics and political science which are so important in framing research questions in the management field. We need to reengage with those disciplines and with other ideas and not just take from them but also contribute to them.

—A. Pettigrew, Professor at Warwick University (Starkey 2002, 25)

A THEORY OF CPD

This book is a consolidation of our ideas on the discourse of corporations viewed from a language-ideology-power perspective. A corporation, we have argued, emerges out of order imposed upon disorder. That which gives order, we have further argued, is power through consent, that is, power practiced through cultural processes such as language and ideology. The fundamental question we have attempted to answer in this book is: how do corporations strategically use discourse to practice power through consent?

A dominant, mostly written, discoursal practice of corporations to practice power through consent is CPD. Serving as a corporation's public statement, CPD positions the corporation in society and supports a specific set of living conditions embodying beliefs, attitudes, and behaviors, social roles and relationships, as well as relations of power. As an artifact, CPD defines social practices within and outside the corporation and determines stakeholders' perception of those practices.

The basic unit of CPD is a communicative event comprising discourse and its participants, the organizational role of that discourse, and the environment of its production and reception, including its historical and cultural associations. Strategic, preplanned, and recorded, a corporate communicative event is constrained by the general communicative purpose of constructing an ideology to practice power through consent, common to all corporate communicative events, and a specific communicative purpose, which is particular to a corporate communicative event. The specific communicative purpose defines a corporate communicative event's propositional content. A class of CPD communicative events sharing the same specific communicative purpose constitutes a CPD genre: a socially recognized frame that links a communicative event to a corporation. Corporate genres that have become stabilized in content and form represent default corporate genres. CPD communicative events, genres, and CPD are brought together as a whole within a CPD continuum that represents actual linguistic choices and potential linguistic choices available to all corporations.

CPD institutionalizes, legitimizes, capitalizes, and inculcates ideas constitutive to a corporation's ideology: a corporation's cognitive and behavioral system that sets priorities among ideas and legitimizes some of those ideas. As a rule, a legitimized idea is rooted in a social value, that itself is a legitimized idea of society. An institutionalized and legitimized idea is a corporation's and corporate management's social, symbolic, cultural, and economic capital to secure "positions of possibility."

A CEO gives legitimacy to a corporation's and her or his ideology through legitimizing herself or himself by disclosing her or his power, leadership, and social position. A corporate manager's right to use CPD to practice power through consent, qualifies her or him as a member of the corporate management discourse community: a social system founded on the common goals of corporate management. As a social system, the CMDC regulates corporations' discourse, of which CPD is an example.

CPD is reproduced through mass media, which makes it a part of the wider social processes of rationalization, commodification, and spectacularization. Rationalized, CPD is made efficient, calculable, predictable, and controllable through nonhuman rather than human technology. Commodified and spectacularized, CPD is constructed to stimulate its own consumption. Through mass media, CPD becomes a medium of virtual witnessing, a medium of compulsory visibility, and a medium of extended mediazation. As a medium of virtual witnessing, CPD replaces the corporation and, in this sense, becomes self-legitimizing. As a medium of compulsory visibility, CPD constitutes legitimate evidence of a corporation's social responsibility, accountability, and transparency. As a medium of extended mediazation, CPD develops a network of references, which has to be managed on the basis of intelligence about that network. Finally, mass media define CPD's audience who, we have said, is increasingly inclined to view their participation in CPD as a key duty of global citizenship. Inevitably, it is the social status of a mass medium, realized through its target audience, that dictates the conditions of consumption of CPD.

EXPLORING CPD

A theory of CPD allows for the exploration of CPD, which can focus on any point along the CPD continuum. In this book we have researched individual communicative events and corporate genres, as well as some more specific CPD-related topics: a CEO's metaphor, globalization, gender, and the promotional function of CPD.

To explore a CPD communicative event, we treated text as a text-world model in which linguistic, cognitive, and social actions converge. Related to social context, text provides evidence of wide social processes within the corporation and society.

To explore a corporate genre, we used a corpus-based approach that involved text corpora compilation, computational analysis of text corpora, and an interpretation of quantitative data. Providing the means for a corporation to continually monitor and manage its CPD continuum as a strategic management resource, a corpus-based approach to CPD, we believe, has the potential to become a powerful tool of a corporation's communication research.

AN INTERDISCIPLINARY APPROACH

By definition, an exploration into CPD has to be interdisciplinary. We, for example, drew upon theories from theoretical linguistics, sociolinguistics, the ethnography of communication, discourse analysis, media theory, the theory of ideology, and organizational studies. Theoretical linguistics offered a theoretical frame for the description of CPD's structure and functions. Sociolinguistics, the study of language as related to its social context, provided an access to CPD as social action, or more specifically, as a means of establishing social relations such as solidarity and power, social networks and social identity. The ethnography of communication, which combines linguistics, anthropology, sociology and folklore studies (Saville-Troike 1990), enabled us to focus on culture-related patterns of communication in corporations. Critical discourse analysis, a "cross-discipline" (Fairclough 1999b, 11), drawing mostly from linguistics, sociology, anthropology, and cognitive psychology, offered the methodology for the systematic exploration of relationships of causality and determination between (a) corporate discursive practices, corporate communicative events, and texts, and (b) wider social and cultural structures, relations, and processes. A theory of ideology founded on social cognition and an understanding of ideology as the basis of the social representation of a group, provided a theoretical access to the relationship between a corporation's ideology and its CPD. Media theory, "the latest arrival amongst the humanities" (Inglis 1996,16), helped us explain the nature of CPD's publicness. Finally, we drew too, upon a number of established theories of organizational studies.

A LAST WORD

OD offers the unique potential of providing organizational studies with what Gaston Bachelard, one of the most influential thinkers of the twentieth century, referred to as an "epistemological break." In his books on the philosophy of modern science, Bachelard analyzed the impact of science upon philosophy, showing how twentieth-century science broke with all previous sciences and all previous philosophy. In opposition to positivistic histories of science, Bachelard's notion of "epistemological break" refutes the continuist, teleological theory of history by denying progress from one scientific theory to another. Rather, successive theories are posited to be radically different from their predecessors, for each establishes its own internal concepts of truth and reality.

Although organizational studies are claimed to be multidisciplinary, they still rely primarily on accredited—and therefore seemingly dependable and orderly—theories, notably, management theory, a theory of organization, human resource management, and organizational behavior. Introducing nonaccredited theories into organizational studies, such as, for example, a theory of CPD as developed in this book, might initially seem to bring chaos to the field of organizational studies and make it unstable. The acknowledgment of such an (unfamiliar) theory by researchers in organizational studies will, we assume, initiate a major shift of organizational studies' research parameters from resistive to such theories toward supportive of them (Fig. 19.1).

Accordingly, organizational studies' theories, which under the currently dominant pradigm are considered supportive, will suddenly start to appear stagnant and regressive. Vice Versa, nonaccredited theories considered resistive will suddenly start to appear creative and progressive. When that happens, an "epistemological break" in organizational studies will take place.

Figure 19.1
A New Organizational Studies Research Paradigm

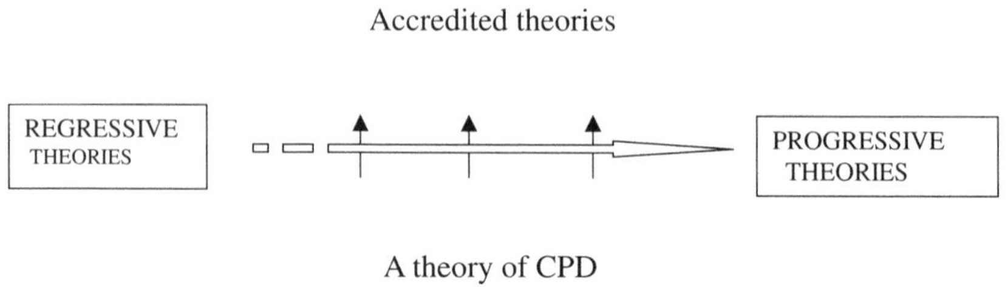

Accredited theories

A theory of CPD

Glossary

accidental knowledge Elements that happen to be true of random instances.

addressee Target audience.

aesthetic function A language function that relates to addressor's and addressee's attitudes and preferences about language, style, and expected rhetorical effect.

androcentric Regarding man or the male sex as central and primary.

androgynous woman A woman claiming or exhibiting both "feminine" and "masculine" characteristics.

applied linguistics A science whose main concern is the application of the concepts and findings of theoretical linguistics to a variety of practical tasks.

attitude The way a person thinks and feels about something. Attitudes are usually based on feelings about attributes, benefits, and objects.

attribute A characteristic or a feature that an object may or may not have.

auditor A member of audience known and ratified as a participant, but not addressed.

authority A leader's right to practice power of position (legitimate power).

average word length Length of the word in a text in orthographic letters. Average word length is an evidence of a text's density of information and exactness of meaning. Greater average word length indicates a careful integration of information and precise lexical choice, typical for discourse with high informational focus.

behavior Social evidence of a person's interaction with the world, which is influenced by various factors.

belief Knowledge and experience a person has of the relations among attributes, benefits, and objects.

benefit The outcome that attributes may provide.

buzzword A word originating in a jargon and acquiring a status of a vogue word in a particular group.

capital (Bourdieu 1985) A power over the field (at a given moment). Capital can be cultural, symbolic, social or economic.

coercive power The leader's power to coerce employees perceived as uncooperative through a system of penalties.

coherence Connectivity of underlying content.

cohesion The connection of words within a sequence.

commissive A type of illocutionary act showing the speaker to be committed to a certain course of action.

communicative competence An individual's ability to use linguistic, pragmatic, and cultural knowledge appropriately to the social situation. In the widest sense, communicative competence is the ability to apply linguistic, pragmatic, and cultural knowledge to create meanings and promote solidarity/power.

community power The leader's power to relate corporate operations and policies to the social environment in ways that are mutually beneficial to both the corporation and society.

composing A process of combining syntactic units into compact and coherent larger structures.

compulsory visibility Visibility as an imperative to which a public person is forced to submit.

concept A configuration of knowledge.

content words (also "lexical words") Content words (nouns, adjectives, adverbs, main verbs) tell us what the text is about.

contextual function Language function that marks setting, purpose, and scene.

corporate artifact A corporate public statement assuming a material form. Artifacts contain a common sense that gives them their acceptability.

corporate communicative event An activity driven by a set of communicative purposes or communicative objectives, which determine the schematic structure of the discourse and constrain choice of content and style.

corporate culture Commonly defined as a system of behaviors, rituals, and meanings, held by members of an organization and distinguishing them from members of other similar units.

corporate genre Class of corporate communicative events sharing the same minor communicative purpose.

corporate inscription devices Corporate communication devices such as discourse, pictures, figures, and graphs.

corporate management discourse community (CMDC) A sociorhetorical network that operates within the corporate world and is aimed at a set of common objectives. The right to membership in the CMDC is attained through a corporate manager's access to the worth of CPD as capital. The CMDC habitat is made up of a macroenvironment encompassing a task environment that contains industries to which corporations belong.

corporate metaphor The dominant metaphorical perspective of corporate management.

corporate public discourse (CPD) A dominant discoursal practice of corporations used to practice power through consent.

corporate public statement Anything from corporate public discourse (CPD) to corporate architecture, office furniture, and dress code.

corporate values A dominant value system, characteristic of an organization.

corporate vision A deep insight into all aspects of life relevant to a corporation combined with a clear idea of a corporation's future.

corporation's symbolic universe A matrix of all social and individual meanings related to a corporation.

critical discourse analysis (CDA) Systematic exploration of relationships of causality and determination between (a) discursive practices, events, and texts and (b) wider social and cultural structures, relations, and processes (Fairclough 1999a).

cultural capital Cultural capital is represented by education and expertise.

declaration A type of illocutionary act in which the speaker alters the status of an object or situation.

default corporate genre A corporate genre, for example, mission statement, financial report, and business guidelines, that has become indispensable for the functioning of the corporation.

determinate knowledge Elements essential to the very identity of a concept.

digital power The ability to develop a new digital infrastructure, to reinvent the way the organization works, and thus provide a competitive edge.

directive A type of illocutionary act by which the speaker tries to induce the hearer to do something.

discourse Language in social action.

dispositive discourse process A discourse process indicating someone's right to dispose of something or deal with something.

domain A particular speaker-audience combination, located in a particular place, related to a particular topic.

eavesdropper A member of an audience not known to be there and not ratified.

economic capital Economic capital has the form of financial assets.

entity That which has identity and properties and is capable of participating in a process of which the basic premise is a state.

ethnography of communication A discipline addressing the structure of communicative behavior and its role in social life. The ethnography of communication combines linguistics, anthropology, sociology, and folklore studies.

event A change from one state to another.

executive power Executive power has been defined in a variety of ways: as "the ability to make things happen" (Kanter 1977), as the capacity to "enhance the organization positively in relation to its 'environment' or key problems" (Pfeffer and Salancik 1997), and as a "resource which enables management to pull together people, technology, time and space" (Morgan 1990). Whereas in the past executive power carried negative connotations, today it is seen as indispensable to the proper functioning of the organization, decision-making processes, and a manager's self-assurance and credibility.

expert power A leader's possession of expert knowledge about a certain area. Subordinates follow because they can benefit from that expertise.

expressive A type of illocutionary act in which a speaker expresses an attitude about a state of affairs.

facunditas The ability to persuasively put a message across to an audience.

felicity conditions (Searle 1976) Constraints on a message that require the message producer to possess authority, show respect for conventions of a message, and assure audiences of her or his sincerity.

field A network of social relations, within which struggles over resources, stakes, and access take place. Fields make up a social site.

frame A configuration of commonsense knowledge.

function words (also "grammatical words") Function words (auxiliary verbs, modal verbs, pronouns, prepositions, determiners, conjunctions) relate content words to each other.

gender polarization Organization of social life around gender distinctions.

gender stereotype A standardized conception associating an exaggerated belief (powerful/powerless) to a gender (man/woman).

general communicative purpose Defines the goal of a corporate communicative event.

glass ceiling An invisible barrier that prevents women (and other minorities) from attaining senior managerial positions. The phrase was apparently coined in 1986 by two Wall Street Journal reporters.

glass wall A functional segregation preventing corporate women from obtaining management experience.

global scrutiny (Thompson 1996) The regime of visibility created by increasingly globalized mass communication, in which television plays a central role.

globalization A continually increasing interdependence between different countries, regions, peoples, and organizations.

habitualization (Berger and Luckmann 1991) Any action that, being repeated frequently, becomes cast into a pattern and can be reproduced with an economy of effort.

habitus (Bourdieu 1989) The set of "mental or cognitive structures through which people deal with the social world." Habitus is a product of a specific set of living conditions embodying social roles and relationships.

hapax legomenon (also "hapax") A word that appears in the text only once.

hapax ratio The ratio (%) of the number of hapax to the number of types.

heuresis The use of one's knowledge to put together that which is appropriate to a message.

ideational function A language function realized through propositional content, that is, the selection of facts.

illocutionary act Refers to the action performed by a communicative event.

institutionalization The process of making something a part of a community's historicity, whereby it is accepted by the majority of the community.

interpersonal function A language function that marks role relationships and attitudes toward participants.

intertextuality The interrelation of texts resulting from people's habit, when composing a text, to consult other texts and adopt elements from those texts.

invenire To make the right conclusions.

jargon A variety of language, created for specific functions, sensitive to the requirements of the activity and both the personal and the social needs of the speaker. One important function of jargon is social bonding. The term "jargon" is often used pejoratively to indicate a too-obtrusive or unnecessary use of professional language.

key word A word expressing central social values of an era.

legitimization The process of ascribing cognitive validity to something in order to make it seem just, valid, correct, and appropriate.

lemma A word considered as its citation form together with all the inflected forms (for example, the lemma "write" includes "write," "writes," "writing," "wrote," and "written").

lemmatization Grouping together the inflected forms of a word for analysis as a single item.

lexical density The proportion (%) of content words in a text.

lexicogrammar The unity of lexical and grammatical resources.

lexicon The vocabulary of a language.

lexis 1. Lexicon. 2. In classical rhetoric, expressive and persuasive language.

lingua franca A language used for communication among people of different mother tongues. Historically, Lingua Franca was the language based on Italian, Spanish, French, Arabic, Greek and Turkish that was spoken from the time of the Crusades to the eighteenth century in the ports of the Mediterranean.

locutionary act Refers to a communicative event having taken place. Locutionary act is evident in communicative event's ideational content.

management ergolect (Fox 1994) A generic term for the language used in corporate management.

meaning The thing or the idea that the word refers to. The meaning of a word is dependent on its use in various linguistic and social contexts.

media literacy A manager's ability to use the public media to construct and manage the visibility of corporate identities.

norm A behavioral rule of conduct specifying what is right and wrong. A norm stands for shared value judgments about how things should be done.

object The place, person, or a thing about which a person holds beliefs.

objectivation (Berger and Luckmann 1991) The ability of human expressivity to manifest itself "in products of human activity that are available both to their producers and to other men as elements of a common world."

organizational discourse (OD) A field of study focused on researching discourse—language in social action—in organizations and its influence upon organizational structure and behavior.

overhearer A member of an audience known to be there but not ratified.

perlocutionary act Refers to the actual effect of a communicative event upon its audience, which may or may not coincide with the illocutionary force of the event.

personal function A language function that marks group membership and attitudes toward facts.

political power: The leader's power of decision to invest into new processes essential for the economical future and welfare of regions and countries.

power of position (also "legitimate power") Authority of the leader to tell subordinates what to do and to direct their behavior.

power over Use of executive power to call on relationships of dominance and submission.

power to Use of executive power to realize personal and collective goals.

process A series of states.

processing function A language function that concerns production- and comprehension-related demands.

productive discourse process A discourse process indicating the creation of something that did not exist before.

professionalisms (also "corporate graffiti" and "business buzzwords") Words of self-description used by corporate management to refer to persons, objects, phenomena, and circumstances of the corporate world.

public Available to all.

referent power Based on appealing personal characteristics and prosocial behavior that has positive consequences for the well-being of others. People with referent power invite admiration and loyalty.

register (sometimes referred to as "style") A language variety according to use, depending on the formality of the occasion, the medium (speech or writing), and the topic. Registers are usually associated with occupational or social groups.

representative A type of illocutionary act showing the degrees of speaker's commitment to the truth of a proposition.

representativeness General applicability of the findings obtained through corpus analysis.

reward power Power that entitles the leader to reward employees she or he perceives as cooperative through attention, praise, access to resources, and material inducements.

scene A part of an event, involving actors and delimited by a change of actors.

schema A global pattern of "events and states in ordered sequences linked by time proximity and causality" (Beaugrande and Dressler 1981, 90).

script A preestablished routine defining situation participants and specifying participant roles and their expected actions in a communicative event (Schank and Abelson 1977).

semiotic discourse processes Semiotic discourse processes are either activity-centered or message-centered. Activity-centered semiotic discourse processes foreground the behavior of entities within a text. Message-centered semiotic discourse processes foreground the communication taking place within a text.

sentence length Measured in the number of words in a sentence. Sentence length is one of the key parameters of text readability, indicating how difficult a text is to read.

social capital Social capital gives access to social networks and positions in social networks.

social class A large-scale grouping of people who share common economic resources, which strongly influence the type of lifestyle they are able to lead.

socialization (of stakeholders by corporations) Presenting stakeholders with a predefined scheme providing them with an institutionalized program for their roles as stakeholders. Processes of stakeholder socialization are either predominantly broad or predominantly narrow. Whereas broad socialization promotes independence, individualism, and self-expression, narrow socialization esteems obedience and conformity and discourages deviation from cultural norms.

social network A social mechanism within which goods and services are exchanged, obligations imposed, and rights conferred. Whereas social class accounts for a person's position in the hierarchical structure of society, social networks deal with the solidarity aspects of a person's everyday contacts.

social status The prestige that a particular group is accorded by other members of society.

sociolinguistics The study of language in relation to society (Hudson 1998, 1).

specific communicative purpose Defines the content of a communicative event.

state A stage in the evolution of an entity.

symbolic capital The capacity to define and legitimize cultural values.

symbolic violence (Bourdieu 1977) Implicit mechanisms of social control, which in developed societies have replaced physical violence.

taxis Constructing discourse.

text The linguistic product of a communicative event.

text cohesion The way words are connected within a sequence.

text concordance (also "KWIC: KeyWord in Context") An alphabetical list of the words in a text, showing them within their natural context, which can vary in size from a few words to two computer lines.

text corpus A representative body of natural texts, enabling identification of central and typical language features.

textual function A language function related to the "packaging" of facts, marking focus and cohesion.

text-world model The total array of knowledge activated while processing a text (Beaugrande 1997, 128).

theoretical linguistics A science studying language to construct a theory of its structure but without regard to any practical applications.

tokens All words in a text.

types Different word forms.

type-token ratio The ratio (%) of different word forms to the total number of words in a text.

typical knowledge Elements true for most but not all instances of the concept constitute.

values Beliefs held by individuals/groups that one mode of behavior is preferable to another.

virtual witnessing (Shapin and Shaffer 1985) A process of accessing scientific evidence through perusal of scientific text (rather than, for example, witnessing an experiment itself).

world model The totality of people's experiences and knowledge.

Bibliography

Achbar, M. (ed.) (1994) *Manufacturing Consent: Noam Chomsky and the Media*. Montreal: Black Rose.

Adams, C. A. (2002) Internal organizational factors influencing corporate social and ethical reporting. *Accounting, Auditing and Accountability Journal*, 15/2, pp. 223–250.

Aijmer, K., and Altenberg, B. (eds.) (1991) *English Corpus Linguistics*. London: Longman.

Althusser, L. (1971) Ideology and ideological state apparatuses. In *Lenin and Philosophy and other Essays*. London: New Left Books.

Alvarez, J. L. (1999) Foreword to Mazza, C. *Claim, Intent, and Persuasion: Organizational Legitimacy and the Rhetoric of Corporate Mission Statements*. Boston: Kluwer Academic Publishers.

An alternative to cocker spaniels. (2001) *The Economist*, August 25, pp. 51–52.

Andersen, E. (1978) Lexical universals of body-part terminology. In J. Greenberg (ed.), *Universals of Human Language*, vol. 3. Stanford, CA: Stanford University Press.

Anderson, B. (1991) *Imagined Communities: Reflections on the Origin and Spread of Nationalism*. London: Verso.

Argyris, C. (1998) Teaching smart people how to learn. In *Harvard Business Review on Knowledge Management*. Boston: Harvard Business School Press, pp. 81–108.

Aristotle (335–323 B.C./1998) *The Nicomachean Ethics*. New York: Dover Publications.

Aristotle (335–323 B.C./1998) *The Politics*. Oxford: Oxford Paperbacks.

Ashford, S. J. (1998) Out on a limb: The role of context impression management in selling gender-equity issues. *Administrative Science Quarterly*, March 1998.

Austin, J. L. (1962) *How to Do Things with Words*. Cambridge, MA: Harvard University Press.

Babcock, L., Laschever, S., Gelfand, M., and Small, D. (2003) Nice girls don't ask. *Harvard Business Review*, October, pp. 14–16.

Bacas, H. (1987) Leaving the corporate nest. *Nation's Business*, March 1987.

Bacharach, S., and Lawler, E. (1980) *Power and Politics in Organizations: The Social Psychology of Conflict, Coalitions and Bargaining*. San Francisco: Jossey-Bass.

Bachelard, G. (2003) *The Formation of the Scientific Mind*. Manchester: Clinamen Press.

Bailyn, B. (1967) *The Ideological Origins of the American Revolution*. Cambridge, MA, and London: Belknap Press of Harvard University Press.

Balmer, J. M. T. (1993) Corporate identity: The power and the paradox. *Design Management Journal*, pp. 39–44.

Balmer, J. M. T. (1997) Corporate identity: Past, present and future. Working paper, University of Strathclyde International Centre for Corporate Identity Studies, Glasgow.

Balmer, J. M. T. (1998) Corporate identity and the advent of corporate marketing. *Journal of Marketing Management*, 14/8, pp. 963–966.

Balmer, J. M. T. and Gray, E. R. (2000) Corporate identity and corporate communications: Creating a competitive advantage. *Industrial and Commercial Training*, 32/7, pp. 256–262.

Balmer, J. M. T. and Greyser, S. A. (eds.) (2003) *Revealing the Corporation*. London: Routledge.

Balmer, J. M. T. and Wilson, A. (1998) Corporate identity and the myth of the single company culture. Working paper, University of Strathclyde International Centre for Corporate Identity Studies, Glasgow.

Barbara, L., Celani, M. A. A., Collins, H., and Scott, M. (1996) A survey of communication patterns in the Brazilian business context. *English for Specific Purposes*, 15/1, pp. 57–71.

Barnes, J. A. (1954) Class and committees in a Norwegian island parish. *Human Relations*, 7/1.

Barnet, R. J. and Cavanagh, J. (1994) *Global Dreams: Imperial Corporations and the New World Order*. New York: Touchstone.

Basi, R. S. (1998) *Contextual Management: A Global Perspective*. New York: International Business Press.

Bateman, T. S. and Zeithaml, C. P. (1993) *Management: Function and Strategy*. Burr Ridge, IL: Irwin.

Beattie, G. W. (1981) Interruption in conversational interaction, and its relation to the sex and status of interactants. *Linguistics* 19, pp. 15–39.

Beaugrande, R. de (1984) *Text Production: Toward a Science of Composition*. Norwood, NJ: Ablex.

Beaugrande, R. de (1997) *New Foundations for a Science of Text and Discourse: Cognition, Communication, and the Freedom of Access to Knowledge and Society*. Norwood, NJ: Ablex.

Beaugrande, R. de and Dressler, W. (1981) *Introduction to Text Linguistics*. London: Longman.

Bell, A. (1991) *The Language of News Media*. Oxford: Blackwell.

Bellah, R. N., Madsen, R., Sullivan, W. M., Swidler, A., and Tipton, S. M. (1985) *Habits of the Heart: Individualism and Commitment in American Life*. Berkeley: University of California Press.

Bendix, R. (1956) *Work and Authority in Industry: Ideologies of Management in the Course of Industrialization*. New York: Wiley.

Benhabib, S. (1997) *Situating the Self: Gender, Community and Postmodernism in Contemporary Ethics*. Cambridge: Polity Press.

Bennis, W. (1996) The leader as storyteller. *Harvard Business Review*. January–February, pp. 154–160.

Bennis, W., and Nanus, B. (1985) *Leaders*. New York: Harper and Row.

Bennis, W. G., and O'Toole, J. (2000) Don't hire the wrong CEO. *Harvard Business Review*, May–June.

Bereiter, C., and Scardamalia, M. (1987) *The Psychology of Written Composition*. Hillsdale, NJ: Lawrence Erlbaum.

Berger, M., and St John, M. J. (1993) Communication, content and skills in intercultural training. *Language and Intercultural Training*, 14, pp. 4–5.

Berger, P. L., and Luckmann, T. (1991) *The Social Construction of Reality: A Treatise in the Sociology of Knowledge*. London: Penguin Books.

Bernard, H. R., E. C. Johnsen, P. D. Killworth, and S. Robinson (1991) Estimating the size of an average personal network and of an event population: Some empirical results. *Social Science Research*, 20, pp. 109–121.

Bernays, P. (1947) Contradiction and non-contradiction. *Dialectica*, 1, pp. 305–309.

Biber, D. (1990) Some methodological issues in corpus-based analyses of linguistic variation. Manuscript. Los Angeles: University of Southern California.

Biber, D. (1991) *Variations across Speech and Writing*. Cambridge: Cambridge University Press.

Biber, D., Conrad, S., and Reppen, R. (1998) *Corpus Linguistics*. Cambridge: Cambridge University Press.

Biber, D., and Finegan, E. (1991) On the exploitation of computerized corpora in variation studies. In K. Aijmer and B. Altenberg (eds.), *English Corpus Linguistics*. London and New York: Longman.

Bijker, W. E., and Pinch, T. (1987) The social construction of facts and artifacts: or how the sociology of science and the sociology of technology might benefit each other. In W. E. Bijker, T. P. Hughes, and T. Pinch (eds.), *The Social Construction of Technological Systems*. Cambridge, MA: MIT Press.

Bing, J. M., and Bergvall, V. L. (1998) The question of questions: Beyond binary thinking. In J. Coates (ed.), *Language and Gender*. Oxford: Blackwell.

BizEthicsBuzz (2000) *Business Ethics Magazine's Online News Report*, Vol. 5, September.

Black, M. (1979) More about metaphor. In A. Ortony (ed.), *Metaphor and Thought*. New York: Cambridge University Press.

Bodenhausen, G. V., and Wyer, R. S., Jr. (1985) Effects of stereotypes on decision making and information-processing strategies. *Journal of Personality and Social Psychology*, 48, pp. 267–282.

Boissevain, J. (1974) *Friends of Friends: Networks, Manipulators and Coalitions*. Oxford: Blackwell.

Boissevain, J., and Mitchell, J. C. (eds.) (1973) *Network Analysis Studies in Human Interaction*. The Hague: Mouton.

Boje, D. M., and Dennehy, R. F. (1994) *Managing the Postmodern World*. Dubuque, IL: Kendall Hunt.

The bottom line: Connecting corporate performance and gender diversity. (2004) Available at: www.catalystwomen.org. Accessed June 7, 2004.

Bourdieu, P. (1977) *Outline of a Theory of Practice*. Cambridge: Cambridge University Press.

Bourdieu, P. (1985) The social space and the genesis of groups. *Theory and Society*, 14, pp. 723–744.

Bourdieu, P. (1989) Social space and symbolic power. *Sociological Theory*, 7, pp. 14–25.

Bourdieu, P. (1990) *The Logic of Practice*. Cambridge, MA: Harvard University Press.

Bourdieu, P. (1991) *Language and Symbolic Power*. Cambridge, MA: Harvard University Press.

Boyle, M., and Tkaczyk, C. (2004) When will they Stop? *Fortune*, May 3, p. 123.

Bradac, J. J., and Mulac, A. (1984) Attributional consequences of powerful and powerless speech styles in a crisis–intervention context. *Journal of Language and Social Psychology*, 3, pp. 1–19.

Bradac, J. J., and Wisegarver, R. (1984) Ascribed status, lexical diversity, and accent: Determinants of perceived status, solidarity and control of speech style. *Journal of Language and Social Psychology*, 3, pp. 239–255.

Bradley, P. H. (1980) Sex, competence and opinion deviations: An expectation state approach. *Communication Monographs*, 47, pp. 101–110.

Brain, D. (1995) Cultural production as "Society in the Making": Architecture as an exemplar of the social construction of cultural artifacts. In D. Crane (ed.), *The Sociology of Culture*. Oxford: Blackwell.

Break your boundaries. (2002) Available at: www. breaktheglassceiling.com. Accessed May 2, 2003.

Bright, W. (1997) Social factors in language change. In F. Coulmas (ed.), *The Handbook of Sociolinguistics*. Oxford: Blackwell.

Brockbank, A., and Traves, J. (1996) Career aspirations: Women managers in retailing. In S. Ledwith and F. Colgan (eds.), *Women in Organisations: Challenging Gender Politics*. London: Macmillan.

Broverman, I. K., Vogel, S. R., Broverman, D. M., Clarkson, F. E., and Rosenkrantz, P. S. (1972) Sex-role stereotypes: A current appraisal. *Journal of Social Issues*, 28/2.

Brown, D. S. (1990) Managers' new job is concert building. *HRMagazine*, September, p. 42.

Brunsson, N. (1986) *The Irrational Organization*. New York: Wiley.

Buchholz, R. E. (1978) The work ethic reconsidered. *Industrial relations*, 31, pp. 450–459.

Buchmann, M. (1989) *The Script of Life in Modern Society: Entry into Adulthood in a Changing World*. Chicago: University of Chicago Press.

Burawoy, M. (1979) *Manufacturing Consent: Changes in the Labor Process under Monopoly Capitalism*. Chicago: University of Chicago Press.

Burrows, P. (2001) Carly's last stand? *BusinessWeek*, December 24, pp. 63–70.

Busch, A. (2000) Unpacking the globalization debate: Approaches, evidence and data. In C. Hay and D. Marsh (eds.), *Demystifying Globalisation*. London: Macmillan.

Butcher, D., and Atkinson, S. (2001) Stealth, secrecy and subversion: The language of change. *Journal of Organizational Change Management*, 14/6, pp. 554–569.

Butcher, D., and Clarke, M. (1999) Politics–the missing discipline of management. *Industrial and Commercial Training*, 31/1, pp. 9–12.

Butler, T. (1995) Gentrification and the urban middle classes. In T. Butler and M. Savage (eds.), *Social Change and the Middle Classes*. London: UCL Press.

Calkins, L. (1986) *The Art of Teaching Writing*. London and Portsmouth: Heinemann.

Cameron, L. (1999) Operationalising "metaphor" for applied linguistic research. In L. Cameron and G. Low (eds.), *Researching and Applying Metaphor*. Cambridge: Cambridge University Press.

Cameron, L., and Low, G. (eds.) (1999) *Researching and Applying Metaphor*. Cambridge: Cambridge University Press.

Campbell, C. (1995) *The Romantic Ethic and the Spirit of Modern Consumerism*. Oxford: Blackwell.

Carli, L. L. (1999) Gender, interpersonal power and social influence. *Journal of Social Issues*, Spring.

Castells, M. (1996) *The Rise of the Network Society*. Malden, MA: Blackwell.

Castells, M. (1997) *The Power of Identity*. Malden, MA: Blackwell.

CCI Corporate Communication: Practices and Trends Study 2003 (2004) Corporate Communication Institute at Fairleigh Dickinson University, Madison, NJ. Available at: www.corporatecomm.org/. Accessed June 22, 2004.

Cerny, P. (1997) Globalisation, fragmentation and the governance gap: Toward a new mediaevalism in world politics. *Globalisation Workshop*, University of Birmingham, March.

Clarkson, M. B. E. (1995) A stakeholder framework for analyzing and evaluating corporate social performance. *Academy of Management Review*, 20, pp. 92–117.

Clegg, S. (1975) *Power, Rule, and Domination*. London: Routledge.

Coates, J. (1998a) Gossip revisited: Language in all-female groups. In J. Coates (ed.), *Language and Gender*. Oxford: Blackwell, pp. 226–253.

Coates, J. (1998b) Introduction to part I: Gender differences in pronunciation and grammar. In J. Coates (ed.), *Language and Gender*. Oxford: Blackwell, pp. 7–11.

Coates, J. (1998c) Introduction to part V: Women's talk in the public domain. In J. Coates (ed.), *Language and Gender*. Oxford: Blackwell, pp. 295–297.

Cohen, A. R., Fink, S. L., Gadon, H., Willits, R. D., and Josefowitz, N. (1992) *Effective Behavior in Organizations*. Homewood, IL: Irwin.

Cohen, M. D., March, J. G., and Olsen, J. P. (1971) A garbage can model of organizational choice. *Administrative Science Quarterly*, March, pp. 1–25.

Coleman, R. P. (1983) The continuing significance of social class to marketing. *Journal of Consumer Research*, 10, December, pp. 265–28.

Colgan, F., and Ledwith, S. (1996) Movers and shakers: Creating organisational change. In S. Ledwith, and F. Colgan (eds.), *Women in Organisations: Challenging Gender Politics*. London: Macmillan.

Collingwood, H., and Coutu, D. L. (2002) Jack on Jack. *Harvard Business Review*, February, pp. 88–94.

Collison, D. J. (2003) Corporate propaganda: Its implications for accounting and accountability. *Accounting, Auditing and Accountability Journal*, 19/5, pp, 853–886.

Colvin, G. (1999) How to be a great CEO. *Fortune*, May 24, p. 104.

Conger, J. A., and Kanungo, R. N. (1988) The empowerment process: Integrating theory and practice. *Academy of Management Review*, 15/3, pp. 471–482.

Cooper, R. L. (1989) *Language Planning and Social Change*. Cambridge: Cambridge University Press.

Cordell, J. (1999) *Business English Activities*. Cambridge: Cambridge University Press.

Corder, S. P. (1973) *Introducing Applied Linguistics*. Harmondsworth: Penguin Education.

Corporate Communication Spending study. (2000) Corporate Communication Institute for the Council for Public Relations Firms, Madison, NJ.

Cossette, P. (1998) The study of language in organizations: A symbolic interactionist perspective. *Human Relations*, 51/11, pp. 1355–1380.

Coulmas, F. (1989) *The Writing Systems of the World*. Oxford: Blackwell.

Coulmas, F. (ed.) (1997) *The Handbook of Sociolinguistics*. Oxford: Blackwell.

Crowther-Alwyn, J. (1999) *Business Roles*, Vol. 1 and Vol. 2. Cambridge: Cambridge University Press.

Crozier, M. (1964) *The Bureaucratic Phenomenon*. Chicago: University of Chicago Press.

Crystal, D. (1991a) Stylistic profiling. In K. Aijmer and B. Altenberg (eds.), *English Corpus Linguistics*. London and New York: Longman.

Crystal, D. (1991b) *The Cambridge Encyclopedia of Language*. Cambridge: Cambridge University Press.

Cyert, R., and March, J. (1963) *A Behavioral Theory of the Firm*. Englewood Cliffs, NJ: Prentice-Hall.

Czarniawska, B. (1997) *Narrating the Organization: Dramas of Institutional Identity*. Chicago: University of Chicago Press.

Dahlgren, K. (1992) Interpretation of textual queries using a cognitive model. In T. W. Lauer, E. Peacock. and A. C. Graesser (eds.), *Questions and Information Systems*. Hillsdale, NJ: Lawrence Erlbaum.

Dauphinais, W., and Price, C. (eds.) (1999) *Straight from the CEO*. London: Nicholas Brealey Publishing.

Davenport, T. H. (1994) Saving IT's soul: Human-centered information management. *Harvard Business Review*, March-April, pp. 41–53.

Davidson, D. (1991) What metaphors mean. In A. P. Martinich (ed.), *The Philosophy of Language*. Oxford: Oxford University Press.

Davies, J. H., Schoorman, F. D., and Donaldson, L. (1997) Toward a stewardship theory of management. *Academy of Management Review*, 22/1.

de Bono, E. (1985) *Atlas of Management Thinking*. Harmondsworth: Penguin Books.

Debord, G. (1994) *The Society of Spectacle*. New York: Zone Books.

De Cock, C. (1998) "It seems to fill my head with ideas": A few thoughts on postmodernism, TQM and BPR. *Journal of Management Inquiry*, 7, pp. 144–153.

Deegan, C. (2002) Introduction: The legitimizing effect of social and environmental disclosures—a theoretical foundation. *Accounting, Auditing and Accountability Journal*, 15/3, pp. 282–311.

Deignan, A. (1995) *English Guides—7: Metaphor*. London: HarperCollins.

Delgado-Gaitan, C. (1990) *Literacy for Empowerment*. London: Falmer Press.

Deluga, R. J. (1990) The effects of transformational, transactional and laissez faire leadership characteristics on subordinate influencing behavior. *Basic and Applied Social Psychology*, June, pp. 191–203.

Demers, C., Giroux, N., and Chreim, S. (2003) Merger and acquisition announcements as corporate wedding narratives. *Journal of Organizational Change*, 16/2, pp. 223–242.

Derewianka, B. (1990) *Exploring How Texts Work*. Rozelle, NSW: Primary English teaching Association, distr. by Heinemann, Portsmouth.

Dhir, K. S., and Gòké-Paríolá, A. (2002) The case for language policies in multinational corporations. *Corporate Communications: An International Journal*, 7/4, pp. 241–251.

Dicken, P. (1998) *Global Shift: The Internationalization of Economic Activity*, 3rd ed. New York: Guilford Press.

Dickson, D., Saunders, C., and Stringer, M. (1993) *Rewarding People: The Skill of Responding Positively*. London: Routledge.

DiMaggio, P. J., and Powell, W. W. (1983) The iron cage revisited: Institutional isomorphism and collective rationality in organizational fields. *American Sociological Review*, 48.

Dixon, R. M. W. (1977) Where have all the adjectives gone? *Studies in Language*, 1/1, pp. 1–80.

Dorfman, P. W., and Howell, J. P. (1988) Dimensions of national culture and effective leadership patterns: Hofstede revisited. *Advances in International Comparative Management*, vol. 3. Greenwich, CT: JAI Press.

Dovey, K. (1997) The learning organization and the organization of learning: Power, transformation and the search for form in learning organizations. *Management Learning*, 28/3, pp. 331–349.

Downs, A., and Eastman, K. K. (2001) Images of quality: Deconstructing the quest for excellence. *Journal of Organizational Change Management*, 14/6, pp. 510–529.

Drew, P., and Heritage, J. (eds.) (1998) *Talk at Work: Interaction in Institutional Settings*. Cambridge: Cambridge University Press.

Dudley-Evans, T., and St John, M. J. (1998) *Developments in ESP: A Multi-disciplinary Approach*. Cambridge: Cambridge University Press.

Eagleton, T. (1985) *Raymond Williams Critical Perspectives*. Cambridge: Polity Press.

Eagly, A., Karau, S., and Makhijani, M. (1995) Gender and the effectiveness of leaders: A meta-analysis. *Psychological Bulletin*, 117, pp. 125–145.

Eagly, A., Makhijani, M., and Klonsky, B. (1992) Gender and the evaluation of leaders: A meta-analysis. *Psychological Bulletin*, 111, pp. 3–22.

Eccles, R., and Nohria, N. (1992) *Beyond the Hype: Rediscovering the Essence of Management.* Boston: Harvard Business School Press.

Eckert, P., and McConnell-Ginet, S. (1998) Communities of practice: Where language, gender and power all live. In J. Coates (ed.), *Language and Gender.* Oxford: Blackwell, pp. 484–494.

Eliot, T. S. (1962) *Notes toward the Definition of Culture.* London: Faber and Faber.

Elyan, O. et al. (1978) RP-accented female speech: The voice of perceived androgyny? In P. Trudgill (ed.), *Sociolinguistic Patterns in British English.* London: Edward Arnold.

Engholm, C. (1991) *When Business East Meets Business West.* New York: Wiley.

Enz, C. A. (1986) New directions for cross-cultural studies: Linking organizational and societal cultures. *Advances in International Comparative Management*, vol. 2. Greenwich, CT: JAI Press.

Enzensberger, H. (1970) Constituents of a theory of the media. *New Left Review*, 64.

Esnault, G. (1925) Imagination Populaire, Métaphores Occidentales. Paris

Evans, D. (1999) *Powerhouse.* London: Longman.

Evans, R., and Russel, P. (1990) *The Creative Manager.* London: Unwin Paperbacks.

An expense by any other name. (2002) *The Economist*, April 6, p. 12.

Faigley, L. (1986) Competing theories of process: A critique and a proposal. *College Composition and Communication*, 48, pp. 527–542.

Fairclough, N. (1995) *Media Discourse.* London: Edward Arnold.

Fairclough, N. (1999a) *Critical Discourse Analysis.* London: Longman.

Fairclough, N. (1999b) *Language and Power.* London: Longman.

Falk, R. (1994) The making of global citizenship. In B. van Steenbergen (ed.), *The Condition of Citizenship.* London: Sage.

Feely, A. J. and Harzing, A. (2003) Language management in multinational companies. *Cross Cultural Management*, 10/2, pp. 37–52.

Fels, A. (2004) Do women lack ambition? *Harvard Business Review*, April, pp. 50–60.

Fierman, J. (1990) Why women still don't hit the top. *Fortune*, July 30, pp. 40–60.

Fillmore, C. J. (1981) Pragmatics and the description of discourse. In P. Cole (ed.), *Radical Pragmatics.* New York: Academic Press.

Firth, A. (1990) "Lingua franca" negotiations: Towards an interactive approach. *World Englishes*, 9/3, pp. 269–280.

Firth, A. (1995) *The Discourse of Negotiation: Studies of Language in the Workplace.* Oxford: Pergamon.

Firth, A. (1996) "Lingua Franca" English and conversation analysis. *Journal of Pragmatics*, April 1996.

Fischer, G., Preissner-Polte, A., Risch, S., and Schwarzer, U. (1993) Der große Unterschied. *Manager Magazin*, 5, pp. 101–115.

Fisher, W. R. (1987) *Human Communication as Narration: Toward a Philosophy of Reason, Value, and Action.* Columbia: University of South Carolina Press.

Fleischer, A., Hazard, G. C., and Klipper, M. Z. (2002) *Board Games: The Changing Shape of Corporate Power.* Frederick, MD: Beard Group.

Fligstein, N. (1990) *The Transformation of Corporate Control.* Cambridge, MA: Harvard University Press.

Fligstein, N. (1997) Social skill and institutional theory. *American Behavioral Scientist*. 40/4, February.

Fligstein, N., and Freeland, R. (1995) Theoretical and comparative perspectives in corporate organizations. *Annual Review of Sociology*, 21.

Fligstein, N., and Mara-Drita, I. (1996) How to make a market: Reflections on the attempt to create a single market in the European Union. *American Journal of Sociology*, 102/1.

Flower, L., and Hayes, J. (1977) Problem-solving strategies and the writing process. *College English*, 39, pp. 449–461.

Flower, L., and Hayes, J. (1984) Images, plans and prose: The representation of meaning in writing. *Written Communication*, 1, pp. 120–160.

Follett, M. P. (1940) Constructive conflict. In H. C. Metcalf and L. Urwick (eds.), *Dynamic Administration: The Collected Papers of Mary Parker Follett*. New York: Harper and Brothers, pp. 71–94.

Ford, J., and Ford, L. (1995) The role of conversations in producing intentional change in organizations. *Academy of Management Review*, 20/3, pp. 541–571.

Foucault, M. (1980) *Power/Knowledge*. Brighton: Harvester.

Foucault, M. (1991) *Discipline and Punish*. London: Penguin.

Foucault, M. (2002) *Archaeology of Knowledge*. London: Routledge.

Fox, J. (2000) Approaching managerial ethical standards in Croatia's hotel industry. *International Journal of Contemporary Hospitality Management*, 12/1, pp. 70–74.

Fox, R. (1994) Structural, semantic and stylistic features of English management ergolect. Unpublished Ph.D. thesis, University of Zagreb.

Fox, R. (1996) Beyond buzzwords. In M. Andrijasevic and L. Zergoller-Miletic (eds.), *Language and Communication*. Zagreb: Croatian Applied Linguistics Society.

Fox, R. (1997) Management ergolect as a separate language variety. *Studia Romanica et Anglica Zagrebiensia*, vol. 42, pp. 113–128.

Fox, R. (1999a) Management ergolect—Language of social power. In B. Robinson and M. Williams (eds.), *ESP Challenges!* Bratislava: British Council, pp. 68–74.

Fox, R. (1999b) The social identity of management ergolect. *English for Specific Purposes*, 18/3, pp. 261–278.

Fox, R. (2003) CEO rhetoric and social identity: Power in the CEO media interview. In B. Lewandowska-Tomaszczyk (ed.), *PALC 2001: Practical Applications in Language Corpora*. Frankfurt am Main: Peter Lang, pp. 365–381.

Fraker, S. (1984) Why women aren't getting to the top. *Fortune*, April 16, pp. 40–45.

Francis, H. (2002) The power of "talk" in HRM-based change. *Personnel Review*, 31/4, pp. 432–448.

Frank, F. and Hamilton, M. (1993) Warm hearts or cool business? Employers' attitudes to workplace basic skills programmes. In K. Forrester, (ed.), *Developing a Learning Workforce*. Conference Proceedings. Leeds: Leeds University.

Freeman, R. E. (1984) *Strategic Management: A Stakeholder Approach*. Boston: Pitman.

French, J. R. P., and Raven, B. (1959) The bases of social power. In D. Cartwright (ed.), *Studies in Social Power*. Ann Arbor, MI: Institute for Social Research.

Friedman, M. (1970) The social responsibility of business is to increase its profits. *New York Times Magazine*, September 13, 1970, pp. 33, 122–126.

Furchtgott-Roth, D. (1999) The myth of the wage gap. *Civil Rights Journal*, Fall.

Gabriel, Y. (1998) Same old story or changing stories? Folkloric, modern and postmodern mutations. In D. Grant, T. Keenoy, and C. Oswick, (eds.), *Discourse and Organisation*. London: Sage, pp. 84–103.

Gabriel, Y. (2000) *Storytelling in Organisations: Facts, Fictions and Fantasies*. Oxford: Oxford University Press.

Gardner, W. L., Van Eck Peluchette, J., and Clinebell, S. K. (1994) Valuing women in management: An impression management perspective of gender diversity. *Management Communication Quarterly*, 8/2, pp. 115–164.

Garvin, D. A. (1995) Leveraging processes for strategic advantage. *Harvard Business Review*, September-October, pp. 77–90.

Gates, W. H. (1999) *Business @ the Speed of Thought: Using a Digital Nervous System*. New York: Warner Books.

Gee, J. P. (1990) *Social Linguistics and Literacies: Ideology in Discourses*, 2nd ed. London: Taylor and Frances.

Gee, J. P. (1994) Quality, science and the lifeworld. *Critical Forum*, 3/1, Leichhardt: ALBSAC.

Gee, J. P., Hull, G., and Lankshear, C. (1996) *The New Work Order*. Sidney: Allen and Unwin.

Gettings, J., and Johnson, D. (2004) Wonder women: Profiles of leading female CEOs and business executives. Available at: www.infoplease.com. Accessed June 7, 2004.

Ghoshal, S. and Bartlett, C. A. (1998) *The Individualized Corporation: A Fundamentally New Approach to Management*. London: Heinemann.

Gibbons, P., Bradac, J. J. and Busch, J. D. (1991) Powerful versus powerless language: Consequences for persuasion, impression formation, and cognitive response. *Journal of Language and Social Psychology*, 10, pp. 115–133.

Giddens, A. (1990) *The Consequences of Modernity*. Cambridge and Oxford: Polity and Blackwell.

Giddens, A. (1991) *Modernity and Self-Identity: Self and Society in the Late Modern Age*. Stanford, CA: Stanford University Press.

Gilbert, D. and Kahl, J. A. (1982) *The American Class Structure: A New Synthesis*. Homewood, IL: Dorsey Press.

Gilligan, C. (1982) *In a Different Voice*. Cambridge, MA: Harvard University Press.

Gioia, D. A., Schultz, M., and Corley, K. (2000) Organizational identity, image and adaptive instability. *Academy of Management Review*, 25/1, pp. 63–81.

Goffman, E. (1981) *Forms of talk*. London: Blackwell.

Goffman, E. (1990) *The Presentation of Self in Everyday Life*. London: Penguin.

Goody, J., and Watt, I. (1963) The consequences of literacy. *Comparative Studies in History and Society*, 5, pp. 304–345.

Gouldner, A. (1960) The role of the norm of reciprocity in social stabilization. *American Sociological Review*, 25, pp. 161–178.

Gowen, S. G. (1996) How the organisation of work destroys everyday knowledge. In J. P. Hautecoeur (ed.), *Basic Education and Work: Alpha 96*. Toronto: UNESCO and Culture Concepts.

Grabe, W., and Kaplan, R. B. (1997) *Theory and Practice of Writing*. London: Longman.

Grant, D., Keenoy, T., and Oswick, C. (eds.) (1998) *Discourse and Organisation*. London: Sage.

Grant, D., and Oswick, C. (eds.) (1996) *Metaphor and Organisations*. London: Sage.

Gratton, L., Hailey, V. H., Stiles, P., and Truss, C. (1999) *Strategic Human Resource Management*. Oxford: Oxford University Press.

Graves, D. (1984) *A Researcher Learns to Write*. London and Portsmouth: Heinemann.

Gray, E. R., and Balmer, J. M. T. (1998) Managing corporate image and corporate reputation. *Long Range Planning*, 31/31, pp. 695–702.

Gray, R., Kouhy, R., and Lavers, S. (1995) Corporate social and environmental reporting. *Accounting, Auditing and Accountability Journal*, 8/2, pp. 47–77.

Greenbaum, S. (1991) The development of the international corpus of English. In K. Aijmer and B. Altenberg (eds.), *English Corpus Linguistics*. London: Longman, pp. 83–91.

Greimas, A. J. (1966) *Sémantique Structurale*. Paris: Larousse.

Guest, D. E. (1990) Human resource management and the American dream. *Journal of Management Studies*, 27/4, pp. 378–397.

Gumperz, J. J. (1992) *Discourse strategies*. Cambridge: Cambridge University Press.

Gunnarsson, B.-L., Linell, P., and Nordberg, B. (eds.) (1997) *The Construction of Professional Discourse*. London: Longman.

Gutek, B. A., and Morasch, B. (1982) Sex-ratios, sex-role spillover and sexual harassment of women at work. *Journal of Social Issues*, 38/4, pp. 55–74.

Habermas, J. (1975) *Legitimation Crisis*. Boston: Beacon Press.

Habermas, J. (2002) *The Structural Transformation of the Public Sphere*. Cambridge: Polity.

Haccoun, D. M., Haccoun, R. R., and Sallay, G. (1978) Sex differences in the appropriateness of supervisory styles: A nonmanagement view. *Journal of Applied Psychology*, 63, pp. 124–127.

Hall, E. (1966) *The Hidden Dimension*. New York: Doubleday.

Halliday, M. A. K. (1978) *Language as Social Semiotic*. London: Edward Arnold.

Halloran, J., Elliott, P., and Murdock, G. (1970) *Demonstrations and Communication*. Harmondsworth: Penguin.

Harragen, B. L. (1977) *Games Mother Never Taught You: Corporate Gamesmanship for Women*. New York: Warner Books.

Hartman, C. (1986) Main Street, Inc. *Inc.*, June.

Harvey, D. (1989) *The Condition of Postmodernity*. Oxford: Blackwell.

Haug, W. F. (1971) *Kritik der Warenästhetik*. Frankfurt am Main: Suhrkamp.

Have fat cats had their day? (2003) *The Economist*, May 24, p. 61.

Heider, F. (1958) *The Psychology of Interpersonal Relations*. New York: Wiley.

Held, D., and McGrew, A. (1998) Globalisation and the end of the world order. In T. Dunne, M. Cox, and K. Booth (eds.), *The Eighty Years' Crisis: International Relations 1919–1999*. Cambridge: Cambridge University Press.

Herman, E., and Chomsky, N. (1988) *Manufacturing Consent: The Political Economy of the Mass Media*. New York: Pantheon.

Herzberg, B. (1986) The politics of discourse communities. Paper presented at the CCC Convention, New Orleans, March.

Hewlett, S. A. (2002) Executive women and the myth of having it all. *Harvard Business Review*, April, pp. 66–73.

Hill, C. W. L., and Jones, T. M. (1992) Stakeholder-agency theory. *Journal of Management Studies*, 29, pp. 131–154.

Hill, L., and Wetlaufer, S. (1998) Leadership when there is no one to ask: An interview with ENI's Franco Bernabé. *Harvard Business Review*, July–August, pp. 81–94.

Hirschman, A. O. (1977) *The Passions and the Interests: Political Arguments for Capitalism before Its Triumph*. Princeton, NJ: Princeton University Press.

Hoey, M. (1991) *Patterns of Lexis in Text*. Oxford: Oxford University Press.

Hogan, P. C. (2001) *The Culture of Conformism: Understanding Social Consent*. Durham, NC: Duke University Press.

Højrup, T. (1983) The concept of life-mode: Aa form-specifying mode of analysis applied to contemporary western Europe. *Ethnologia Scandinavica*, pp. 1–50.

Holden, N. (1987) The treatment of language and linguistic issues in the current English-language international management literature. *Multilingua*, 6/3, pp. 233–246.

Holden, B. (1993) Analysing corporate training needs: A three way approach. *Language and Intercultural Training*, 14, 4–6.

Hudson, R. A. (1998) *Sociolinguistics*, 2nd ed. Cambridge: Cambridge University Press.

Hui, C. H. (1990) Work attitudes, leadership styles, and managerial behaviors in different cultures. In R. W. Brislin (ed.), *Applied Cross-cultural Psychology, Cross-cultural Research and Methodology Series*, vol. 14. Newbury Park, CA: Sage, pp. 186–208.

Humphreys, M. (2002) Narratives of organizational identity and identification: a case study of hegemony and resistance. *Organization Studies*, May-June.

Hymes, D. (1972) On communicative competence. In J. B. Pride and J. Holmes (eds.), *Sociolinguistics*. Baltimore: Penguin Books, pp. 269–293.

Ihalainen, O. (1991) The grammatical subject in educated and dialectal English: Comparing the London-Lund corpus and the Helsinki corpus of English dialects. In S. Johansson and A. Stenström (eds.), *English Computer Corpora*. Berlin: Mouton de Gruyter.

Inglis, F. (1996) *Media theory*. Oxford: Blackwell.

Internet infrastructure spending continues to grow: U.S. businesses to spend nearly $200 billion in 2004. (2003) Available at: www.instat.com. Accessed on October 17, 2003.

Irresponsible. (2002) *The Economist*, November 23, p. 60.

Ivancevich, J. M., Lorenzi, P., and Skinner, S. J. (1994) *Management: Quality and Competitiveness*. Burr Ridge, IL: Irwin.

Jackall, R. (1996) The social structure of managerial work. In B. Castro (ed.), *Business and Society*. Oxford: Oxford University Press.

Jakobson, R. (1960) Linguistics and poetics. In T. Sebeok (ed.), *Style in Language*. Cambridge, MA: MIT Press, pp. 350–377.

Johnson, M. (1990) *Business Buzzwords: The Tough New Jargon of Modern Business*. Oxford: Basil Blackwell.

Jost, J. T., and B. Major (2001) *The Psychology of Legitimacy*. New York: Cambridge University Express.

Kane, E. J. (2004) Continuing dangers of disinformation in corporate accounting reports. *Review of Financial Economics*, 13, pp. 149–164.

Kanter, R. M. (1977) *Men and Women of the Corporation*. New York: Basic Books.

Kanter, R. M. (2001) *Evolve!* Boston: Harvard Business School Press.

Kapalka, G. M., and Lachenmeyer, J. R. (1988) Sex-role flexibility, locus of control, and occupational status. *Sex Roles*, 19, pp. 417–427.

Kapferer, B. (1969) Norms and the manipulation of relationships in a work context. In J. C. Mitchell (ed.), *Social Networks in Urban Situations*. Manchester: Manchester University Press.

Kawakami, C., and White, J. B. (2000) Mindful and masculine: Freeing women leaders from the constraints of gender roles. *Journal of Social Issues*, Spring.

Keenoy, T. and Anthony, P. (1992) HRM: Metaphor, meaning and morality. In P. Blyton and P. Turnbull (eds.), *Reassessing Human Resource Management* London: Sage, pp. 233–255.

Keizer, J. and Post, G. (1996) The metaphoric gap as catalyst of change. In C. Oswick and D. Grant (eds.), *Organisation Development: Metaphorical Explorations*. London: Pitman, pp. 90–105.

Kelley, R. E. (1988) In praise of followers. *Harvard Business Review*, November-December.

Kelly, M. (2001) *The Divine Right of Capital*. San Francisco: Berrett-Koehler.

Kilduff, M., and Tsai, W. (2003) *Social Networks and Organisations*. London: Sage.

Killworth, P. D., Johnsen, E. C., Bernard, H. R., Shelley, G. A., and McCarty C. (1990) Estimating the size of personal networks. *Social Networks*,12, pp. 289–312.

Kjellmer, G. (1984) Some thoughts on collocational distinctiveness. In J. Aarts, and W. Meijs (eds.), *Corpus Linguistics*. Amsterdam: Rodopi.

Klaehn, J. (2002) A critical review and assessment of Herman and Chomsky's propaganda model. *European Journal of Communications*. 17/2, pp, 147–182.

Knights, D., and Morgan, G. (1991) Corporate strategy, organizations and subjectivity: A critique. *Organization Studies*, 12, pp. 251–273.

Kotter, J. P. (1979) *Power in Management*. New York: AMACOM.

Kramer, R. M. (2002) When paranoia makes sense. *Harvard Business Review*, July, pp. 62–69.

Kreitner, R., and Kinicki, A. (1992) *Organizational Behavior*, 2nd ed. Burr Ridge, IL: Irwin.

Labov, W. (1966) *The Social Stratification of English in New York City*. Washington: Center for Applied Linguistics.

Labov, W. (1972) *Sociolinguistic Patterns*. Philadelphia: University of Pennsylvania Press.

Labov, W., and Waletzky, J. (1967) Narrative analysis: Oral versions of personal experience: In J. Helms (ed.), *Essays on the Verbal and Visual Arts*. Seattle: University of Washington Press.

Lakoff, G., and Johnson, M. (1980) *Metaphors We Live By*. Chicago and London: University of Chicago Press.

Lakoff, G., and Turner, M. (1989) *More Than Cool Reason: A Field Guide to Poetic Metaphor*. Chicago and London: University of Chicago Press.

Lakoff, R. (1973) Language and woman's place. *Language in Society*, 2, pp. 45–80.

Lakoff, R. (1975) *Language and Woman's Place*. New York: Harper and Row.

Landau, S. I. (1989) *Dictionaries: The Art and Craft of Lexicography*. New York: Scribner.

Lankshear, C. (1994) Self-direction and empowerment: Critical language awareness and the "new work order." In P. O'Connor (ed.), *Thinking Work*. Sydney: ALBSAC.

Lankshear, C. (1998) Introduction to C. Holland, F. Frank, and T. Cooke, *Literacy and the New Work Order*. Leicester: National Institute of Adult Continuing Education (England and Wales).

Lankshear, C., and Lawler, M. (1987) *Literacy, Schooling and Revolution*. London: Falmer Press.

Lawrence, P. R., and Lorsch, J. (1967) *Organization and Environment*. Homewood, IL: Irwin.

Leech, G. N. (1971) *English in Advertising*. London: Longman.

Leech, G. N. (1981) *Semantics*. Harmondsworth: Penguin.

Leech, G. (1991). The state of the art in corpus linguistics. In K. Aijmer and B. Altenberg (eds.), *English Corpus Linguistics*. London: Longman, pp. 8–29.

Leet-Pellegrini, H. M. (1980) Conversational dominance as a function of gender and expertise. In H. Giles, W. P. Robinson, and P. M. Smith (eds.), *Language: Social Psychological Perspectives*. Oxford: Pergamon.

Legge, K. (1995) Human *Resource Management: Rhetorics and Realities*. London: Macmillan.

Limaye, M. R., and Victor, D. A. (1991) Cross-cultural business communication research: State of the art and hypotheses for the 1990s. *Journal of Business Communication*, 28, pp. 277–299.

Linstead, S. (1993) Deconstruction in the study of organisations. In J. Hassard and M. Parker (eds.), *Postmodernism and Organisations*. London: Sage.

Lippman, W. (1922) *Public Opinion*. New York: Macmillan.

Livesey, S. M. (2002) The discourse of the middle ground. *Management Communication Quarterly*, 15/3, pp. 313–349.

Lomnitz, L. A. (1977) *Networks and Marginality*. New York: Academic Press.

Loudon, D. L. and Della Bitta, A. J. (1993) *Consumer Behavior*. New York: McGraw-Hill.

Lyons, J. (1978) *Semantics*, 2 vols. Cambridge: Cambridge University Press.

Machiavelli, N. (1532/1998) *The Prince*. Oxford: Oxford Paperbacks.

Machiavelli, N. (1517/1983) *The Discourses*. London: Penguin.

MacKay, D. G. (1980) Language, thought and social attitudes. In H. Giles, P. Robinson, and P. M. Smith (eds.), *Language: Social Psychological Perspectives*. Oxford: Pergamon, pp. 89–96.

Maitland, K., and Wilson, J. (1987) Ideological conflict and pronominal resolution. *Journal of Pragmatics*, 11, pp. 495–512.

Makimoto, T., and Manners, D. (1997) *Digital Nomad*. Chichester: Wiley.

Mann, M. (1993) *The Sources of Social Power*, vol. 2. Cambridge: Cambridge University Press.

Marsden, P. V. (2002) Egocentric and sociocentric measures of network centrality. *Social Networks*, 24, pp. 407–422.

Marshak, R. (1993) Managing the metaphors of change. *Organizational Dynamics*, 22/1, pp. 44–57.

Martin, J. (1989) *Factual Writing: Exploring and Challenging Social Reality*. Oxford: Oxford University Press.

Marwick, N., and Fill, C. (1997) Towards a framework for managing corporate identity. *European Journal of Marketing*, 31/5–6, pp. 396–409.

Marx, K. and Engels, F. (1974) *The German Ideology*. London: Arthur.

Maslow, A. H. (1970) *Motivation and Personality*, 2nd ed. New York: Harper and Row.

Mathews, M. R. (1997) Twenty-five years of social and environmental accounting research: Is there a silver jubilee to celebrate? *Accounting, Auditing and Accountability Journal*, 10/4, pp. 481–531.

Matoré, G. (1951) *Le Vocabulaire et la société sous Louis-Philippe*. Geneva: Lille.

Matoré, G. (1953) *La Méthode en Lexicologie*. Paris: Domaine Français.

Matthews, R. (1998) The myth of global competition and the nature of work. *Journal of Organizational Change Management*, 11/5, pp. 378–398.

Mattis, M. C. (2001) Advancing women in business organizations. *Journal of Management Development*, 20/4, pp. 371–388.

Mattis, M. C. (2004) Women entrepreneurs: Out from under the glass ceiling. *Women in Management Review*, 19/3, pp. 154–163.

Mazza, C. (1999) *Claim, Intent, and Persuasion: Organizational Legitimacy and the Rhetoric of Corporate Mission Statements*. Boston: Kluwer Academic.

McClelland, D. C. (1963) *The Achieving Society*. Princeton, NJ: Van Nostrand.

McClelland, D. C. (1971) *Motivational Trends in Society*. Morristown, NJ: General Learning Press.

McCourt, W. (1997) Using metaphors to understand and to change organizations: A critique of Gareth Morgan's approach. *Organization Studies*, 18/3.

McElhinny, B. S. (1998) "I don't smile much anymore": Affect, gender and the discourse of Pittsburgh police officers. In J. Coates (ed.), *Language and Gender*. Oxford: Blackwell.

McKern, B. (ed.) (2003) *Managing the Global Network Corporation*. London: Routledge.

McLeish, K. (1996) Editor's introduction. In R. Graves, *The Greek Myths*. London: The Folio Society.

Mead, G. H. (1962) *Mind, Self and Society: From the Standpoint of a Social Behaviorist*. Chicago: University of Chicago Press.

Meijer, I. (1998) Advertising citizenship: An essay on the performative power of consumer culture. *Media, Culture and Society*, 20, pp. 235–249.

Merleau-Ponty, M. (1962) *Phenomenology of Perception*. London: Routledge.

Meyerson, D. E., and Fletcher, J. K. (2000) A modest manifesto for shattering the glass ceiling. *Harvard Business Review*, January-February, pp. 127–136.

Michels, R. (1915) *Political Parties: A Sociological Study of the Oligarchical Tendencies of Modern Democracy*. New York: Free Press.

Mills. C. W. (1956) *The Power Elite*. New York: Oxford University Press.

Milroy, J. (1992) *Linguistic Variation and Change*. Oxford: Blackwell.

Milroy, J., and Milroy, L. (1997) Varieties and variation. In F. Coulmas (ed.), *The Handbook of Sociolinguistics*. Oxford: Blackwell.

Milroy, L. (1989) *Language and Social Networks*. Oxford: Blackwell.

Mitchell, J. C. (ed.). (1969) *Social Networks in Urban Situations*. Manchester: Manchester University Press.

Mittelman, J. H. (2000) *The Globalization Syndrome: Transformation and Resistance*. Princeton: Princeton University Press.

Mohler, P., and Züll, C. (1998). TEXTPACK PC, Release 7.5, Mannheim: ZUMA.

Monbiot, G. (2004) *The Age of Consent*. London: Harper Perennial.

Money for nothing? (2001) *The Economist*, August 18, p. 51.

Morgan, G. (1980) Paradigms, metaphors and puzzle solving in organisation theory. *Administrative Science Quarterly*, 25/4, pp. 605–622.

Morgan, G. (1986) *Images of Organization*. London: Sage.

Morgan, G. (1990) *Organisations in Society*. Houndmills: Macmillan.

Morgan, G. (1993) *Imaginisation*. London: Sage.

Morison, I. (1997) Breaking the monolithic mold. *International Journal of Bank Marketing*, 15/5, pp. 153–162.

Mukerji, C. (1995) Toward a sociology of material culture: Science studies, cultural studies and the meaning of things. In D. Crane (ed.), *The Sociology of Culture*. Oxford: Blackwell.

Muller, C. (1969) Lexical distribution reconsidered: The Waring-Herdan formula. In L. Dolezel et al. (eds.), *Statistics and Style*. New York: American Elsevier, pp. 42–56.

Mumby, D. K., and Clair, R. (1997) Organisational discourse. In T. A. van Dijk (ed.), *Discourse as Structure and Process*, vol. 2. London: Sage.

Munro, R. (1994) Governing the new province of quality. In A. Wilkinson and H. Willmott (eds.), *Making Quality Critical*. London: Routledge.

Murrell, A. J. (2001) Gender and diversity in organizations: Past, present, and future directions. *Sex Roles: A Journal of Research*, September.

Musson, G., and Cohen, L. (1999) Understanding language processes: A neglected skill in the management curriculum. *Management Learning*, 3/1, pp. 27–42.

Naisbitt, J. and Aburdene, P. (1990) *Megatrends 2000*. New York: William Morrow.

Nash, W. (1992) *Rhetoric: The Wit of Persuasion*. Oxford: Blackwell .

Newman, M. E. J. (2003) Ego-centered networks and the ripple effect. *Social Networks*, 25, pp. 83–95.

Ng, S. H., (1996) Language and control. In H. Giles and W. P. Robinson (eds.), *Handbook of Language and Social Psychology*. Chichester: John Wiley and Sons, pp. 271–285.

Ng, S. H. and Bradac, J. J. (1993) *Power in Language*. Newbury Park: Sage.

Nickerson, C. (1998) Corporate culture and the use of written English within British subsidiaries in the Netherlands. *English for Specific Purposes*, 17/3, pp. 281–294.

Nieva, V., and Gutek, B. (1981) *Women and Work: A Psychological Perspective*. New York: Praeger.

Nogales, P. D. (1999) *Metaphorically Speaking*. Stanford, CA: CSLI Publications.

Nonaka, I. (1998) The knowledge-creating company. In *Harvard Business Review on Knowledge Management*. Boston: Harvard Business School Press, pp. 21–45.

Oakes, L. S. (1998) Business planning as pedagogy: Language and control in a changing institutional field. (Special issue: Critical Perspectives on Organizational Control). *Administrative Science Quarterly*, June.

Oates, J. (1986) *Babylon*, revised ed. London: Thames and Hudson.

O'Barr, W. M., and Atkins, B. K. (1998) "Women's language" or "powerless language"? In J. Coates (ed.), *Language and Gender*. Oxford: Blackwell.

Ochs, E. (1979) Planned and unplanned discourse. In T. Givón (ed.), *Discourse and Syntax*. New York: Academic Press, pp. 51–80.

Ong, W. J. (1986) Writing is a technology that restructures thought. In G. Baumann (ed.), *The Written Word: Literacy in Transition*, Oxford: Clarendon Press.

Opportunity 2000 (1988) Indianapolis: Hudson Institute.

Oswick, C., and Grant, D. (1996) The organisation of metaphors and the metaphors of organisations: Where are we and where do we go from there? In C. Oswick, and D. Grant (eds.), *Metaphor and Organizations*. London: Sage.

Oswick, C., Keenoy, T., and Grant, D. (1997) Managerial discourses: Words speak louder than actions? *Journal of Applied Management Studies*, 6/1, pp. 5–12.

Oswick, C., and Montgomery, J. (1999) Images of an organization: The use of metaphor in a multinational company. *Journal of Organizational Change Management*, 12/6, pp. 501–523.

Öztel, H., and Hinz, O. (2001) Changing organisation with metaphors. *Learning organisation*, 8/4, pp. 153–168.

Palmer, I., and Dunford, R. (1996) Conflicting uses of metaphors: Reconceptualizing their use in the field of organizational change. *Academy of Management Review*, 21/3, pp. 691–717.

Parsons, T. (1958) Authority, legitimation and political action. In C. J. Friedrich (ed.), *Authority*. Cambridge, MA: Harvard University Press.

Perrow, C. (2002) *Organizing America: Wealth, Power and the Origins of Corporate Capitalism*. Princeton, NJ: Princeton University Press.

Peters, T., and Austin, N. (1986) *A Passion for Excellence: The Leadership Difference*. New York: Warner Books.

Peters, T. J., and Waterman, R. H. (1984) *In Search of Excellence: Lessons from America's Best-run Companies*. New York: Harper and Row.

Pfeffer, J., and Salancik, G. (1978) *The External Control of Organizations: A Resource Dependency Perspective*. New York: Harper and Row.

Pfeffer, J., and Salancik, G. (1997) Who gets power and how they hold on to it. *Organizational Dynamics*, Winter.

Phillips, R. (2003) *Stakeholder Theory and Organizational Ethics*. San Francisco: Berrett-Koehler.

Pickett, D. (1989). The sleeping giant: Investigations in business English. *Language International*, 1.1, pp. 5–11.

Pinder, C. C., and Bourgeois, V. W. (1982) Controlling tropes in administrative science. *Administrative Science Quarterly*, 27/4, pp. 641–652.

Potter, J., and Wetherell, M. (1987) *Discourse and Social Psychology: Beyond Attitudes and Behaviour*. London: Sage.

Powell, G. N. (1993) *Women and Men in Management*, 2nd ed. Newbury Park, CA: Sage.

Powell, G. N. and Butterfield, D. A. (1979) The "good manager": Masculine or androgynous? *Academy of Management Journal*, 22, pp. 395–403.

Propp, V. (1971) *Morphology of the Folk Tale*. Austin: University of Texas Press.

Punnett, B. J., and Shenkar, O. (1996) *Handbook for International Management Research*. Cambridge, MA: Blackwell.

Quirk, R. (1968) *The Use of English*. London: Longmans.

Rafoth, B. (1988) Discourse communities: Where writers, readers and texts come together. In B. Rafoth and D. Rubin (eds.), *The Social Construction of Written Communication*. Norwood, NJ: Ablex, pp. 131–146.

Redfern, W. (1989) *Clichés and Coinages*. Oxford: Blackwell.

Reich, R. B. (1991) Who is them? *Harvard Business Review*, March-April, pp. 77–88.

Reichheld, F. F. (1996) *The Loyalty Effect*. Boston: Harvard Business School Press.

Reid, E. (1995) Virtual worlds, culture and imagination. In S. Jones (ed.), *Cybersociety*. London: Sage.

Rice, B. (1978) Measuring executive muscle. *Psychology Today*, December 1978.

Ritzer, G. (2000) *Modern Sociological Theory*. Boston: McGraw-Hill.

Robinson, W. I. (1996) *Promoting Polyarchy: Globalization, U.S. Intervention, and Hegemony*. Cambridge: Cambridge University Press.

Robinson, W. and Harris, J. (2000) Toward a global ruling class? Globalization and the transnational capitalist class. *Science and Society*, 64/1, pp. 11–54.

Rokeach, M. (1979) *Understanding Human Values*. New York: The Free Press.

Rosen, M. (1988) You asked for it: Christmas at the bosses' expense. *Journal of Management*, 11/2, pp. 31–48.

Rosener, J. B. (1990) Ways women lead. *Harvard Business Review*, May-June, pp. 103–111.

Rubinstein, S., and Kochan, T. (1996) Toward a stakeholder theory of the firm: The case of the Saturn Fellowship. Working paper, MIT.

Ruskin, J. (1905) *Sesame and Lilies*. Ginn and Company.

Saggs, H. W. F. (1999) *The Babylonians*. London: The Folio Society.

Sapir, E. (1921) *Language*. New York: Harcourt Brace and World.

Saturday morning fever. (2001) *The Economist*, December 8, p. 60.

Saville-Troike, M. (1990) *The Ethnography of Communication*. Oxford: Basil Blackwell.

Schank, R. C., and Abelson, R. (1977) *Scripts, Plans, Goals and Understanding*. Hillsdale, NJ: Lawrence Erlbaum.

Schein, E. H. (1985) *Organizational Culture and Leadership*. San Francisco: Jossey Bass.

Schein, V. E., and Mueller, R. (1992) Sex role stereotyping and requisite management characteristics: A cross-cultural look. *Journal of Organizational Behavior*, 13, pp. 439–447.

Schermerhorn, J. R., Hunt, J. G., and Osborn, R. N. (2002) *Organisational Behaviour*. Chichester: John Wiley and Sons.

Schiff, L. R. (2003) *Informed Consent: Information Production and Ideology*. Lanham, MD: Scarecrow Press.

Schiffrin, D. (1994) *Approaches to Discourse*. Oxford: Blackwell.

Schilling, M. A. (2000) Decades ahead of her time: Advancing stakeholder theory through the ideas of Mary Parker Follett. *Journal of Management History*, 6/5, pp. 224-242.

Schmidt, K. (1995) *The Quest for Identity*. London: Cassell.

Schudson, M. (1995) Culture and the integration of national societies. In D. Crane (ed.), *The Sociology of Culture*. Oxford: Blackwell, pp. 21–43.

Schwartz, F. N. (1992) Women as a business imperative. *Harvard Business Review*, March-April, pp. 105–113.

Scollon, R., and Scollon, S. W. (1995) *Intercultural Communication*. Oxford: Blackwell.

Scott, J. (1988) Social network analysis. *Sociology*, 22/1, February 1988.

Searle, J. R. (1976) A classification of illocutionary acts. *Language in Society*, 5, pp. 1–23.

Senge, P. (1990) *The Fifth Discipline: The Art and Practice of the Learning Organization*. New York: Doubleday.

Sexual harassment charges. (2003) EEOC and FEPAs Combined: FY 1992–FY 2002. Available at: www.eeoc.gov/stats/harass.html. Accessed May 25, 2003.

Shapin, S., and Shaffer, S. (1985) *The Leviathan and the Air Pump*. Princeton, NJ: Princeton University Press.

Shaw, B. (1946) *Preface to Plays Pleasant*. Harmondsworth: Penguin Books.

Shenkar, O., and Luo, Y. (2002) *International Business*. Chichester: John Wiley and Sons.

Sheppard, D. L. (1989) Organizations, power and sexuality: The image and self-image of women managers. In J. Hearn, D. L. Sheppard, P. Tancred-Sheriff, and G. Burrell (eds.), *The Sexuality of Organisation*. London: Sage.

Shrivastava, P. (1986) Is strategic management ideological? *Journal of Management*, 12/3, pp. 363-377.

Sinclair, J. (1991) *Corpus, Concordance, Collocation*. Oxford: Oxford University Press.

Sinclair, J., and Coulthard, M. (1975) *Towards an Analysis of Discourse: The English Used by Teachers and Pupils*. London: Oxford University Press.

Sisson, K. (1994) Personnel management paradigms, practice and prospects. In K. Sisson (ed.), *Personnel Management*. London: Blackwell.

Sklair, L. (1995) *Sociology of the Global System*. 2nd rev. ed. Baltimore: Johns Hopkins University Press.

Sklair, L. (2000) *The Transnational Capitalist Class*. Oxford: Blackwell.

Solomon, C. (1990) Careers under glass. *Personnel Journal*, April, pp. 97–105.

Solomon, R. (1992) *Ethics and Excellence: Cooperation and Integrity in Business*. Oxford: Oxford University Press.

Soysal, Y. (1994) *Limits of Citizenship*. Chicago: University of Chicago Press.

Stafford, B. M. (1994) *Artful Science*. Cambridge, MA: MIT Press.

Starik, M. (1994) Should trees have managerial standing? *Journal of Business Ethics*, 14/3, pp. 207–218.

Starkey, K. (2002) Andrew Pettigrew on executives and strategy: An interview by Kenneth Starkey. *European Management Journal*, 20/1, pp. 20–25.

Statham, A. (1987) The gender model revisited: Differences in the management styles of men and women. *Sex Roles*, 16, pp. 409–429.

Steel, D. (1994) *They Can Kill You but They Can't Eat You: Lessons from the Front*. New York: Pocket Books.

Stephens, C. (1994) Saved by a metaphor! *Executive Development*, 7/4, pp. 7–9.

Stevens, D. P. (1993) Avoiding failure with total quality. *Quality (QUA)*. December, pp. 18–22.

Stevenson, N. (1997) Globalization, national cultures and cultural citizenship. *Sociological Quarterly*, 38, pp. 41–66.

Stiver, I. P. (1991) Work inhibitions in women. In J. V. Jordan, A. G. Kaplan, J. B. Miller, I. P. Stiver, and J. L. Surrey, *Women's Growth in Connection*. New York: The Guilford Press.

St John, M. J. (1996) Business is booming: Business English in the 1990s. *English for Specific Purposes*, 15/1, pp. 3–18.

Stock, B. (1983) *The Implications of Literacy: Written Language and Models of Interpretation in the Eleventh and Twelfth Centuries*. Princeton, NJ: Princeton University Press.

Storey, J. (1992) *Developments in the Management of Human Resources*. Oxford: Blackwell.

Strindberg's nightmare. (1996) *The Economist*, June 8, 1996, p. 35.

Stubbs, M. (2001) *Words and Phrases: Corpus Studies of Lexical Semantics*. Oxford: Blackwell.

Surrey, J. L. (1991) Relationship and empowerment. In J. V. Jordan, A. G. Kaplan, J. B. Miller, I. P. Stiver, and J. L. Surrey, *Women's Growth in Connection*. New York: The Guilford Press.

Swales, J. M. (1991) *Genre Analysis: English in Academic and Research Settings*. Cambridge: Cambridge University Press.

Swales, J. and Feak, C. B. (2000) *English in Today's Research World: A Writing Guide*. Ann Arbor: University of Michigan Press.

Tajfel, H. (1978) *The Social Psychology of Minorities*. London: Minority Rights Group.

Tajfel, H. (1981) Human Groups and Social Categories. Cambridge: Cambridge University Press.

Tannen, D. (1990) *You Just Don't Understand: Women and Men in Conversation*. New York: William Morrow.

Tayler, A. (1986) Why women managers are bailing out. *Fortune*, August 18, pp. 16–23.

Taylor, W. (1991) The logic of global business: An interview with ABB's Percy Barnevik. *Harvard Business Review*, March-April, pp. 90–105.

Testimony of Christine Stolba, Senior Fellow, Independent Women's Forum, before the Committee on Government Reform, Subcommittee on Government Efficiency, Financial Management, and Intergovernmental Relations, U.S. House of Representatives. (2002) Available at: www.iwf.org/news/001129.shtml. Accessed May 26, 2003.

Thank you and goodbye. (1999) *The Economist*, October 30, p. 77.

Thompson, J. B. (1996) *The Media and Modernity: A Social Theory of the Media*. Cambridge: Polity Press.

Thucydides (423 B.C.E./1998) *History of the Peloponnesian War*. Cambridge, MA: Hackett Publishing Co. Inc.

Tietze, S., Cohen, L., and Musson G. (2003) *Understanding Organisations through Language*. London: Sage.

Tjosvold, D. (1984) The dynamics of positive power. *Training and Development Journal*, June.

The Tower of Business Babel. (1991) Parker Pen Company, Janesville, Wisconsin.

Trier, J. (1931) Der Deutsche Wortschatz im Sinnbezirk des Verstandes. *Die Geschichte eines sprachlichen Feldes. I: Von den Anfangen bis zum Beginn des 13. Jh*. Heidelberg.

Troemel-Ploetz, S. (1998) Selling the apolitical. In J. Coates (ed.), *Language and Gender*. Oxford: Blackwell, pp. 446–458.

Trompenaars, F. (1993) *Riding the Waves of Culture: Understanding Cultural Diversity in Business*. London: Nicholas Brealey.

Trudgill, P. (1988) *Sociolinguistics*. London: Penguin Books.

Tsoukas, H. (1993) Analogical reasoning and knowledge generation in organization theory. *Organization* Studies, 14/3, pp. 323–346.

Ullmann, S. (1983) *Semantics: An Introduction to the Science of Meaning*. Oxford: Blackwell.

Ure, J. (1971) Lexical density and register differentiation. In G. E. Perren and J. L. M. Trim (eds.), *Applications of Linguistics: Selected Papers of the 2nd International Congress of Applied Linguistics, 1996*. Cambridge: Cambridge University Press.

Urry, J. (2000) *Sociology beyond Societies*. London: Routledge.

van Dijk, T. (1988) *News as Discourse*. Hillsdale, NJ: Lawrence Erlbaum.

van Dijk, T.A. (1996) Social cognition and discourse. In H. Giles and W. P. Robinson (eds.), *Handbook of Language and Social Psychology*. Chichester: John Wiley and Sons, pp. 163–183.

van Dijk, T.A. (1997) The study of discourse. In T. A. van Dijk (ed.), *Discourse as Structure and Process*, vol. 1. London: Sage.

van Dijk, T. A. (2000) *Ideology*. London: Sage.

van Leeuwen, T. (1987) Generic strategies in press journalism. *Australian Review of Applied Linguistics*, 10/2, pp. 199–220.

Vision quest. (2003) UNESCO Asia and Pacific Regional Bureau for Education, Bangkok. Available at: www.unescobkk.org/. Accessed June 21, 2004.

Wallerstein, I. (1987) Patterns and perspectives of the capitalist world-economy. In P. R. Viotti and M. V. Kauppi (eds.), *International Theory: Realism, Pluralism, Globalism.* New York: Macmillan.

Warner, A. (1962) *A Short Guide to English Style.* Oxford: Oxford University Press.

Watson, G. W. (2003) Ideology and the symbolic construction of fairness in organizational change. *Journal of Organizational Change Management,* 16/2, pp. 154–168.

Weber, M. (1918/1968) *Economy and Society* (ed. G. Roth and C. Wittich). Berkeley: University of California Press.

Weber, M. (1970) *From Max Weber: Essays in Sociology.* London: Routledge.

Weber, M. (1976) *The Protestant Ethic and the Spirit of Capitalism.* London: Allen and Unwin.

Weihrich, H., and Koontz, H. (1993) *Management: A Global Perspective.* New York: McGraw-Hill.

Weinrich, H. (1968) Thesen. In *Die Metapher (Bochumer Diskussion), Poetica* 2, pp. 100–130.

Weinrich, H. (1976) *Sprache in Texten.* Stuttgart: Klett.

Weiss, E. H., and Fisher, B. (1998) Should we teach women to interrupt? Cultural variables in management communication courses. *Women in Management Review,* 13/1, pp. 37–44.

Weiss, L. (1998) *The Myth of the Powerless State.* Ithaca, NY: Cornell University Press.

Wells, G. (1979) Variation in child language. In V. Lee (ed.), *Language Development.* London: Croom Helm.

Wernick, A. (1991) *Promotional Culture.* London: Sage.

Westwood, R., and Linstead, S. (eds.) (2001) *The Language of Organisation.* London: Sage.

Wetlaufer, S. (1999) Organizing for empowerment: An interview with AES's Roger Sant and Dennis Bakke. *Harvard Business Review,* January-February, pp. 111–123.

Wetlaufer, S. (2000) Who wants to manage a millionaire? *Harvard Business Review,* July-August, pp. 53–60.

Wiener, Y. (1988) Forms of Value Systems: A Focus on Organizational Effectiveness and Cultural Change and Maintenance. *Academy of Management Review,* October, pp. 534–545.

Wierzbicka, A. (1999) *Emotions across Languages and Cultures: Diversity and Universals.* Cambridge: Cambridge University Press.

Wilson, G. K. (1985) *Business and Politics: A Comparative Introduction.* London: MacMillan.

Wilson, J. (1990) *Politically Speaking.* Oxford: Blackwell.

Wilson Nelson, M. (1998) Women's ways: Interactive patterns in predominantly female research teams. In J. Coates (ed.), *Language and Gender.* Oxford: Blackwell.

Winn, J. (2004) Entrepreneurship: not an easy path to top management for women. *Women in Management Review,* 19/3, pp. 143–153.

Wong, P. T. P., Kettlewell, G., and Sproule, C. F. (1985) On the importance of being masculine: Sex role, attribution, and women's career achievement. *Sex Roles,* 12, pp. 757–769.

Wood, T. (2002) Spectacular metaphors. *Journal of Organizational Change Management,* 15/1, pp. 11–20.

Woolard, K. A. (1998) Language ideology as a field of inquiry. In B. B. Schieffelin, K. A. Woolard, and P. V. Kroskrity (eds.), *Language Ideologies: Practice and Theory.* New York: Oxford University Press.

A world fit for women. (1999) *The Economist,* December 31, 1999, p. 44.

Yang, H. (1986) A new technique for identifying scientific/technical terms and describing science texts. *Literary and Linguistic Computing,* 1, pp. 93–103.

Young, M. A. (2001) *A Philosophy of Business Negotiation from Practical Reason*. Westport, CT: Quorum Books.

Zaleznik, A. (1992) Managers and leaders: Are they different? *Harvard Business Review*, March-April.

Zbaracki, M. J. (1998) The rhetoric and reality of total quality management. *Administrative Science Quarterly*, Sept.

Zelditch, M., Jr. (2001) Theories of legitimacy. In J. T. Jost and B. Major (eds.), *The Psychology of Legitimacy*. New York: Cambridge University Press, pp. 33–53.

Zipf, G. K. (1949) *Human Behavior and the Principle of the Least Effort*. Cambridge, MA: Addison-Wesley.

Zukov, G. (1980) *The Dancing Wu Li Masters*. London: Fontana.

Index

About the Authors

RENATA FOX is associate professor at the University of Rijeka, Croatia, where she teaches English, German, and business communication.

JOHN FOX holds a doctoral degree in communication and media and has taught English at a number of universities.